W9-AMB-800
Library
Congregation Ner Shalom

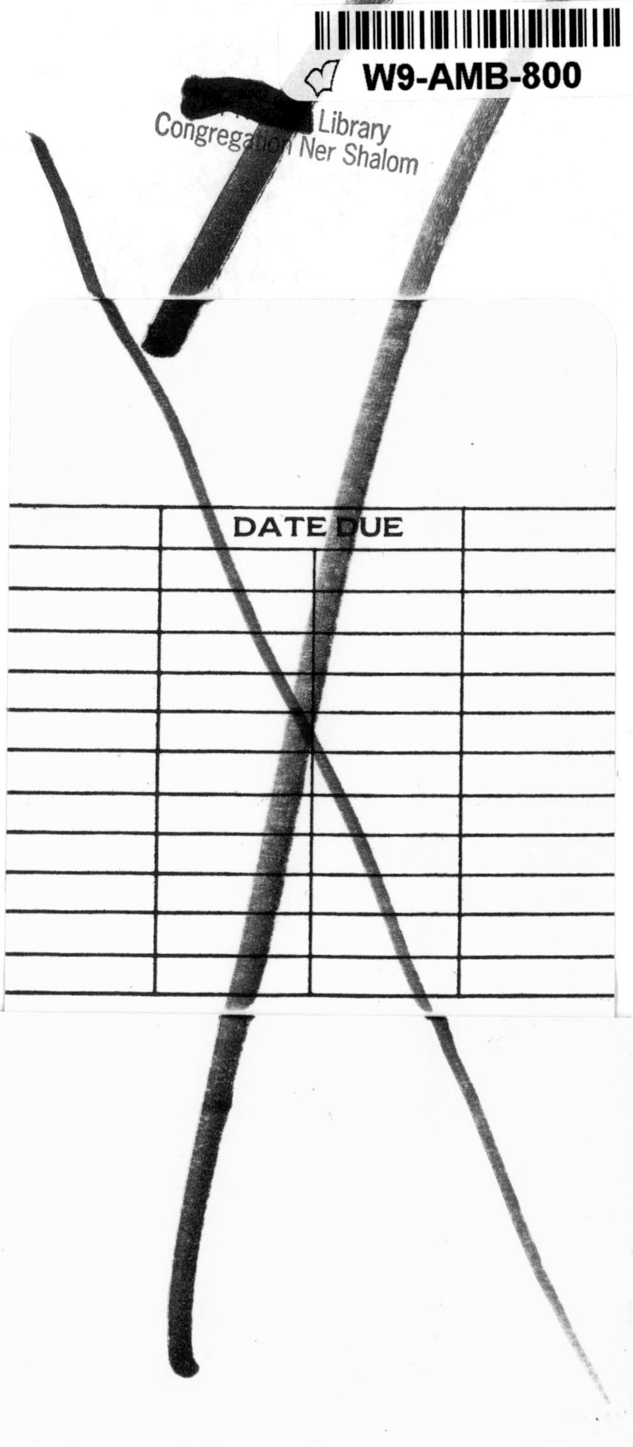

DATE DUE

JEWISH WOMEN SPEAK OUT:

EXPANDING THE BOUNDARIES OF PSYCHOLOGY

EDITED BY
Kayla Weiner and Arinna Moon

FOREWORD BY
PHYLLIS CHESLER

CANOPY PRESS
SEATTLE

Copyright © 1995 Kayla Miriyam Weiner and Arinna Moon. Printed and bound in the United States of America. All rights reserved. No part of this book may be reproduced or transmitted in any form or by any means, electronic or mechanical, including photocopying, recording or by an information storage and retrieval system, except by a reviewer who may quote brief passages in a review to be printed in a magazine or newspaper, without permission in writing from the author of the chapter to be quoted.

Canopy Press, P.O. Box 46252, Seattle, WA 98146.

An earlier version of the work by tova "does it hurt?" appeared in *Bridges: A Journal for Jewish Feminists and our Friends.* (1990). 1 (2).

Logo design by Sharla Kibel and Lilian Bern for the *First International Conference on Judaism, Feminism and Psychology: Creating a Shelter in the Wilderness* presented by the Jewish Women's Caucus of the Association for Women in Psychology, October 1992 in Seattle, WA.

Back cover photograph by Geoff Manasse, Seattle, WA.

ISBN: 0-9645878-0-7
LCCN: 95-68925

First Printing: 1995

DEDICATION

I wish to dedicate this work to my grandmothers: Rebecca Baker whose ability to provide for her family of eight children despite the social oppression inherent in being poor, female and Jewish sparked my feminist consciousness; Dora Weiner who gave me unconditional love and helped to instill in me a deep connection to my Jewish roots; and Ann Weiner whose love of people, refreshing openness, and joy in living continue to be an inspiration to me.

Kayla Miriyam Weiner

I wish to dedicate this work to my grandmother, Daisy Newmark, who loved me "no matter what" and gave me a sense of belonging and pride about being Jewish, and to my grandmother, Pauline Connor, born in Russia in a different century, who has passed her heritage on to me. For my mother, Fran Connor, who left Judaism because she refused to accept the inequality for women, I offer this book as an affirmation that things can change.

Arinna Moon

ACKNOWLEDGMENTS

We gratefully acknowledge the help of the organizers, presenters and participants of *The First International Conference on Judaism, Feminism and Psychology: Creating a Shelter in the Wilderness*; the women who submitted papers for consideration for this volume; Florence Howe of Feminist Press for her guidance and support in the early stages of this project; Laurie Slatin, Tammy Lianu, Marian Broida, Alison Sands, Margaret Bergmann-Ness, Michael Gross and Jackie Gollan for their help in proofreading the manuscript; and Shari Steiner, Clyde Steiner and Goldy VanDeWater for typesetting and countless pieces of helpful advice.

TABLE OF CONTENTS

FOREWORD

This is a wonderful anthology, full of wisdom, information, and steady, quiet courage. I warmly welcome it. However, I am also deeply saddened, sobered, by its existence, or rather, by the *need* for its existence. *Jewish Women Speak Out, Expanding The Boundaries of Psychology*, edited by Kayla Weiner and Arinna Moon, exists because anti-Semitism still exists. Among educated folk. Among feminist folk. Among feminist therapist folk. Among *Jewish* feminist therapist folk. In America.

Despite all the "progressive" movements Jews have joined and led, despite all the Jewish pre- and post-Holocaust attempts to assimilate, to become Jewishly invisible, to understand things from the "other" person's point of view (à la Freud), 55 years after the rise of European Nazism, American Jewish feminists found it necessary to create a *Jewish* caucus within a feminist, professional organization. This anthology is an outgrowth of their first conference.

The Jewish Caucus is part of the Association for Women in Psychology (AWP), an organization I co-founded in 1969-1970. The Association has endured for more than 25 years, proof, perhaps, of the enduring sexism and hostility towards feminism within the professions, as well as to women's natural/conditioned gravitational pull towards each other.

In 1989, some Jewish members of AWP formed a Jewish caucus. Perhaps the increased feminist awareness of the importance of ritual, or the feminist reclamation of "sacred space" within Judaism, compelled Jewish AWP members to do so; perhaps the increase in anti-Semitism which always accompanies the rise of fundamentalism in history, also spurred them on. Whatever explanation applies, I'm glad they exist, and I'm glad they're publishing this collection. Sadly, though, *Jewish Women Speak Out* proves how little has changed since I first encountered anti-Semitism among radical feminists and lesbians in the early 1970's.

That encounter sent me straight to Israel for the first time a few months after *Women and Madness* was first published in 1972. I remember browsing in a Tel Aviv shop and unexpectedly coming upon *Time* magazine's review of the book in January of 1973. At the time, I was shocked more by the blatantly anti-Semitic illustration that accompanied the review than by the anti-feminist review itself. Freud was caricatured as a big-nosed, ugly, pygmy-midget, clearly "in lust" with the tall, blonde, Viking princess on his couch. The pure racism just leapt off the page. In 1982, in Vienna, I visited the Freud Museum; they closed it, briefly, so that I could be there quietly. I lay down on that famous, faded red couch of his, and I let Freud tell me all his problems! Sigmund moved me, he talked to me: Jew to Jew.

When I returned to America, I started wearing big Jewish stars to the most radical rallies—my version of an Afro, or a dashiki. I waited for someone to challenge me, publicly, on The Jewish Question. Few ever did. More often, that took place behind closed doors, sometimes behind my back. I was either accused of being the wrong kind of Jew (too pushy, too verbal, too visible, too sexy, too smart), or a too-typical kind of Jew (reactionary, racist, capitalist, imperialist, sectarian). In short, I was sometimes viewed as a betrayer of feminism because I dared to identify anti-Semitism as racism, and to therefore identify myself both as a Jew and as a Zionist.

Between 1973 and 1975, I tried, but failed, to interest other Jewish feminists in meeting, on a continuous basis, to discuss the problem of anti-Semitism. At the time, one rising feminist light said: "Phyllis, it may be a problem, but it's not my problem." Another said that "she didn't identify as a Jew anyway—and hoped I'd give it up too." (Within a decade, both women would have important things to say on this very subject, and would even become quite successful as "professional" Jewish feminists.)

I began to hear stories from other feminists about their experiences of anti-Semitism within the movement. (Of course, the stories of sexism/racism/homophobia within the Jewish and Israeli communities, never stopped coming my way either). As a radical feminist I didn't know what to do. I felt it was important to act on my analysis of anti-Semitism. I feared that to do so would irreparably slow us down in terms of feminist progress. I was right on both counts. Within a few years, other Jewish feminists began to talk about the "Problem that dared not speak its name." In 1975-1976, I participated in the first National Jewish Feminist Conference, which took place at the McAlpin hotel in New York City. It was a thrilling and energizing conference.

I remember spending hours with Aviva Cantor, who, together with Susan Weidman Schneider, founded *Lilith* magazine in 1976. *Lilith* published my conversation with Aviva in the winter of 1976/77. Although I'd been quoted at length on feminism and Judaism at the McAlpin Hotel conference, this was really my first "out" interview as a Jew and a Zionist. When my friend Naomi Weisstein, also a co-founder of AWP, published her paper "Woman as Nigger," I told her, "Try 'Woman as Jew'" because that would take us back 5,000 years of being without land, in exile, without any means of self-defense or economic independence.

As a feminist, I was also learning from Jewish and Israeli history. I began to think about the importance of feminist sovereign space, of a feminist government in exile. I had in mind something far beyond a coffee house, magazine, shelter for battered women, or Women's Studies program. I was thinking about the creation of feminist sovereign space psychologically, legally, economically and militarily.

I told Aviva that feminists would have to learn how to fly planes, use and control technology, defend ourselves and each other, i.e., to do all the things that men do. Dreamer that I am, I said that I believed a feminist government would be the only solution to The Woman Problem. Not just in one little territory, but world-wide, everywhere. Incredulous, Aviva asked me: "But is it possible?" And I, Jewish-style, answered a question with a question. "Do you think the State of Israel seemed possible, in say, 1820?" "No," said Aviva. "Well," said I, "I learned from the State of Israel that the impossible is possible."

In 1975, together with New York Jewish feminists Esther Broner, Edith Issac-Rose, Bea Kreloff, Letty Cottin Pogrebin and Lily Rivlin, we began to hold feminist *seders*. With feminist pride, and love, many of our members wrote about us; Lily made a wonderful and inspiring film about us. We were enormously privileged. History—and our own unaffiliated, grassroots nature—allowed us to be radically Jewish and feminist with each other, at no cost. All gain, no pain. Our venture was both splendid and flawed. We had more media coverage than sisterhood, more celebrities per square inch than *Yiddishkeit*. We were the keepers of the flame of our own growing myth. Sadly, we had no "hands-on" connection to other, similar, grassroots groups, around the country or around the world. We never managed to include sons as well as daughters, we had little institutional influence, and we did not collectively create an evolving *Haggadah*, complete with specific rituals. (We were so creative, so madcap, that each year we dared to have different rituals, and to focus on different themes.) Lily Rivlin, Esther Broner and myself, also created Jewish feminist New Year's and *Yom Kippur* rituals, as well as rituals for other rites of passage, such as giving birth, having a hysterectomy, losing a loved one, etc.

In 1980, I attended the Conference on Women in Copenhagen sponsored by the United Nations. In Copenhagen, Israel officially became the "Jew of the world", the scapegoat for the West, the cause of every country's plagues. It was not a conference about or for women; it was really a conference about Palestinian and other so-called Third World rights. I heard women, most of whom had been trained by Russia, and/or who were members of their own countries' ruling-class elite, thunder, chant, repeat, over and over again: "Our problems—drought, famine, tyranny—are due to Apartheid in South Africa and Zionism." The anti-Semitism, masquerading as anti-Zionism, was truly staggering. More important, I saw what absolute pushovers other, presumably "pushy Jewish women" were, when confronted with shouted hatred, oft-told lies, propaganda.

In 1980-81, I did three things: I persuaded the Israeli government to allow me to organize a really radical feminist conference and hold it in Jerusalem; I wrote about the Copenhagen Conference for *Lilith*, but under a pseudonym, so as to not jeopardize the safety of feminists from Arab and Islamic countries whom I was inviting, to this conference-that-never-was; and I coordinated a panel on Feminism and Anti-Semitism for the National Women's Studies Association meeting in

Storrs, Connecticut. I did so, because I did not want to talk about anti-Semitism among feminists alone, or behind closed doors. I wanted to present the facts publicly, to other American feminists.

I remember "coming out" again, as a Zionist, at this panel. I talked about Zionism as the national liberation movement of the Jewish people. I described how feminist reports of anti-Semitism in our ranks were often seen as exaggerated, groundless, lies. I loved this group of women. I said: "If we understand why women need separate shelters for battered women, coffee houses, music festivals, land trusts, Women's Studies programs, can't we also understand why Jews might need a Jewish state?"

I asked my assembled feminist sisters: "Who'd hide me and all the other Jewish feminists and our families in their attics when the Nazis come to get us?" "I will, I will," promised an earnestly distraught Susan Griffen. Some Christian and Jewish feminists were not at all amused; some women of color were a lot less than amused. From 1981-1990, I would have many passionate conversations with individual Christian feminists, both white, and of color, who emotionally seemed to believe that 20th century Jews and Zionists were more responsible than anyone else for the death of the Goddess two to three more thousand years ago and for the slave-trade four centuries ago; that Zionism was responsible for racism in America today—and for all forms of American and Western imperialism; that all Jews are rich, powerful, racists, etc.

Mainly, many feminists truly believed that Jewish women, most of whom were white-skinned were, unjustifiably, trying to jump on, profit from, even halt feminist, revolutionary, progress against racism, imperialism, or colonialism, and to "ruin it" for women of color. World-wide, they were no more accepted among their African, Hispanic and Asian brothers than we were, among our Jewish brothers, but like the rest of us, they found it easier to fight with other women than to take on the brothers.

Post-Storrs, I turned over our panel tapes to Letty Cottin Pogrebin, who incorporated some of the information into her important article on anti-Semitism among feminists. The article, which appeared in *Ms* magazine in 1982, caused quite a stir. A number of feminists asked me, privately, whether I thought Letty was exaggerating, grand-standing, merely applying for a position in the Jewish establishment, etc. I told them she was neither exaggerating nor grandstanding, and might only be *forced* to apply for a "position" as a feminist among Jews if the career-path was too heartbreaking for her as a Jew among feminists.

In 1988, I was one of the women who *davenned* for the first time ever at the *Kotel* in Jerusalem with a *Torah.* In fact, I had the great honor of *opening* the Torah for the women that morning on December 1, 1988. It wedded me to the action. I helped form the International Committee for Women at the *Kotel*, and became a name-plaintiff in the historic lawsuit on behalf of Jewish women's religious rights. After seven years the matter is still pending. The suit was heard by the Israeli Supreme Court and deserves a separate article entirely. I often tell people that what we did was the equivalent of Catholic women taking over the Vatican and officiating at Mass; and that I believed that women's mental health would vastly improve, as a result of actions like this.

In the beginning, many Jewish and Israeli feminists, secularists, and radicals, tried to pry me loose from what they saw as an unimportant, or even reactionary struggle. Didn't I see that we were only arguing for a piece of a tainted pie, that we were settling for too little, and for the wrong thing? They had a point—but they were also wrong. Women have as much right as men do to exercise our rights as Jews—even if, from the feminist point of view, all patriarchal religions need to be transformed/overthrown. In the course of this struggle I have seen how a moderate, liberal, demand for women's civil and human rights, is treated as if it's a revolutionary demand. Which, in a sense makes it revolutionary.

I will stop here. There's more, but this is enough. My point is this: that given this history, imagine how moved, angered, saddened, validated I felt when I read what Evelyn Torton Beck has to say about the "resistance to including Jews in the developing field of multicultural psychology," and about the numerous "unacknowledged acts of anti-Semitic complicity on the part of lesbian feminists." Beck describes numerous instances of blatant anti-Semitism in the published works of psychoanalysts, most notably, Thomas Szasz and M. Masud R. Khan, which have gone unchallenged. (I guess once you've read about Carl Gustav Jung's profound and virulent anti-Semitism, there's really no cause for surprise, is there? And yet one is still always a little surprised). Beck also describes how difficult it still is to call others on their anti-Semitism—at least, not without risking hostility and failure.

The collection is rich, very rich, and contains unique and creative suggestions about Jewish experience, both sacred and secular, and has implications for Jewish psychological suffering, clinical theory and practice. I could go on, but here's the anthology itself, waiting to be read. Please do so. Use it, dialogue with it, challenge it, embrace it, dance with it, keep it by your bedside, add to it.

To the editors and the contributors: *Yasher Koach!*

Phyllis Chesler Ph.D.
Brooklyn, New York
1995

PREFACE

Jewish women's voices have been silent too long. Lost in the wilderness of male dominated religion, politics and psychology, Jewish women, until recently, haven't had a place to make our voices heard. We have lacked an audience who cared to listen or even a way to connect with each other to begin the sometimes joyous, sometimes painful, process of uncovering our realities. During the holiday of *Sukkot*, modern Jews construct a *Sukkah* (shelter) to remind us of the temporary huts built while wandering in the desert following our Exodus from Egypt. These shelters provide a safe place in which to live and celebrate. The First International Conference on Judaism, Feminism and Psychology, held during *Sukkot* in Seattle, WA, October 29 to November 1, 1992, created a symbolic shelter in the current psychological wilderness in which Jewish women live. Having a safe place enabled us to begin to uncover and explore the psychological implications of being Jewish women. We began to make our voices heard.

The conference was an outgrowth of the Jewish Women's Caucus of the Association for Women in Psychology. The caucus formed in 1989 to address the psychological issues significant to Jewish women that were not being addressed at the organizational level or within professional mental health communities. The purpose of the conference was to bring together clinicians, academics and activists, both Jewish and non-Jewish, to learn to help Jewish women deal with issues of external and internalized anti-Semitism, assimilation, isolation, visibility, invisibility and over visibility, and women's roles in the Jewish community and in the non-Jewish world. The goals of the conference were: (1) to integrate our identities as Jews, feminists and mental health professionals; (2) to raise awareness of Jewish issues among mental health practitioners, academics and community activists; (3) to examine the realities for Jewish women living in a predominantly male-centered, homophobic, non-Jewish world; (4) to celebrate the strengths and diversity of Jewish women and build bridges of understanding; and (5) to offer a "shelter in the wilderness," a safe place for the exploration of complex, painful and sensitive realities related to being Jewish and female.

It is estimated that 150,000 people were made aware of the conference and its issues. Approximately 350 women from across the United States and Canada were in attendance, with interest and queries coming from all over the world. The participants covered the spectrum of diversity within the Jewish community: *Ashkenazi* and *Sephardic*, differing class backgrounds, the entire gamut of religious observance, differing sexual orientations, differences in age and more. At times it seemed the differences were greater than the similarities. Yet, women who wouldn't ordinarily get to meet each other came together in an environment of exploration, learning and support for one another. The conference was designed to feed women on a mental, emotional and spiritual plane. In addition to providing the space for that magical coming together, and also providing access to highly intelligent women addressing topics relevant to our lives, the conference provided a place for women to experience Judaism in a feminist context.

This book is an outgrowth of that groundbreaking event. The editors of this volume, Kayla Weiner and Arinna Moon, were the coordinator and registration chair, respectively, for the conference. We share a deep commitment to enlightening the lives of Jewish women, in a psychological context and in the larger world. While the conference was a great success, it still only reached a limited number of people. We saw the need to reach a much larger audience and so the idea for the book was conceived. This book is not presented as a definitive analysis of the psychological issues for Jewish women. Many important Jewish topics are not covered which have an impact on the psychology of Jewish women such as history, class, African-American and Jewish relations, Israeli and Palestinian questions and more. Also, each paper does not exhaust its individual subject. Nevertheless, a great deal of material is being covered to enlighten and educate a wide audience about the relationship of the disciplines of Jewish studies, women's studies and psychology.

Professionals in other disciplines, as well as lay people, will find this volume useful as a tool to help them understand the feelings, attitudes and behaviors of Jewish women. The book will provide nourishment to the many people clamoring for information about the psychology of Jewish women. It is our hope that these essays encourage continued study in related areas and inspire others to publish their work. Jewish women must continue to speak out.

Kayla Weiner and Arinna Moon

SETTING THE FRAME

Kayla Weiner and Arinna Moon
Evelyn Torton Beck

INTRODUCTION

KAYLA WEINER AND ARINNA MOON

Jewish culture is over four thousand years old. Most texts related to Jewish life that were available until recently were written by men, about men and addressed to men. Even the conceptualization of God is traditionally male. Despite the presence of women in the *Torah*, the stories of the Jewish people and the commentaries about those stories are really about Jewish male experience. Rarely do we learn of women's experience or hear women's voices.

Despite the achievement or privilege of some individual women, all women have been oppressed physically, sexually and emotionally just by virtue of living in a patriarchal culture: our voices have been silenced at every opportunity. The non-Jewish world has made it unsafe for Jewish women to be visible about Jewish concerns through persecution and through pressure to assimilate. In the Jewish community, Jewish women have been additionally oppressed as we have faced silencing by Jewish men who have historically controlled the community and who have not been interested in our life experiences. Our traditional role as mother and the one with the responsibility for transmitting the faith and the culture, left little time to be public about our concerns. Additionally, because women lacked access to education we were not provided a means to express ourselves in a scholarly way. Only in the very recent past has some progress been made in illuminating Jewish women's experiences.

This book is intended to end our silence and let the world know about our lives from the inside. Four thousand years of patriarchal oppression have taken their toll; many of us have been wounded by our experiences. The inability to speak and have our feelings fully acknowledged has compounded the pain. Women are no longer tolerating this oppression. Our search for healing has taken many paths. Speaking out, writing, creating new rituals and transforming old rituals are just some of the ways that Jewish women are seeking to overcome our pain and at the same time stay connected to our Jewish heritage and culture. Women are not only talking about our own individual experiences, but making connections between what happens to us and what happens in the world. We are questioning tradition and addressing global concerns. For Jewish women this means changing core practices in our culture and it means addressing the ways in which we are ignored or persecuted by the non-Jewish world.

Jewish Women Speak Out focuses on the psychological issues specific to Jewish feminists and contains material that integrates the three disciplines of Jewish studies, women's studies and psychology. We include some well-known Jewish scholars and authors and introduce important new writers who are making valuable contributions to these fields. The chapters include a mix of theoretical, clinical and experiential approaches to the psychology of Jewish women. The book has been divided into four broad categories entitled: *Setting the Frame, Identity Development, Therapeutic Encounters* and *Contemporary Topics*. Several threads tie these sections together: making ourselves known, questioning standard practices and traditional ways of thinking, and writing a feminist version of our lives as Jewish women. Some authors struggle with issues of identity: defining ourselves as people both in the Jewish world and in the larger society. Others grapple with issues of fear: dealing with the realities of external and internalized anti-Semitism. The issues of visibility, invisibility and over visibility weave through all the sections. The exploration of these themes helps to make Jewish women understood from our own perspectives rather than from the perspectives of other people who have attempted to define us. Taken individually, each section of the book illuminates a specific aspect of modern Jewish thought. As a whole, the book expands the boundaries of Jewish women's psychology.

The first section, *Setting the Frame*, includes this introduction and an article by Evelyn Torton Beck. Here Beck explores more fully the relationship between Judaism, feminism and psychology. She offers examples of the resistance to the inclusion of Jews in the developing field of multicultural psychology and describes several instances of flagrant anti-Semitism in recent experiences with professional psychologists. Beck makes it clear why feminists in the field of mental health must become culturally literate about Jewish women. Competent professionals are called to recognize that Jewish women are an oppressed minority and to understand the psychological implications of that oppression for Jewish women. Beck makes it evident that the inclusion of the psychology of Jewish women in feminist theory development and in the practice of feminist therapy is crucial. This opening section prepares the reader to delve further into the thinking, behavior and practices of Jewish feminists.

The second section of the book, *Identity Development*, addresses some of the complex questions Jewish women face in defining ourselves. Who are we? What is our role? Can we change roles? Can we be Jewish leaders? How does it feel to have been circumscribed for so long? Deborah Engelen-Eigles examines the sense of Jewishness, self-concept and experiences in the daily lives of three generations of Jewish women. She shows how internal and external forces in self and society intertwine to shape and influence each woman's unique Jewish identity and Jewish practice. She illuminates how practice and underlying beliefs are not necessarily the same, and that to make assumptions in this regard gives an incomplete picture of any given woman's Jewish identity. Rachel Josefowitz Siegel addresses how the relationship Jewish women have to our bodies may be a result of Jewish laws and customs that are often understood to portray women negatively. She elaborates on how these laws and customs combine with the dominant culture's portrayal of women and contribute to low self-esteem in Jewish women. She presents ways in which Jewish women can begin thinking about our relationship to our bodies and our sense of self in the world. Nora Gold's paper explores the phenomenon of Jewish women who espouse strong commitment to feminist principles and to women's right to full participation in Jewish religious life, yet never lead their communities in prayer. She elaborates on research she did in several communities and offers illustrations to show why the belief and practice of women are often dissonant. She offers strategies for overcoming the obstacles identified in order to increase Jewish women's participation in prayer leadership.

This section looks at three different aspects of Jewish women's identity. The first of these papers is a qualitative research paper based on interviews with three generations of Jewish women, the second is a theoretical presentation and the third is a quantitative research paper. They offer significantly different ways of examining the experiences of Jewish women; each a marvelous illustration of feminist scholarship. Although not a complete analysis of this topic, nevertheless, the papers in this section illustrate some of the many facets of the complexity of Jewish women's identity formation. Other aspects need to be illuminated through further research.

The next section, *Therapeutic Encounters*, presents some of the methods women have chosen to work on their healing process, with a particular emphasis on feminist therapy. Robin Zeiger's paper explores the question of infertility and she tells of her personal experiences attempting to conceive. She also provides insights useful to the therapist working with women struggling with infertility. Of particular significance to the Orthodox Jewish woman, her words will resonate on some level for all Jewish women. In an essay that evolved from a personal account written on the day of her divorce, Sara Horowitz examines the *get* (the Jewish divorce) as a ritual of separation, grief and renewal. In this traditionally male controlled legal process, she found ways to make the often demeaning experience meaningful to her as a feminist. In an analytic section she considers the need for a new woman's divorce ritual and provides ideas to help women empower themselves in a situation where they traditionally have no control. The powerful poem by tova, accompanied by her essay, poignantly describes her experience of being abused by her Jewish family. She also expresses the impossibility of separating her abuse from her Jewishness and likewise the need for connection between her healing and her Jewish identity. tova's work and Yonah Klem's paper are a wonderful complement to the other. Klem presents a case study and a discussion of how the ancient tradition of the *mikvah* (the Jewish ritual bath) can be helpful in healing the adult Jewish woman who is a survivor of incest or similar abuse. She also suggests ways in which elements of the ritual can be used for non-Jewish survivors of abuse. Melissa Schwartz discusses how Jewish issues for women in therapy may often be overshadowed by the content of the material presented by the client. She presents a number of specific issues which may be embedded in the problems with which the client struggles. She demonstrates how these Jewish issues can be unveiled by the sensitive clinician. Barbara Breitman discusses the therapeutic process of several clients and includes her personal reflections on the therapeutic relationship. She shows the ways in which gender, ethnicity and culture have an impact on the identity of an individual. Her work demonstrates that it is necessary to unravel these strands of identity to allow each woman to know herself and enable her to develop into a fully functioning human being.

Infertility, divorce and abuse are problems for women in all cultures. What makes these papers unique, in addition to the fact that they deal with the issues in terms of Jewish women, is that the analysis, the therapeutic interventions, the ways of looking at the psychological issues and the manner of being in a therapeutic relationship, are consciously and intentionally Jewish. A Jewish essence shines through in the writing of each author. This lens can be applied to any number of therapeutic topics and will yield a greater understanding of the similarities and differences between Jewish and non-Jewish women.

The last section of the book, *Contemporary Topics*, addresses four areas of political significance to Jewish women. Miriam Pollack challenges Jewish feminists to examine their position on male circumcision. She maintains that this practice is unnecessary both medically and *halachically* and is a form of sexual abuse. She argues that childhood male circumcision contributes to alienation between adult men and women. Pollack advocates for a new covenant ceremony for male children that eliminates the severing of the foreskin. Michele Clark urges all Jewish activists to make their Jewishness known as part of their activism. She suggests that forming alliances with other oppressed groups is critical for protection of the Jewish individual in times of racial oppression. She explains that making one's Jewishness visible also helps to preserve the Jewish community. Barbara Hammer presents a theoretical paper that contends all Jewish women are suffering from some degree of post traumatic stress syndrome because world wide anti-Semitism in general, and the Holocaust in particular, are experienced as trauma. She supports her theory with numerous illustrations of how trauma is manifested in individual Jews. She proposes that this condition contributes to the diminishment of the Jewish community because of the assimilation of Jews into the dominant culture in a misguided attempt to find safety. Kayla Weiner suggests that many women who have not had direct personal contact with the Holocaust, Jewish and non-Jewish, may nonetheless have been traumatized by it. Often neither the woman nor her therapist recognizes the trauma. Weiner presents a case study to demonstrate the need for therapists to listen to all women with a filter that sifts through each woman's pain and gleans the part that has resulted from the hidden, societally transmitted Holocaust trauma.

This final section helps to illuminate the inherent contradictions women face being Jewish in the non-Jewish world and being feminists within Judaism. The papers in this section present these contradictions from a personal perspective, a political perspective and a therapeutic perspective. They challenge Jewish feminists to rethink their positions on a number of issues. Together these papers are a call for further analysis of the socio-political-psychological reality of being a Jewish feminist. This section gives the reader a taste of the possibilities of topics to be explored and hopefully will stimulate further thinking and discussion in areas that affect large groups of people.

The fifteen authors in this book are affiliated with all the major designations of Jewish religiosity: Orthodox, Conservative, Reform, Reconstructionist and Jewish Renewal. Some have no religious affiliation and clearly identify themselves as secular Jews. Their life experiences and lifestyles encompass a broad range: differing class backgrounds, ages, physical abilities and sexual orientations. The diversity of the authors is a direct reflection of the diversity within the Jewish community and that diversity is represented in this book. For example, some authors use Yiddish words while others use Hebrew. We retain individual preferences as much as possible in each manuscript, such as the exclusive use of lower case letters by tova and the journal writing style of Horowitz. In the use and spelling of non-English words we allowed for each author's preference in spelling. The first time the author uses a non-English word in her paper that word is italicized and defined. Subsequent uses of the word are italicized only. In addition, all the non-English words used in the papers are defined in a common glossary.

This book furthers the process of Jewish women reclaiming our voices and making our individual and collective realities heard within the male dominated field of psychological theory and practice. We must now do the difficult work needed to maintain the relationship between Judaism, feminism and psychology. It is essential we continue to look at painful issues in Jewish homes such as incest, violence and substance abuse, as well as controversial issues of Jewish practice such as circumcision and Jewish divorce. There must be additional research and writing about the psychological effects of being a woman within the patriarchal structure of Judaism. It is critical to maintain connection between Jewish women, in all of our diversity, in order to address the issues that have damaged us. It is only as Jewish feminists that we can expand the boundaries of psychology to include us all.

JUDAISM, FEMINISM AND PSYCHOLOGY: MAKING THE LINKS VISIBLE

EVELYN TORTON BECK

We only see what we look at
To look is an act of choice.
John Berger

You hear me speak
But do you hear me feel*?*
Gertrud Kolmar

The links between Judaism, feminism and psychology do not need to be manufactured: they are already there. Yet, all too often, they have been either ignored or trivialized, even by Jews. It has become the chosen task of Jewish feminists to make these links known to ourselves and visible to others.

Because Jews constitute about 2% of the world's population and less than 3% of the United States, Jewish women represent only a small minority that is itself far from homogeneous or monolithic. Jewish women are both "one and many", and it is context, above all, that determines how "one" and how "many" at any given moment. It therefore seems appropriate to consider the contexts in which we must work together as Jewish women in all of our diversity, toward an integration of feminist perspectives with the spectrum of psychological theories and practices.

In some ways it feels as if I have been on the road to this moment for a very long time. The journey to here began on the day of my birth in January, 1933. It is true that if Hitler had not invaded Austria in 1938, if my father had not been arrested and sent to Dachau and Buchenwald, if he had not been released a year later, if my small nuclear family had not managed to escape from Vienna—first to Italy and finally (in 1940) to the safety of the United States—if none of this had happened, my path might not have led me here. I might not have spent my life coming to voice as a woman, a lesbian, and a Jew, categories that still carry meaning, both in theory and in everyday life.

I hear in the rhythms of this paper the cadence of a kind of reverse *dayenu*: not as we say on Passover, "if only this, it would have been enough," but, "if not this, if not this, if not that." My fate, like that of many Jews, was both completely chance and also overdetermined.

I might also not be writing this today if I had not (after twenty years of a heterosexual marriage) come out as a lesbian in the 1970's within a welcoming feminist and lesbian liberation movement that refused in those years to recognize its own complicity in perpetuating anti-Semitism by acts of commission and omission which have since been documented (Beck, 1982/1989, 1988). Finally, I would not be writing in this way if I had not engaged in a long, arduous and ultimately liberating therapy process with a guide who could tolerate the ambiguities, contradictions and pain. With her I could finally, after fifty years, face the shame associated with being marked for annihilation, and the shame of the sexual and psychological abuse from within the very same nuclear family that saved me from the Holocaust. If none of this had happened, I might really not be here today.

I tell my life story in its specificity, not because I am an anomaly, but because I believe that in my story each Jewish woman can find a piece of herself. I do not see myself as separated or separate, but integrated within myself and connected to all Jewish women.

I feel more whole and safe at a gathering of Jewish women than I do anywhere in the world. By this I do not mean to suggest that we are all necessarily going to agree—far from it, *khas v khulile* (God forbid) but there is so much that I will not have to explain. That freedom from explanation, at least about Jewish issues, is a palpable lightening: it makes light our load, it lights the way, and it is a lightning rod for change. I have mentioned my own process of therapy, not only because I feel safe to do so in the context of other Jewish feminists, but because the complex layerings of this work have helped me to fathom on a deeper, more visceral level what the philosopher Polanyi called "tacit knowing", knowing beyond words, knowing in and through the body (1958/1962). I am not simply talking about the importance of putting together Judaism, feminism and psychology, but the necessity of so doing, not for the sake of theory, but for ourselves and for our clients.

Why necessary? To the extent that Jewish identity is not theorized in the psychological literature, nor brought to consciousness in clinical practice, nor taken into account in research projects (especially those who unthinkingly equate Jewish identity with white Christian identity as if there were no psychological differences, as if the long history of anti-Semitism did not exist), to that extent will therapeutic opportunities be lost. For example, this past year I heard a case presentation of a young professional woman from a large Eastern city, in her early thirties, who had, over six or seven years of ongoing psychodynamic psychotherapy, been experiencing serious difficulties figuring out who she was, what she was capable of, and how she could form an intimate bond with a man. Many details of the client's family history were presented, including the highly significant comment that her mother had made on learning that her daughter was in therapy—"You would benefit more from a nose job!" In the course of the presentation, this remark was neither interpreted nor commented upon, but my antennae went up. Nose job? Who has nose jobs? Is this young woman a Jew? If so, how does it matter? The presenter continued: Her client had expressed the desire to go with her father to Ellis Island to celebrate his birthday. He at first refused, and then finally agreed to go. Immediately, my antennae were up again: Ellis Island? Was she searching for her roots? Her *Jewish* immigrant roots? The presenter said nothing about this possibility.

Finally, during the question period, I had the opportunity to ask the question that had been nagging at me: "*Was* the client Jewish, and if so, was her Jewishness an issue?" Sure enough, it was. The woman had in fact been working on her anger toward the family's superficial relationship (bordering on denial) to their Jewish heritage. She was figuring out what it meant to be a *Jewish* woman, and in the process was turning toward religious observance. While I was gratified to be such a "good reader" of the text of this case, I was also horrified that had I not raised the question, the client's Jewishness would very likely have gone unnamed. As Audre Lorde (1984) reminds us, "The unspoken soon becomes the unspeakable." More to the point, in this case I was worried about the therapy process itself. Was this therapist capable of working with difficult Jewish identity issues, and could she recognize their importance? How far could this young woman go with this therapist, who had not bothered to name so significant a factor about her client in making this detailed presentation? I have often observed in discussions of other cases, that whether a client is or is not Jewish is often not even known with any certainty by the therapist, as if Jewish identity carried no real significance and had no bearing on the therapy process, or the developing relationship with the therapist.

In the case described above, the therapist was herself probably not a Jew, but the same thing could well have happened if she had been. I have seen it happen. Jews are not exempt from forgetting ourselves. Our ignorance, discomforts, and unworked-through places can seriously limit the therapeutic process. What we do not see or consider important for ourselves (or do not recognize in others), we will never see as important in our clients who are, of course, the ones who ultimately pay for the slippage.

In the swiftly growing body of multicultural psychology, Jews are often omitted. In one widely cited text, typical of many others, Sue and Sue's *Counseling the Culturally Different* (1990), the authors' definition of "difference" includes only the four groups of "people of color" within the United States: in their own words, and their ordering: "American Indians, Asian Americans, Black Americans, Hispanic Americans." Even though most *Ashkenazi* Jews (Jews of European origin) are "whitish" in skin color, many are actually darker than light-skinned Blacks or Hispanics. I would like the real reasons why Jewish Americans are excluded from the discussion to emerge. Aren't Jews "different" enough? Or doesn't our difference matter? (Schlossberg, 1989; Beck, 1991b and forthcoming). Jews are still a minority, still an ethnic (and also religious) group subject to anti-Semitism and still misrepresented and oppressed by the myths and stereotypes of the dominant Christian culture.

Two recent examples point out the seriousness of anti-Semitism in multicultural psychology. The first episode occurred at a small seminar on multicultural issues in psychology in which experts in this field were offering case presentations of working with diverse cultural groups. We had been addressing the need for the therapist to be especially attentive to the reticence of recent Latin American immigrants to speak about their war experiences, and I had compared this phenomenon with the reticence of Holocaust survivors (and even their children born after the war) to talk about their traumas and concentration camp experiences. Up to this point, no professionals had been identified by any ethnic or racial descriptors. Immediately following my observation, the case presenter remarked, with a good deal of angry affect, that the only doctor who had not returned her many calls when she needed him desperately, was the *Jewish* psychiatrist, an epithet she repeated several times, smiling oddly and looking directly at me as she spoke.

Since this was a small group sitting around a seminar table, the gesture toward me was quite unmistakable. I was highly unsettled by her remark and tuned her out momentarily while trying to figure out how to respond—she was, after all, a guest—when I heard her continue, "And there were so many Jewish psychiatrists in the hospital, I thought I had better change my name [it was Fong]. I'd better call myself 'Fongowitz' or 'Fongstein' or 'Fongberg' just for self-protection." At that point, I was impelled to speak. My response was surprisingly calm and measured as I called attention to what had just happened, though I did choke up a little. After I spoke, she seemed surprised that I had taken offense at her "joke." Her defense was an embarrassingly blatant cliché. She actually said, "But some of my best friends are Jews, my neighbors, have been for 18 years."

When it became clear to me that I could not get through to her, I gave up trying, but some of my colleagues pursued the matter and pointed out the significance of her inconsistency in naming. If they had not come to my support, I think I would have walked out and possibly not continued in the group since I was the only Jew in it. Perhaps it was fortunate that I had just the evening before made a presentation to this very group (before the guests arrived) on the necessity of including Jews in the multicultural psychology curriculum. This incident was a perfect illustration of my point that Jews often feel safer when Jewish material is *not* brought up, because to do so often evokes anti-Semitism.

The second episode concerned a decision made not to include Jews on a reading list for the newly developing area of multicultural psychology at the institute where I am training. Determined to be proactive, I had contacted the faculty member while she was still in the process of putting together this bibliography, alerting her to the significance of anti-Semitism and urging her to include Jews as part of this knowledge area. In response to my urging, she sent me a letter with the draft copy of the bibliography, saying that she regretfully had decided not to include Jews "after much agonized thinking," though she did think that we "probably did belong." I noticed, with pained irony, that there was a long section on homosexuality which did not include either *Nice Jewish Girls* (1982/1989) or *Twice Blessed* (1989), the only two texts that focus entirely on lesbian and gay Jews. After my initial shock (which was greater because this is a woman known for her integrity and support of oppressed peoples), my next response was: why the "agony?" What made it so difficult to include Jews? Does the inclusion of Jews harm others? Does it discredit the person who includes us? And if so, why? And in making this decision, whose agony really matters? To be fair to my correspondent, she did invite me to prepare a bibliography which might be added to the study guide at a later time, but that did not explain why she felt obliged to leave Jews out even after our discussion. What if I were not studying at this institute? Who is responsible for doing the work? Was the exclusion really due only to lack of information? That would hardly be cause for agony. That would only require the kind of homework anyone would expect to have to do when they are embarking on the project of multicultural psychology.

At an earlier period of my life I believe I would have felt defeated, perhaps even ashamed, and would have stopped at this point. Now I felt strong enough not to let the matter go. In some ways I felt as if I were once again fighting for my life. I responded by expressing my disappointment, and sent her copies of my written work on the subject (Beck 1982/1989, 1988, 1991a, 1991b). I am happy to report that she not only responded by "implementing inclusion", but also apologized for her initial insensitivity. The knowledge that it is sometimes possible to move people to new understandings and actions fuels what often feels like my continuing battle.

While these incidents may appear to be minor to some, and others may use the fact that I am a child survivor to suggest that I overreacted to these episodes, I doubt that I am an anomaly. I believe that many (perhaps most) second and third generation post-Holocaust Jews (and also some non-Jews) would have been as hurt, angry and discouraged as I was by these incidents.

Yet in spite of these recent events, I feel hopeful. It is out of this sense of hope that I attempt to close the triangle: Judaism, feminism, psychology. When I heard myself thinking, "triangle" in this context, I became especially nervous. Are the three elements I named in a triangulated relationship with each other? Is that why there is so much resistance to bringing them together? The more I pondered the image of the triangle, the less I liked what I was thinking, the more forcefully the thought persisted. Finally, I developed the following associations among the three points:

1. Feminist challenges to patriarchal Jewish institutions have had a powerful impact and have resulted in feminist transformations of Jewish religious and cultural practices. Women are more vocal and more visible in Jewish life than ever before.

2. Feminist challenges to patriarchally-dominated psychology have been powerful and have been similarly effective. Women are more vocal and more visible in the field of psychology than ever before. Our numbers are growing in the field in general so that some are actually alarmed by what they view as the "feminization of psychology."

3. According to absolute numbers in the population, psychology has a disproportionate number of Jews as theorists and practitioners, especially in psychoanalysis, psychodynamic psychotherapy and group psychotherapy. The latter didn't surprise me much, once I learned that the main function of a group is to maintain itself. Jews are highly visible in the field of psychology, but are not necessarily named as Jews or concerned with Jewish issues, except the effects of the Holocaust. We could speculate as to why that is the one Jewish issue singled out. Is it possible that it is less threatening in the "here and now" to focus on dead Jews?

4. The fields of psychology named above developed in a climate of virulent, open anti-Semitism which marked the period in which Freud lived, studied and worked in Vienna. Freud was first called a pervert because of his unorthodox ideas, and was ultimately forced to flee Vienna because he was a Jew.

Freud's Jewish identity has been a source of anti-Jewish attack even in the contemporary period. Thomas Szasz, in *The Myth of Psychotherapy*, a book that was published in 1978, reprinted in 1988, and still quite widely read, includes a chapter ominously entitled, Sigmund Freud: The Jewish Avenger, in which Szasz attacks Freud as "a proud and vengeful Jew who developed the fields of psychiatry and psychoanalysis as revenge against anti-Semites." Szasz cites as proof of Freud's malicious intent, the contradiction between Freud's rejection of Judaism as a religion, and his "profound commitment to Jewishness from which he drew strength, in spite of his alleged repudiation of religious belief." Szasz cites Freud's attachment to Jews as his proof of his "anti-Gentilism." This attack rests on Freud's "love of Yiddish and Hebrew, his sympathy for Zionism and respect for Herzl, his interest in Moses, his joining *B'nai Brith* [a Jewish fraternal society], his sending greetings to his family when he was away from home on the high holidays." Szasz clearly fails to understand the interrelationship of Jewish religious practices, Jewish culture and Jewish identity issues. Moreover, it seems obvious that Freud's minimal expressions of secular Jewish identity make him much too much of a Jew for Szasz's comfort.

It would be easy to write off Szasz's attack as the irresponsible words of a fringe thinker, but Szasz is not alone in the field of psychology. If his words did not resonate, they would not be taken seriously. There are other such anti-Jewish voices, as for example the highly respected work of psychoanalyst M. Masud R. Khan, whose deep hatred of Jews and gays is blatantly manifest in a case he describes in *The Long Wait* (1989), a book in which Khan claims to be more candid than he had ever been before. Khan had at first refused to treat Luis, who correctly sensed Khan's disdain for Jews, but Luis nonetheless pleaded for his help. Although Khan became increasingly provocative in the years of his last illness, this can hardly serve as a credible excuse for the abuse he heaps on his patient. For example, Khan states, "One more personal remark about me, my wife, my staff or my things, and I will throw you out, *you accursed nobody Jew.* Find your own people then. Shoals of them drift around, just like you. *Yes, I am anti-Semitic. You know why Mr. Luis? Because I am an Aryan and had thought all of you Jews had perished when Jesus, from sheer dismay—and he was one of you—had flown up to Heaven, leaving you in the scorching care of Hitler, Himmler and the crematoriums.* Don't fret, Mr. Luis; like the rest of your *species*, you will survive and continue to harass others, and lament, and bewail yourselves. Remarkable how Yiddish/ Jewish you are" (p. 92-93). (emphasis mine)

Luis' non-Jewish lover Dave is described by Khan as being, "Like me [Khan], everything Mr. Luis was not" (p. 93). To my knowledge, this blatant self-revelation of Jew-hating has in no way diminished Khan's stature in the field nor led to a questioning of any aspect of his work.

In fact, Szasz, Khan and others speak in exaggerated form what many in the field may say only to themselves, which is one reason that there is silence from so many, including Jews. Szasz and Khan expose feelings about Jews and psychology that are alive today as witnessed in the encounter I described previously. No wonder many Jews walk around with a subliminal fear of anti-Semitism the way many women walk around with a subliminal fear of rape. No wonder so many Jewish psychologists do not want to be visibly Jewish in the field of psychology. To be visible as a woman, a feminist, *and* a Jew makes you multiply vulnerable to attack on those counts. No wonder major Jewish theorists are stripped of their Jewishness in histories of psychology. No wonder we have had difficulty in putting together the three points of the triangle: feminism, Judaism and psychology.

Given this dilemma, could it be that Jewish psychologists have somehow been complicit in making Jewish themes unspeakable in psychology? Is this a form of self-protection? How outside the institutions are we willing to be? While there has been wide support from the women's liberation movement for feminist correctives to psychology and to Judaism, where is the support for a Jewish visibility that also concerns itself with Jewish issues? Do we have the strength to take on multiple disloyalties to those very institutions which helped make us who we are? Can we convince ourselves and others to keep bringing up the connections in our separate spheres and in institutions where we are sometimes really alone as Jews?

Let me not paint an entirely bleak picture. There are some theorists, practitioners and resources in psychology that do take Jewish voices into account. I am thinking, for example, of the wide inclusivity of Monica McGoldrick's *Ethnicity and Family Therapy* (1982), one of the few anthologies focusing on ethnicity that does include a useful essay on Jewish families (Herz and Rosen). Theirs is a thoughtful overview of the characteristics of *Ashkenazi* Jews, mostly middle class, and all heterosexual, it would seem from the discussion. What I find especially useful about this book is that McGoldrick correctly recognizes that any extrapolation about ethnicities could itself lead to new forms of stereotyping. Her introduction acknowledges that *Ashkenazi* Jews themselves are not a monolithic group, but the chapter on *(Ashkenazi)* Jewish families nonetheless provides a useful template which allows both Jews and non-Jews to think about specific ways in which being an *Ashkenazi* Jew might enter the therapy room.

Herz and Rosen in McGoldrick provide a long list of possible factors to consider when working with Jewish families. If we were to discuss each of these one by one, it is quite possible, even likely, that we would not agree with all of them as they are listed, but these are not intended to be characteristic of every *Ashkenazi* family. These represent a composite portrait whose details inform *Ashkenazi* Jewish families differently. To summarize their thinking, I will briefly mention a few of the characteristics that Herz and Rosen discuss. One of the primary markings they cite is the centrality of family and loyalty to the family of origin, to the structure of Jewish life.

When I first read Herz and Rosen's essay, their words immediately resonated and helped me to understand what had always been a puzzling episode in my own life. Years after I had separated from my husband, my father continued to be disturbed about my divorce. When, to reassure him, I said, "Poppa, do not worry, I am so happy now. I have never been happier in my life!" He looked me straight in the eye and, with angry passion, said without smiling, "Happiness? What's that? Family is what matters!" At the time I was quite horrified at his way of thinking, and was able to make sense of it only if I understood it as part of his pathology, but Herz and Rosen provide a frame which contextualizes his value system within Eastern European Jewish norms.

Another example concerns the deep resentment often shown by Jewish families when a sibling or other close relative does not attend a *bar/bat mitzvah* (coming of age ritual) or wedding, no matter what the circumstances are. Siblings have been known not to talk to each other for years because of such perceived slights. If the therapist does not know that this response is deeply embedded in Jewish culture, she might very well interpret it as pure pathology. It may well be, but if so, it is also part of a socially shared pathology. If this is the case, how can we use such knowledge most constructively? In the light of the value system in which such events occur, their interpretation has to be contextualized and perhaps modified.

Another extremely significant issue which I had not thought about as pertaining to my family, although we were refugees, is the centrality of suffering within Jewish families and the way that suffering is used as a means of creating bonds among Jews. Related to this is the centrality of the *Shoah* (Holocaust) for post-Holocaust Jews. Even Jewish psychologists may not fully appreciate the meanings of the Holocaust and its repercussions, not only to families who lived through it, but to Jews who did not experience its events themselves (though most American families lost some family members). The Holocaust has transformed what it means to be a Jew, no matter how old or young one is. The individual and collective psychic pain being caused by the Holocaust denial movement has yet to be tallied (Lipstadt, 1993; Hammer, this volume).

Possibly related to the high incidence of public catastrophe in the history of Jewish life is the high incidence of hypochondria among Jews, another factor I always thought was peculiar to my own family. It never occurred to me in the years following our immigration, that my own panic attacks, my father's false alarms of heart failure, my mother's depressions, and their frequent out-of-control rages might have anything to do with his concentration camp experiences or the murder of her mother (and other relatives) in Auschwitz. In retrospect it seems clear that my parents, and probably our entire family, were suffering from undiagnosed post-traumatic stress disorder. Reading Herz and Rosen's chapter helped me put these behaviors into better perspective.

Another important observation is the paradox of Jews' reliance on and belief in "experts" (especially doctors), accompanied by deep suspicion and disbelief. Other characteristics are: the centrality of intellectual achievement, the high value placed on education, and the importance of financial success (*parnosse*, the old country imperative to "make a living") which could also help Jews escape persecution of all kinds. Related to the focus on education is the centrality of verbal expression. Jews are not only the "People of the Book", but also an oral people who relish the spoken word; among Jewish men we find the historical tradition of public argumentation which in modern times is also shared by Jewish women. As a result, I have a difficult time with people who do not speak much, and I know that when I work with clients whose cultures are different from my own, I have to figure out what their silence means to them in their context. This is, of course, a characteristic of all good therapy, but it takes on added significance across cultural differences.

I also tend to be disturbed when people do not look me in the eye when speaking to me; but there are cultures, for example some Asian and Asian-American groups and African-Americans from the rural South, in which it is considered impolite for a young person to look an elder directly in the eye or to initiate conversation. So we have to take special care to understand what is and is not our own. While some surface aspects of Jewish culture (such as foods and concepts like *chutzpah* (gutsy, courageous)) have permeated American society, therapists should take responsibility for a deeper familiarity with the spectrum of Jewish customs and values which can become critical when working with Jewish clients.

In this connection it is essential to highlight the effects of stereotyping and internalized anti-Semitism. The ridicule heaped on the "Jewish mother" (whose worries are, in fact, typical of all immigrant mothers), or the viciousness of the more recent misogyny and anti-Semitism that lead to the typing of the "Jewish American Princess" as "J.A.P." (Beck, 1991; Siegel, 1986) must be understood in its contemporary context. The stereotype that associates Jews and money is historically one of the most persistent, and it has resurfaced with particular force in the past two decades as a direct result of the legacy of Bush/Reagan policies. The increasing disparity between rich and poor has led to serious class antagonism in which Jews are once again singled out as scapegoats for those at the very top of the economic ladder (most of whom are *not* Jews, although as a group Jews have moved solidly into the middle-class).

These prejudicial ways of thinking have ramifications in our practice. I have noted in the recent group therapy literature that some psychologists (Gans, 1992) argue that money and issues of non-payment must become a subject of discussion within the therapy group, not punitively, but as an appropriate part of the group process which includes the therapist's fees. While I can understand this argument, I wonder how the subject of money might affect Jews differently as therapists and/or as clients. How might the question of money color the interaction when the therapist is Jewish and the client is not? Or vice-versa? Is it possible that the issue might have a different meaning to a Jew? Or to a non-Jew in the presence of a Jew?

To make theory concrete, I will give an example, not from therapy, but from my work as director of a Women's Studies program. When, at a meeting of administrators, the dean acknowledged my fundraising skills, I was at first proud, but almost simultaneously my heart sank when I realized that in the course of my tenure at the university I had made myself very visible as a Jew. Pride quickly turned to fear as I began to worry that my colleagues would associate me (and Women's Studies) with Jews and money in the old stereotyped way. Another example in this vein concerns the demographics of the Women's

Studies Program: we are seven core faculty of whom five identify as heterosexual, three as women of color, three as Jews, and two as lesbians. The word around the university is that there are too many Jews in Women's Studies. Clearly the three Jews are visible in a very particular way, while the "over-representation" of lesbians runs a close second.

The centrality of food in Jewish culture (including its meaning in communal rituals like the Passover *seder*) is fairly widely known. Equally known is women's complicated relationship to food and body image, yet little attention has been given to the ways in which Jewish ethnicity complicates the issue of food for women. I doubt that the Jewish dimension is given serious attention even in discussions of eating disorders; clearly, such a focusing is long overdue. In a similar vein, I note the absence of theorizing about Jewish women's sexuality in the many current discussions of the meanings of race and ethnicity for women's sexual development. Nor is the impact of the Jewish family on Jewish women's sexuality taken into account. The meaning of Jewish themes should also be kept in mind when working with non-Jewish clients; anti-Semitism, as well as its opposite, philo-Semitism, can find their way into the psychic economy of non-Jews in powerful and surprisingly significant ways.

This brief summary does not nearly exhaust the issues, nor does it take into account the lives of Jews in different parts of the world whose circumstances will affect the meanings of Jewish identity differently. Most *Ashkenazi* Jews in the United States (and here I do not exempt myself) know very little about Jews of color and *Sephardic* Jews (Jews of Spanish origin) the world over, or the effects of intermarriage across lines of ethnicity and religion (Kaye/Kantrowitz & Klepfisz 1989; Krakauer, 1991). Incorporating such sensitivities into the framework of hypotheses as we work with clients will bring us closer to creating a Jewish feminist psychology and a feminist psychology of Jewish women.

It is too soon to say where such inquiries will lead us. Anthologies like Siegel and Cole's *Jewish Women in Therapy* (1991) as well as the writings of many others have made a start. Our task is to figure out how the Jewish dimensions of our lives influence us in ways that are similar or different, depending on our location in time, space, geography, social class, age, sexuality, dis/ability and other differences among us. We must learn to talk about a unified concept without obliterating the very real differences among us as women and as Jews.

Perhaps if we create a series of Jewish feminist psychologies, the way we now speak of feminisms, we may be on more sound and safe ground. In this process of creation there are no unambiguous answers, only the continual process of paying close attention to details, and a willingness to work with contradictions without trying to reconcile or flatten them out. It is a process without an end. For those who are even minimally consciously Jews, by birth or by choice, culturally or religiously, there is no turning back. (This parallels women's coming to consciousness as women in the late 1960's and early 70's.) It is easier to divorce a spouse than to divorce yourself from your people. As Lee Knefelkamp (1989) has formulated so well, "If you make yourself dead to your past, you make yourself dead to the future" (p.92). We owe it to ourselves, our history, and to our Jewish clients not to forget to keep Jewish identity issues alive in all their complexity.

The following quotation is taken from a poem by Muriel Rukeyser (1913-1980), a life-long social activist Jew who near the end of her life also acknowledged her lesbian identity. "Letter to the Front" was written in 1944, near the end of World War II, during the Jews' darkest hours in Europe. In making visible the links between Judaism, feminism and psychology, these words serve as a reminder, a meditation, a challenge, and an offer of hope:

To be a Jew in the twentieth century
Is to be offered a gift. If you refuse,
Wishing to be invisible, you choose
Death of the spirit, the stone insanity.
Accepting, take full life. Full agonies:
Your evening deep in labyrinthine blood
Of those who resist, fail, and resist; and God
Reduced to a hostage among hostages.

The gift is torment. Not alone the still
Torture, isolation; or torture of the flesh.
That may come also. But the accepting wish,
The whole and fertile spirit as guarantee.
For every human freedom, suffering to be free,
Daring to live for the impossible (p. 239).

REFERENCES

Balka, C., & Rose, A. (1989). (Eds.). *Twice blessed: On being lesbian or gay and Jewish.* Boston: Beacon Press.

Beck, E. T. (Ed.). (1989). *Nice Jewish girls: A lesbian anthology.* (Rev. ed.). Boston: Beacon Press.

Beck, E. T. (1988). The politics of Jewish invisibility. *National Women's Study Association Journal, 1*(1), 93-102. Also anthologized in Beck, E.T. (1991). The politics of Jewish invisibility in women's studies. In J.E. Butler & J.C. Walker (Eds.), *Transforming the curriculum: Ethnic studies and women's studies.* (pp. 187-330). Albany: The State University of New York.

Beck, E. T. (1991a). Therapy's double dilemma: Anti-Semitism and misogyny. In R. Siegel & E. Cole (Eds.), *Jewish women and therapy: Seen but not heard.* New York: Haworth Press.

Beck, E. T. (1991b). Multiculturalism in the university and beyond: How "multi?" whose "cultures?" and why? *Carrying it on: A national conference organizing against anti-Semitism and racism for Jewish activists and college students.* Philadelphia: New Jewish Agenda.

Beck, E. T. (in preparation). The Jewish stake in the multicultural agenda. *Proceedings of the First National Conference of Anti-Defamation League.* Anti-Defamation League: Los Angeles.

Berger, J. (1972). *Ways of seeing.* London: British Broadcasting System, Penguin Books.

Gans, J. S. (1992). Money and psychodynamic group psychotherapy. *International Journal of Group Psychotherapy, 42*(1), 133-152.

Hammer, B. (1995). Anti-Semitism as trauma: A theory of Jewish communal trauma response. In K. Weiner & A. Moon (Eds.), *Jewish women speak out: Expanding the boundaries of psychology.*

Herz, F. M. & Rosen, E. J. (1982). Jewish Families. In M. McGoldrick, J.K. Pearce, & J. Giordano (Eds.), *Ethnicity and family therapy.* (pp. 364-392). New York: Guildford Press.

Kaye/Kantrowitz, M. & Klepfisz, I. (Eds.). (1989). *Tribe of Dina: A Jewish women's anthology.* Boston: Beacon Press.

Khan, M. M. R. (1989). A dismaying homosexual. In *The long wait and other psychoanalytic narratives.* (pp. 87-116). New York: Summit Books.

Klein, D. B. (1981). *Jewish origins of the psychoanalytic movement.* Chicago: University of Chicago Press.

Knefelkamp, L. L. (1989). Living in the in-between. In *Nice Jewish girls: A lesbian anthology.* (pp. 91-99). Boston: Beacon Press.

Kolmar, G. (1975). *Dark soliloquy: Selected poems.* New York: Seabury Press.

Krakauer, H. Y. L. (1991). *Lilith: The Jewish women's magazine, 16*(4), 5.

Lipstadt, D. (1993). *The growing assault on truth and memory.* New York: Free Press.

Lorde, A. (1984). *Sister/outsider: Essays and speeches.* Trumansburg, N.Y.: Crossing Press.

Luepenitz, D. A. (1988). *The family interpreted: Feminist theory in clinical practice.* New York: Basic Books.

McGoldrick, M., Anderson, C.M., & Walsh, F. (Eds.). (1989). Women and ethnicity. In *Women in families: A framework for family therapy.* New York: W.W. Norton & Co.

Polanyi, M. (1958/1962). *Personal knowledge.* Chicago: University of Chicago Press.

Rukeyser, M. (1982). *The collected poems of Muriel Rukeyser.* New York: McGraw Hill.

Schlossberg, N. (1989). Marginality and mattering: Key issues in building community. *New Directions for Student Services, 48.* San Francisco: Jossey-Bass.

Siegel, R. J. (1986). Anti-Semitism and sexism in stereotypes of Jewish women. *Women and Therapy, 5*(2/3), 249-257.

Siegel, R. J. (1995). *Jewish women's bodies: Sexuality, body image and self-esteem.* In K. Weiner & A. Moon (Eds.), *Jewish women speak out: Expanding the boundaries of psychology.*

Sue, D. W., & Sue, D. (1990). *Counseling the culturally different.* New York: Wiley.

Szasz, T. (1979/1988). Sigmund Freud: The Jewish avenger. In *The myth of psychotherapy.* Syracuse, N.Y.: Syracuse University Press.

IDENTITY DEVELOPMENT

Deborah A. Engelen-Eigles
Rachel Josefowitz Siegel
Nora Gold

DIFFICULT QUESTIONS: UNDERSTANDING HOW JEWISH WOMEN CONSTRUCT THEIR IDENTITIES

DEBORAH A. ENGELEN-EIGLES

INTRODUCTION

What does "being Jewish" mean to women who identify as such? Is this aspect of "self" woven into the fabric of daily life, and if so, in what ways? How does it shape, and how is it shaped by, women's experiences and ideals? This paper is an initial effort to understand these issues.

Much social science research on Jewish "identification" in the United States has taken a broad demographic approach or concentrated on Jews as an ethnic/immigrant group in the larger society. Using primarily survey research techniques (e.g., Cohen, Woocher, & Phillips, 1984; Mayer & Sheingold, 1979), "commitment" to a Jewish identity has been measured by such indicators as synagogue membership, presence of Jewish ritual objects, books and posters in the home, and rates of intermarriage.

This work is often founded on the assumptions of the assimilation paradigm. This paradigm takes the *shtetl* culture of the immigrant generation, the 19th century Jewish communities of the Eastern European Pale of Settlement, as a baseline against which to measure contemporary Jewish American practice and identification. On this basis,

American Jews are usually found to be "less" Jewish with each successive generation and their commitment waning.

This approach tends to ignore the ways that the *shtetl* culture itself was not a single uniform culture, but many. It disregards the ways that many diaspora communities, not only 20th century American Jewry, have changed in response to the particular cultural and social contexts in which they existed across the centuries. This body of work tends not to focus on the meanings of Jewish identity, symbols and practices to individual Jewish women. As such, it is often limited in allowing new dimensions of Jewish identity to emerge. It inhibits the ability to gain insight into the different and changing ways individuals understand their identities as Jews (e.g., Cohen, 1988).

The makeup and place of Jews as a group within the larger society are useful background for understanding the context in which individuals' experiences unfold. The characteristics of the group, however, cannot necessarily be attributed to any given person. Focusing on the meaning of any individual woman's Jewish identity may help her to understand her relationship to the community in a relevant and meaningful way.

Qualitative, in-depth interviews can provide insight into meaning and identity since participants relate experiences in their own words. The following narratives, examined in the social and historical context in which the speakers' lives unfold, offer an alternative to measurement against a *shtetl* culture baseline and its limitations.

Nine *Ashkenazi* Jewish American women from each of three families in the Minneapolis/St. Paul metropolitan area participated in this study. Three generations in each family were represented: maternal grandmother, mother and daughter. I conducted qualitative, in-depth interviews individually with each woman, meeting with her twice for about an hour each time. With her permission, I taped the interviews.

I analyzed the women's narratives by listening to the interview tapes multiple times, each time noting themes and issues each woman raised and listening for what I might not have heard before. I decided not to transcribe the interviews as a response to concerns I have had in my previous work as well as those raised by other researchers. Smith (1987), for example, notes how the transcript is an inadequate representation of what transpires in the particular context of the interview. DeVault (1990) stresses the importance of pauses, verbal "crutches" and repetitions as indicators of concepts that are difficult for the narrator to express, for lack of language appropriate to her experiences. Added to these are my particular concerns for the meaning embedded in the speaker's intonation and rhythm, differences in narrative styles that may be harder to discern when the speech is rendered in print form (see also Riessman 1987 on culture and different narrative styles), and the contextual nature of particular statements made within a specific narrative sequence. These cues often disappear in a print rendition, making it easy to unintentionally isolate and extract particular ideas from their context.

DISCUSSION

The women's narratives focus on Jewish identity, meaning and experience. In discussing these below, particular attention is paid to constraints and opportunities specific to the 20th century United States and how, in this context, Jewish women construct identity in their daily lives. The names I use to refer to each speaker are pseudonyms.

Jewishness, ideals and experience

In the United States, synagogue affiliation is often considered an important indicator of personal commitment to a Jewish identity as well as commitment to and involvement in the larger Jewish community. Furthermore, the denomination of the group to which one belongs may also be taken as a shorthand description of one's "level" of ritual observance. In trying to map identity in relation to the organized or formal Jewish community, synagogue affiliation may seem like a useful starting point. This can appear to be a relatively unproblematic category from which to orient an understanding of Jewish American women's identities: it might be assumed that an individual identifies most with the community of which she is a part (or has chosen to become a part of the community with which she identifies most). As in the following case, however, knowing that Marsha belongs to a Reform synagogue is not enough.

Marsha, a homemaker, has three adult children, two sons and one daughter, now living on their own. Growing up, her parents' household was Orthodox, though her mother now considers herself a Conservative Jew. Unlike her mother, Marsha does not follow the Jewish dietary laws. She describes the decision she made about synagogue affiliation early in her marriage:

> I chose to join a Reform synagogue with [my husband] because that's where he was most comfortable. And I thought as a father someday, I want him to be a very good role model for our children, and I don't have to twist his arm to get him to go to synagogue or to enjoy his time there and praying and so forth and his Jewishness, so perhaps we're better off to go to a Reform [synagogue] where he's comfortable and can understand things. And so I sacrificed that, and I was never happy there. So what I did was on the second day of the holidays, I went to a Conservative synagogue so that I had the feeling that I had prayed, if I wanted to, which I never felt in the Reform synagogue.

With her own sense of Jewishness as a starting point, Marsha tried to actively create an environment in which she could share and pass on that identity to her future children; this involved the participation of her husband as father and role model. What was a given for her (going to synagogue, enjoying her time there, praying) was not a given for her husband. By choosing a setting in which he was most at home, Marsha thought she had the best chance of enlisting his participation and creating the atmosphere she envisioned would foster a sense of Jewishness in her children. Ironically, this compromise interfered with her own experience of being Jewish, the original impetus that led her to choose a Reform congregation.

Marsha's description of how she chose to affiliate with a Reform synagogue and how she felt about her subsequent participation there is integral to interpreting a seemingly straightforward piece of information like synagogue membership. Knowledge of her affiliation with a Reform synagogue alone reflects neither the community she most identifies with, her ideals regarding raising Jewish children, nor the estrangement she feels in the Reform congregation.

The role of experience in shaping identity can be far reaching. Introspective self-evaluation, memories and unconscious emotions that are difficult to articulate, and multiple, competing feelings can all be tied up in one's sense of being Jewish. Tracey's experiences surrounding her *bat mitzvah* suggest how this seemingly common event, in which a child is welcomed as an adult in the Jewish community, deserves closer examination for the ways it can shape identity within both the Jewish and secular spheres.

Tracey, Marsha's daughter, is a student in her early twenties. Her family belonged to a Reform synagogue as she was growing up; she attended Saturday and Sunday school for her formal Jewish education. Tracey remembers her *bat mitzvah* as follows:

> I really screwed up! I didn't know my prayers well, and I had it all written in English phonetically, and I agreed to wear this, this outfit that was too dressy that my mom bought me, which I really regretted afterwards. I mean it really made me look young. And my aunt gave me a permanent, and, I mean, I really looked awkward. And, I had a lot of non-Jewish junior high friends there. And it was just like, why am I inviting these girls, they're my friends, but they're my sch—I mean why am I bringing them into it? Nothing seemed normal, nothing seemed normal at all. Like, gosh, I think I didn't know part of a prayer at one point and I didn't know what to do so I started giggling, and that was, you know, I felt like I was in way over my head, like I went about it totally prematurely. Like, because I am this age, that this ceremony happens, does not mean that I'm in mind or that I understand it...it was really an occasion that set a lot of my social feelings around my relatives for the next few years...because of being on the stage and being awkward.... Sunday school didn't tell me what it was all about.

Tracey's description of her experience of, and feelings about, her *bat mitzvah* touch on issues of self-esteem and her feelings about her place in the Jewish community as well as her interactions with non-Jewish friends at school. They speak to the difficulties of negotiating identity in two communities, sometimes separate, sometimes overlapping.

Jewishness, self-concept and daily life

For many of the women, Jewish identity was part of their self-concept and woven into daily life. As such, it was the object of both change and continuity over the life course. Each woman's idea of "change" and her characterization of how meaningful or profound that change was, often evolved over the course of the discussion. The narrative of Anne, one of the women in her eighties, is an example.

Anne immigrated with her family from Russia when she was ten years old. She grew up in an Orthodox home and today continues to keep a kosher home and not ride on the Sabbath. She attends services infrequently at an Orthodox synagogue, primarily for *yizkor*, the memorial service for the dead. She describes the change in her practices over her lifetime as follows:

> I didn't change, but maybe I changed a little, too. Many years ago, we never ate out. Never. Who ever thought of eating out? Today, we eat out. I never eat meat, but I go out.... Oh, it's changed, even with me it changed a lot.... It's changed, people don't like to cook. They buy everything. Today you go into the store, you don't have to cook. They don't, if you tell 'em "Oh, you bake?" they don't believe in that.

It is hard to know from her narrative how Anne might have characterized her sentiments on a seven-point Likert scale, a common survey question format. Does her assessment of change lie closer to number one, "not changed at all", or is it nearer the other end of the scale at number seven, "changed completely"? Interpreting her response in a meaningful way, or reconstructing how she arrived at that response and what "change" meant to her, would be all the more difficult. Anne suggests that she sees change not only in terms of her own practices, but also in terms of her social environment, including the practices of people with whom she comes in contact.

Attention to change over the life course highlights another way in which constructions of identity vary. The narratives of the participants here suggest that "change" happens in differing degrees over different lengths of time, at different stages in the life course. Thus even choosing a "theoretically meaningful" point, such as marriage, may not be a useful axis around which to examine change in identity, experience, and practice. Anne's daughter, Helene, raised in an Orthodox home, gives an example:

> First few years I got married I didn't ride [on the Sabbath]. I still thought I was going to be struck down or something, you know, if I rode...but then, as the years went by, we were forced to drive.... [Also,] I started out keeping really strictly kosher, everything. And now I'm to the point where I only have one set of dishes, one set of dishtowels, but everything in my house as far as food is kosher.... Somewhere along the line, I don't know, I sort of lost that. But I don't mix meat and milk, or anything like that...I have glass dishes, and I just make that, I don't know

> why, I just all of a sudden one day I just gave up separate dishes and silverware. But my real good china, and my real good dishes, for some odd reason, I've never mixed them.

Helene's narrative suggests that change, when it comes, may be partial or full, gradual or sudden. Though she mentions marriage as a marker of time in reference to the changes, she is clear that riding on the Sabbath and using only one set of dishes did not coincide with beginning her married life. Thus, not only do individuals' experiences vary, but they are not always neatly contained within a particular life course stage.

An understanding of change depends on the particular context of an individual woman's life; so too may a single practice have very different meanings to different individuals. This is illustrated in the narratives of three women, each from a different family and a different generation, on their practice of the traditions of *kashrut*, the Jewish dietary laws. These perspectives do not represent a linear progression, but rather three different ways of understanding one's practice of traditions, which the particular historical and social context of each woman's experience at some level likely plays a part in shaping.

Marsha's mother, Edie, is an American-born woman of eighty-five. Raised in an Orthodox home like many of her friends, she explains why she still follows the Jewish dietary laws, though many of her friends have long since given them up:

> It isn't that I'm that religious, I do it because I can't change. I don't know if it's respect for my mother and my father, or it's just me, but I cannot change.

The way Edie speaks of *kashrut*, "I cannot change," suggests that the practice itself is embedded in her self-concept. To change this practice is to change a fundamental part of her identity, which she feels unable to do.

In a different way, Susan, a woman in the middle generation, relates *kashrut* to her Jewish identity. Though her mother kept kosher when Susan was a small child, she gave it up when Susan was still young. Susan discusses her conclusions as to why she herself began keeping a kosher home just a few years ago, after her own children were grown and out of the house:

> I began to realize that I could lose my identity as a Jew because of the things I no longer did. I no longer go to synagogue as often as I used to, I'm not involved as I used to be, and so keeping kosher was a way for me to continually remind myself what I am.... I think some people think I do it because I, I must be very religious because I do it. And I'm not. I don't do it for that reason.

Susan, thus, speaks of *kashrut* itself less as a part of her self-concept, and more as a way to keep part of her identity, her being a Jew, in the forefront of her consciousness.

The third woman, Judy, a single professional in her early thirties, did not grow up in a kosher home. Her grandmother, Anne, was a source of information and a role model for the kosher home Judy has kept since she moved out on her own. She describes her practices and her attitudes toward them in this way:

> I go through cycles where I think that there's no point to religion at all, that there's no, I mean *kashrut* is crazy and the whole thing is crazy and then I go though cycles where I, I go to synagogue with my grandma, I go to her Orthodox synagogue and I, I get into it more.... As the years go on now, I guess I'm getting less and less in terms of religion and that, I still keep a kosher home and I'll always keep a kosher home, but my strong feelings are dwindling.

Unlike the first two women, Judy doesn't give a sense of a link between *kashrut* and her identity. The relation between her practices and the strong religious feelings she suggests in some way underlie those practices, is unclear: in fact, the two seem to exist somewhat independently of each other.

Particularly striking is the commonality among all three women of expressly dissociating the practices of *kashrut* and considering oneself to be "religious." Two ways of understanding this come to mind. First, the label "religious" might connote a degree of intensity or spirituality incongruous with practices that are, for the women involved, a comfortable and familiar part of their everyday routines. Second, religious feelings may simply not be an accurate description of the connection the women feel to these traditions and their practice of them.

The women's common rejection of the categorization "religious" by no means implies that *kashrut* has a similar significance to each, as their own words, above, clearly demonstrate. For example, Edie's narrative suggests family ties, specifically intergenerational relationships, as an important factor. Adhering to particular traditions such as *kashrut*, or not dating/marrying a non-Jew out of respect for parents and family, was often mentioned, particularly by the oldest generation.

What does "being Jewish" mean?

In some cases, the women had difficulty articulating the way in which a particular practice was meaningful to them. For example, while Judy distinguished between stable practices and her fluctuating feelings toward them in the last passage above, she gives no reason for keeping a kosher home. She addressed this issue specifically later in our interview:

> I can say the Jewish "why," okay, but.... Does that make sense for today? I'm not sure. How does that affect my life? I can't answer those type of questions.

This raises an issue that surfaced often in the interviews. Many of the women said directly that I was asking "difficult questions." The "difficulty" apparently lay not in remembering details from childhood or getting me to understand the importance of particular aspects of their experiences, but in what might be termed "expressing meaning in words." In many instances, what I asked of these women was to articulate the meanings they attached to certain aspects of themselves. While social psychologists have long utilized personal narratives to get at meanings, when those meanings are so intertwined with other aspects of the self-concept, grasping and isolating them so as to be able to articulate them in words (in a sense, scrutinizing and objectifying them) becomes difficult.

In the above example, Judy says that she has no answer. She does that, however, by posing rhetorical questions and responding to them. In addition to suggesting that these issues are at the core of the self-concept, such exchanges allude to an additional dimension of Jewish women's identities: the subconscious aspects of connection and meaning. The women's characterization of these questions as "difficult," rather than, for example, irrelevant, suggests to me how important these issues are. They may involve early experiences not readily remembered, or emotions or spiritual feelings not easily put into words. Thus, even where women say that they practice a particular tradition and that it is meaningful to them, it may be difficult for them to consciously express how this is so. These traditions are not any less meaningful because they are hard to articulate. How to understand their significance remains an important issue for future exploration.

CONCLUSION

Jewish women's narratives give insight not only into the traditions and practices they carry out, but also to the meanings they attach to these actions, conflicts and ambivalent feelings surrounding them, and their attitudes toward and motives for doing them. It is then possible to question and go beyond even seemingly reasonable assumptions, as in the case of synagogue affiliation.

The specific personal context and experience of events such as a *bat mitzvah* may be integral to understanding a woman's construction of her Jewishness. Unstructured interviews allow the participant's experiences, narrative styles and concerns to guide the discussion. Changes over the life course and between generations then become salient as they are woven into each individual woman's experience. Meanings associated with a single practice such as *kashrut*, and how they relate to identity, can be examined in their diversity.

These insights may be particularly useful in exploring Jewish women's responses to and away from assimilation. Where a woman could be considered to have taken a step toward assimilation, as my interviews with Tracey suggest, exploring her feelings surrounding her *bat mitzvah* can help understand her apparent weakening association with Jewish traditions. Where little engagement with Jewish practice seems to point to a waning Jewish identity, women's narratives may show ways that this is not the case. Because the self is often seen to embody a history of experiences, interactions, and responses (as in the case of self-schemata (Markus, 1977)), ethnic identity could be salient even where specific traditions and rituals are not part of an individual's current practice. Conversely, where Susan seems to have taken a step away from assimilation by beginning to keep a kosher home, her narrative allows us to see this in the context of her and her family's previous practices as well as her own understanding of her actions.

The narratives also suggest ways in which women have experienced and responded to exclusion within the Jewish community, as two final examples illustrate. Dora, Susan's mother, immigrated with her family from Eastern Europe at age two. Her father was a rabbi, and she remembers what often happened in the Orthodox synagogue she attended as a child, where women were obliged to sit apart from the men, up in a balcony:

> We all attended services at the synagogue, and for certain prayers, my sisters and I would run downstairs and sit with my father. And all the Jewish men would...look like this, [as if] to say "you don't belong here," and my father...would say, "you just stay put." That's the way he felt: you just stay.

This experience may have given Dora and her sisters a glimpse of a possible community in which women and men could pray and celebrate together, taking equal part.

In a second excerpt, Marsha's sentiments suggest how deeply entwined women's traditional exclusion in Judaism may be with Jewish-American women's identities today:

> I guess I'm kind of old-fashioned. I'm not comfortable with the pregnant female rabbi on the pulpit, holding a *Torah*, and her pregnant stomach. [laughs] I, you know, so for me it's not comfortable. I'm not, I'm not judging it as right or wrong, but for me it's, it's not right.

The work of constructing identity, both individually and collectively, as Jews, as women, and especially as Jewish women, is a complex task. Shared experience between researcher and participant, counselor and client, can be an important resource in research and therapy. This common ground can be the basis for a more holistic and contextualized understanding of a woman's experiences and concerns than might be possible in its absence. Shared experience can facilitate the communication and integration of issues surrounding Jewish identity within the professional relationship.

That both therapist and client, or researcher and participant, may identify as Jewish, however, does not necessarily presuppose shared experience: the particular meanings and experiences each individual brings to her construction of "Jewishness" need to be examined. "Labels" and categories that provide shorthand references to aspects of Jewish life need to be explored in the specific context of each individual's experience, as the narratives above illustrate. If the Jewishness of Jewish women is to be attended to as part of understanding one's identity, it is particularly important that people interacting with Jewish women have an appreciation for the diversity and individuality of ways this Jewishness becomes (or fails to become) meaningful for the women involved.

REFERENCES

Cohen, S. (1988). *American assimilation or Jewish revival?* Bloomington: Indiana University Press.

Cohen, S., Woocher, J., & Phillips, B. (Eds.). (1984). *Perspectives in Jewish population research.* Boulder: Westview Press.

DeVault, M. (1990). Talking and listening from women's standpoint: Feminist strategies for interviewing and analysis. *Social Problems, 37*, 96-116.

Markus, H. (1977). Self-schemata and processing information about the self. *Journal of Personality and Social Psychology, 35*, 63-78.

Mayer, E. & Sheingold, C. (1979). *Intermarriage and the Jewish future: A national study in summary.* New York: American Jewish Committee, Institute of Human Relations.

Riessman, C. (1987). When gender is not enough: Women interviewing women. *Gender and Society, 1*, 172-207.

Smith, D. (1987). *The everyday world as problematic: A feminist sociology.* Boston: Northeastern University Press.

ACKNOWLEDGMENTS

I wish to thank the nine women who so generously shared their time, experiences, and ideas about Jewish identity with me, and without whose participation I could not have undertaken this work. Thank you also to Barbara Laslett and Susan Zeller, for their comments at earlier stages of this work, and to the women who attended and enthusiastically participated in this session at the First International Judaism, Feminism, and Psychology conference. This work benefited from support through a University of Minnesota Graduate School Fellowship and from a travel grant from the University of Minnesota Department of Sociology.

JEWISH WOMEN'S BODIES: SEXUALITY, BODY IMAGE AND SELF-ESTEEM

RACHEL JOSEFOWITZ SIEGEL

INTRODUCTION

A woman's feelings about her body and her sexuality are intertwined and have a significant impact on her self-esteem. Conversely, a woman's sense of self and her self-esteem can significantly affect her feelings about her body and her sexuality.

Messages about sex and the female body are culturally transmitted, and in the case of a minority group, are conveyed by the host culture as well as by the minority group's own cultural, historical and religious customs. The negative attitudes and biases of a host culture are frequently expressed by means of stereotyping the physical attributes and sexuality of the more marginal group. Such caricaturing, when directed at women, is likely to be more socially acceptable than when it is directed at men, because it is couched in woman-blaming and woman-ridiculing language that is pervasive in both cultures (Siegel, 1987).

While women of all ethnic and cultural backgrounds are similarly affected, and Jewish men also feel the impact of anti-Jewish body stereotyping (Gilman, 1991), this article will focus on the specifically Jewish aspects of Jewish women's sense of body, sexuality and self-esteem, which also include matters of reproductive choice and heterosexual imperatives.

The scope of this article does not permit a full exploration of the complexity and variety of views among Jewish women in North America today, nor does it address the experience of Jewish women in Israel, who are not exposed to the forces of a differing host culture. Within the framework of her own feminist perspective, however, the author will attempt to present at least some of the differing observations that have recently been published by Jewish feminists about this topic. Hopefully this preliminary work can be used as a springboard for further study and discussion.

LOOKS AND SELF-ESTEEM

Women of all ages, Jewish and non-Jewish, are preoccupied with looks and body image. A woman's physical appearance is associated with her sexual attractiveness, her social status, employability and even her mental health. These concerns are so much a part of our general culture, that their very obviousness makes them invisible. A woman may not even notice how much of her time and emotional energy are tied up in dealing with her appearance. Women are bombarded by media images, advertisements, art and literature that set up standards of beauty and attractiveness to live up to or to be judged by. While feminists have drawn attention to the tyranny of this pervasive over-investment in how women look, most women are still caught up to some degree in wondering what they can do to become more attractive.

Since "Jewish traits" have negative or ambivalent connotations in predominantly non-Jewish countries, the Jewish woman has the additional burden of wondering whether her appearance conveys an image that is "too Jewish" or "not Jewish enough." She wonders if she will be avoided by others because her looks convey Jewish ethno-religious messages.

These concerns may evoke strong and often disturbing emotions. A woman's most private feelings about her body and about her Jewish identity can be very intense, and comprise a significant part of her self-esteem, and her sense of worth or worthlessness. When a woman is troubled by low self-esteem or general emotional discomfort, she may not be aware that her feelings about "looking Jewish" could be a major part of the problem. If she seeks therapy, her therapist may not attribute her discomfort to the ethnic factors that interact with her body image and her sexuality.

MIXED MESSAGES AND CHANGING VALUES

The messages that the Jewish woman gets about her looks, her reproductive functions, her sexuality and her physical attractiveness to others, come from two separate but overlapping sources. One set of messages is unique to her own Jewish family and community, and to the Jewish culture, traditions and religious or secular teachings to which she has been exposed. Another set of messages comes from her non-Jewish and sometimes anti-Jewish environment.

The messages about a Jewish woman's body must also be understood within the broad context of the historical time in which she lives. Today is a time of mixed and conflicting value systems, rapid social change, and tumultuous, almost chaotic innovations in family values and sexual norms. The nuclear, two parent, heterosexual family with a paternal breadwinner and maternal homemaker can no longer be considered typical. Gender roles are in a state of flux. Women are portrayed in contradictory images; they are perceived as either liberated or oppressed, as victims or castrating and dominating villains. The motherhood imperative continues as strong as ever while career goals demand other priorities. Jewish women are caricatured as spoiled and selfish princesses or as overly demanding, anxious and overprotective mothers. It is difficult indeed for the Jewish woman to make sense of these conflicting images, to choose her role models, and to figure out not only who she is but who she wants to be and how she wants to look.

RANGE OF PERSPECTIVES

Attitudes about diversity in general, and Jewish identity in particular, encompass the broadest possible range of options. Jewish women come from diverse backgrounds and can choose many ways of being Jewish. The possibilities include a continuum that ranges from total return to traditional Jewish customs and *Halacha* (Jewish law) at one end, to complete absorption into a generalized, somewhat nameless majority culture at the other end. It is in this context then, that the Jewish woman struggles with or celebrates her physical appearance, her sexuality, and her deepest feelings about her body.

Jewish views of women's sexuality are diverse. According to Lynn Davidman (1986), there is probably more variety on this topic among Jews than between Jews and non-Jews. In her article *Sex and the modern Jewish woman: An overview*, she identifies a wide range of observations, attitudes, teachings and behaviors among Jewish women and among those who write about Jewish women. Feminist scholar and theologian Susannah Heschel (1990), notes that traditional sources and biblical commandments about Jewish women still have an effect on the modern Jewish woman today, no matter what her Jewish upbringing or her present level of Jewish observance or identification. In her well documented statement, she points out that the ancient commandments regulating woman's intimate behavior all center around the needs of man, and that the *mitzvoth* (religious obligations) that are expected of observant Jewish women are stated in terms of a woman's relationship to man. Such male-centeredness does not teach the Jewish woman to value her own sexuality or even to recognize the legitimacy of her body rhythms and desires.

Another viewpoint is presented by Blu Greenberg (1981), a practicing Orthodox feminist, and Debra Kaufman (1991), a feminist sociologist. They report that Orthodox observant Jewish women today can find personal and positive meaning, as well as enhanced self-esteem, in observing the religious laws concerning menstruation and heterosexual intercourse, known as *taharat hamishpacha* (family purity).

If we are to understand how Jewish sources affect a Jewish woman's feelings about her body and her sexuality, we need to keep in mind that the same teachings and practices can have opposite meanings for different Jewish women and that the individual woman's interpretation must be respected as legitimate for her. Conflicting meanings can and do co-exist within a particular relationship or family, as well as within the Jewish woman herself. She can experience significant tensions if her partner or her family disagree with her. She may be under pressure to conform to their convictions concerning her own body. Matters of religious observance or interpretation are felt very deeply. Adherence or non-conformity to Jewish teachings about *taharat hamishpacha* are often interpreted by family members as symbols of acceptance or rejection of Judaism and Jewish identity. Such inner conflicts and family disagreements can undermine the Jewish woman's self-assurance and lower her self-esteem in ways that she finds hard to identify or to describe. It is incumbent upon the clinician to tread carefully, and to remain non-judgmental while the client unravels her feelings and attitudes about these issues within her own value system.

TRADITIONAL JEWISH VIEWS ON WOMAN'S SEXUALITY AND REPRODUCTION

Religion is one of the strongest forces defining a woman's sexuality, even when she herself does not believe or practice religiously, or has not been brought up in a religious home (Siegel, Choldin, & Orost, in press). Some attitudes and behaviors may continue to be conveyed long after the belief system has changed.

Traditional Jewish messages about sexuality are somewhat ambivalent, though on the whole, positive. Among Jews, sex is definitely not considered a sin, and celibacy is not a virtue. Sexual behavior is considered a necessary, important and pleasurable activity that should be practiced within acceptable and clearly defined boundaries. It is to be enjoyed by both woman and man within heterosexual marriage. Blessings said on the occasion of the naming of a girl or at her *bat mitzvah* (coming of age ritual), traditionally include the phrase: "may she be brought to the wedding canopy." Married heterosexual activity is encouraged, and a man is expected to respect and satisfy his wife's sexual needs.

The injunction to avoid sexual activity before marriage has openly been ignored by the Conservative and Reform Jewish communities and their rabbis, at least since the sexual revolution of the sixties. The heterosexual imperative, however, is still very strong. Traditional positive messages about sex are consistently heterosexual and marriage oriented.

The existence of lesbian and gay congregations and rabbis remains mostly unmentioned within the Jewish establishment and its publications. There is no specific biblical injunction against lesbianism, but the very absence of any mention of a lesbian option carries a powerful message of disapproval. Jewish lesbians have written extensively about the difficulties of their position (Balka & Rose, 1989; Beck, 1982/1989; Kaye/Kantrowitz, 1990). The bisexual or lesbian Jewish woman often feels the subtle or overt non-acceptance of the Jewish community. Like her non-Jewish sisters, she is constantly exposed to pervasively heterosexual assumptions within Jewish organizations and congregations, which may cause her to feel even more invisible than her non-lesbian counterparts. She may also be in great pain and feel unacceptable as a Jew. Anti-lesbian biases within the Jewish community can cause her to feel ambivalent about her sexuality and about her Jewish identification and participation.

In biblical literature and Jewish religious practice, woman, since Adam and Eve, is portrayed as the ultimate sexual temptress whose body must be hidden from man's eyes, for his sexuality is considered both innocent and uncontrollable. In Orthodox synagogues, women sit behind a curtain called a *mehitza*, or in the balcony, lest their visible presence distract the men from their prayers. An Orthodox woman is expected to keep her arms and legs covered. She has the option of covering her hair or shaving her head when she gets married. She is told that her voice is considered lascivious and must be silenced. Orthodox custom forbids a man from touching or even looking upon any woman other than his wife. The Jewish woman who is exposed to these customs and who is also exposed to current norms of sexual freedom and expressiveness, can feel conflicted between her Jewish sense of shame or modesty and her wish to go along with more liberated patterns.

Contradictory meanings have been attributed to the *halachic* requirements concerning woman's impurity during menstruation or after childbirth. Woman is considered ritually and sexually unclean or impure during menstruation as well as after childbirth. She may not touch the *Torah* (scrolls containing the Five Books of Moses) or other ritual objects, and she must immerse her body in a ritual bath called *mikvah* before resuming sexual relations, lest she defile her male partner's body with her impurity. Susan Weidman Schneider (1984) observes: "There are two distinct schools of thought on this issue among Jewish women: those who believe that the laws of ritual purity hark back to a primitive blood taboo and reflect male fear and loathing of women; and those who believe that the laws and rituals surrounding *mikvah* are sensual, spiritual, expressive, allow room for women to experience a symbolic rebirth every month..." (p. 207).

While the literal meanings can be argued at length, many Jewish women, far removed from these customs, still carry the sense of bodily shame and uncleanness that these practices taught their mothers and foremothers, and many Jewish men still carry an attitude of avoidance toward the bodily secretions of women. Rabbi Laura Geller, quoted in *Jewish and Female* (Schneider, 1984, p. 209), states that, "Menstrual taboos are responsible for real damage to Jewish women's views of themselves and their bodies." My mother, a rabbi's daughter, no longer practiced these customs, yet she conveyed to me and my sisters, a strong sense of modesty about any sexual display of our bodies, and a concomitant sense of responsibility for unduly arousing men's sexual responses. On the other hand, Debra Kaufman (1991) writes that Orthodox Jewish women who observe the laws of *taharat* (purity) report that they gain a sense of dignity and self-respect in taking control of their own body through this self-caring ritual, especially if they are part of a community that fully supports these practices.

The Jewish woman's sexuality and self-esteem also interact with the powerful Jewish imperative to reproduce and to insure the genetic survival of the Jewish people. She learns that the survival of the Jewish people depends on her getting married and having Jewish children. Since the Holocaust, the burden of Jewish survival is felt deeply by many Jews. "Be fruitful and multiply" (Genesis 1) assumes new meaning when an ethnic group has lost over six million members, creating a strong motherhood expectation. The Jewish woman's decisions about sexual activity, dating and choosing a life partner can all be influenced by her feelings about Jewish survival. Her self-esteem may be severely shaken when she falls in love with the "wrong" person, or is faced with the choice or the inevitability of not producing her own children. On the other hand, she may feel resentful of her parents' role in conveying these pressures, and make her sexual and affectional choices out of a powerful urge to resist parental or communal pressures.

The responsibility for Jewish survival, being placed on a woman's reproductive function, directly increases and perpetuates Jewish biases against the single woman, the childless woman, and the lesbian woman. The fear of Jewish annihilation or disappearance also affects Jewish attitudes about intermarriage. The Jewish woman confronted with reproductive choices, with infertility, with abortion, with intermarriage or interdating, or even with menstruation and menopause, may well be unaware of how the Jewish expectation that she will produce Jewish children has affected her feelings and her decisions.

The pressure to reproduce does not, in Jewish law or custom, translate into rigid measures or attitudes against abortion or contraception, except in fundamentalist Orthodox communities, where birth control is abhorred and large families are the norm. In Jewish religion, the saving of a life overrides all other religious injunctions, and this concept is applied to the life of the mother, rather than the fetus. While abortion is generally not viewed as the method of choice, the necessity for keeping that option available has been defended by all but the most Orthodox. Even among the ultra-Orthodox, abortion is viewed as an option, but it is reserved for extreme circumstances and to be regulated by male rabbis and physicians.

THE IMPACT OF NEGATIVE STEREOTYPES ON JEWISH WOMEN

Idealized images of the American woman and caricatured images of the Jewish woman abound in the non-Jewish environment of North America. Jewish women are frequently confronted by anti-Jewish and anti-woman messages that are perceived as accurate, non-objectionable and humorous. Both Jews and non-Jews seem to find the baiting of Jewish women acceptable, when they would be up in arms if Jewish men were similarly ridiculed. While this is true for women in general, in the case of Jewish women it is compounded by external and internalized Jew hating and Jew deprecating.

The Jewish woman is surrounded by artificial images of the ideal American woman who is portrayed as white skinned, with straight, blond hair and blue eyes, thin, athletic, young and sometimes dumb. In contrast, the negative stereotypical image of the Jewish woman has darker skin, curly dark hair, a large nose, rounded contours, a loud voice, a Long Island accent and too much gold jewelry. She is accused of being too rich, too smart and too earnest. Even the eating disorders and preoccupation with weight, that are so common among all women, are frequently attributed to Jewish patterns of hospitality and blamed on Jewish mothers, though other factors may be much more salient. So-called Jewish features are unfavorably compared to media messages about the white, middle-class, successful American woman.

Jewish assimilation into the American host culture puts Jewish women face to face with an artificial standard of female attractiveness, based on privileges of class and race, that causes them to feel inferior and less attractive than their non-Jewish counterparts. Tensions have developed between generations and between genders in the drama of wanting to look and to be American, while also wanting to remain Jewish. The ambivalence about Jewish identity is often externalized and directed against Jewish women, who then become the scapegoats, excluded from intimate relationships because their potential partners found them to be or look "too Jewish."

Jewish women do not necessarily look different than non-Jewish women from the same geographic areas. Some Jewish women have dark-skinned Mediterranean or Near Eastern features; some have the tall, elegant bearing and black skin that signify their Ethiopian origins; others are blond, red-haired and light skinned. Many do not have stereotypical Jewish features at all, though some do. However, certain stereotypical traits have been portrayed as Jewish and unattractive, and Jewish women have been sensitized to being perceived or compared to these stereotypes. Having absorbed some of the negative judgements about so-called Jewish features, it is nearly impossible not to participate to some extent in conveying and perpetuating the stereotypes, unless a serious effort is made to raise consciousness and to exercise extreme vigilance. Jewish women are deeply affected by this pervasive devaluation of so-called Jewish features, and could benefit from addressing these feelings among themselves or with a sympathetic and well-informed therapist.

Large numbers of Jewish women have had nose jobs, or gone to great lengths to differentiate themselves from "New York Jews." Jewish women from New York or Long Island are generally presumed to be more aggressive, loud and pushy than Jewish women from other areas who have taken on the more ladylike demeanor of white middle class females. Every Jewish woman has developed strategies for coping with the daily assaults on her "Jewish looks" or "Jewish traits." She may brazenly own and even exaggerate her so-called Jewish traits, and this may temporarily feel good to her, or she may try to hide or deny them and find some relief in that tactic. She can surround herself with friends who also look and act Jewish, and feel at home among her own kind, or she can avoid other Jews, or she can vacillate between these choices, or retreat into feelings of unexplained embarrassment. Whatever she does, it is often without conscious awareness, and in response to being perceived as "other." There is no way for her to feel neutral about whether she "looks Jewish" or not.

The Jewish woman who lives among non-Jews almost invariably has some issues about where and how she fits or does not fit into her own environment by looking or acting Jewish. These issues have an effect on her intimate relationships, her choice of partner, her friendships and her work associations. She may have strong feelings about her hair, her nose, her voice, her figure. She may find it very difficult to voice these feelings because she might be embarrassed, or deeply angry, at herself or someone else, for making her feel this way.

Some environments, non-Jewish as well as Jewish, are more friendly to Jewish women than others; yet a Jewish woman never knows when she might have to deal with an anti-Jewish, anti-female slur. Jewish men and the Jewish community in general continue to participate in ridiculing and even harassing Jewish women. Jewish male comedians were the first to institutionalize the jokes about Jewish Mothers and the Jewish American Princess, and Jewish audiences are still laughing. The Jewish woman may feel the way women have felt about other types of harassment; she may feel that there is something wrong with her if she can't take the joke.

The misogynistic, anti-Jewish stereotyping of the Jewish woman is particularly vicious in finding fault with contradictory aspects of the Jewish woman's style, looks or behavior. As Jewish American Princess, she is caricatured as too selfish, too demanding, too loud and pushy, either over-sexed or too frigid; as Jewish Mother, she is misportrayed as too self-less, too nurturing, too unassertive and desexualized (Beck, 1991; Siegel, 1987). Either way, she falls short of what she is expected to be. These stereotypes carry some grossly exaggerated grains of truth, and they make fun and devalue those aspects of the Jewish woman that are threatening to men, or that do not match the model of the white middle class American "lady." The Jewish woman may well respond with self-doubts and lowered self-esteem, especially if she is lesbian or bisexual. She may be caught in the bind of having to choose between hiding her feelings from herself, hiding her Jewishness, or retreating from painful situations. If she objects to the stereotyping or calls attention to the harassment, she risks being perceived as even more stereotypically Jewish by appearing too loud, too pushy, and making an unnecessary fuss.

Repeated incidents of misogynist and anti-Jewish devaluation can cause the Jewish woman to constantly remake these decisions, living with ambivalence and compromise, expressing or swallowing her anger, often afraid to rock the boat for fear of exposing herself or her community to external anti-Semitism. Furthermore, the Jewish woman is often unaware that it is these demeaning messages that have undermined her self-esteem; she then tends to attribute her symptoms and discomfort to individual shortcomings or her own pathology.

CLINICAL CONSIDERATIONS

Therapists, both Jewish and non-Jewish, are not immune to the biases about Jewish women that exist in the culture at large. Even those therapists who have worked hard at examining and overcoming their own stereotypical assumptions can still have some automatic and unexamined reactions to Jewish women, especially when the woman's looks or behavior have triggered some unconscious biases. Efforts to recognize and monitor personally biased reactions toward Jewish clients who "look Jewish" or "not Jewish enough" must be ongoing.

Therapists are also frequently unaware and insufficiently informed about the variety of Jewish content that could and should be brought into the therapy. The therapy can be improved and enriched by being alert to the cultural, ethnic or religious components of the work, and by continuing to learn more about such aspects of clients' lives.

A clinician's first task is to examine and discuss her/his attitudes and feelings toward Jewish women, or certain types of Jewish women, with colleagues, and a consultant or supervisor. In a non-Jewish, male-centered environment, no therapist, Jewish or non-Jewish, can ever be totally free of some traces of anti-Jewish/anti-female bias, no matter how much work she/he has already done in this area. Biases even persist among Jewish professionals and in Jewish settings. Therapists need to make a habit of repeatedly naming the particulars of their own biases against certain kinds of Jewish women. Jewish therapists need to clarify and come to terms with their feelings about their own Jewish features, bodies, and sexuality in the context of their own Jewish identity.

The second task is to apply this information and self-awareness to the work with Jewish women. Therapists can draw attention to the interaction between Jewish identity and body image, sexuality and self-esteem. They can help their clients to identify and work through the negative and conflicting voices that have become part of the client's internal Jewish dialogue. They can introduce the client to self-affirming patterns of integrating a positive Jewish self-concept with a positive body image. These therapeutic goals, if they are in keeping with the client's own goals, can be implemented creatively within the therapist's usual therapeutic modes.

GUIDELINES FOR CLINICAL WORK WITH JEWISH WOMEN

In my own work with individual Jewish women and in groups and workshops, I have found it useful to keep some guidelines in mind, not necessarily in any specific order, yet I generally try to end each session with a brief and positive client affirmation. The following guidelines can be applied not only to body image and sexuality, but also to other specific or more general areas of the Jewish client's life:

1. Identify the sources of Jewish pain, anger and conflict about Jewish identity, including specific incidents and situations.

2. Identify the sources of Jewish joy and healing, including role models of Jewish women.

3. Identify positive experiences of individual and communal Jewish celebration and introduce Jewish self-affirmations.

QUESTIONS FOR LAUNCHING WORKSHOP DISCUSSIONS

In workshops on Jewish body image I have used some of the following questions to launch the discussion:

1. What aspects of your life have been affected by Jewish and non-Jewish messages about your body and your sexuality?

2. Which of these are positive and which of these are negative?

3. When you hear "she looks Jewish," what comes to your mind?

4. What parts of your face or your body do you consider Jewish, and how do you feel about these?

5. Can you think of a situation or incident that made you feel bad as a Jewish woman?

6. Can you think of a situation or incident that made you feel good about being a Jewish woman?

These questions can be posed in small groups, dyads or with the entire group. Negative biases may emerge, as well as painful or angry feelings and memories, which need to be accepted with respectful empathy. It is wise to follow the expression and discussion of such negative material with an active and more positive exercise. It is at this time that I might ask: "When you think of your Jewish mothers and foremothers, what are some of the endearing qualities you would like to emulate?" The group can also be encouraged to share strategies for coping with the anti-Jewish and anti-woman biases of their internal and external environments. The workshop can end on a note of celebration, with positive and healing self-affirmations.

CONCLUSION

Many Jewish women have felt the impact of Jewish and non-Jewish attitudes toward their looks, their bodies, their sexuality and self-esteem, without being fully aware of it. The mental health professionals who work with them have also, on the whole, been insufficiently aware, or poorly informed, of the connection between the client's self-esteem and the manner in which her looks, her body, and what she does with her body, are viewed by her and her community in the context of her Jewish identity.

In this article I have begun to examine some of the sources of stress in this intimate and emotionally significant area of Jewish women's experience. I have indicated the range and variety of possible responses and the need to respect the individual Jewish woman's attitude toward these issues, based on her specific background and value system. I have also offered some suggestions for enriching the therapeutic experience by including and focusing on this content area. Jewish women can gain Jewish and personal self-esteem and self-acceptance when they can clarify their Jewish values, name and work through their negative or conflicted feelings about "looking Jewish," and integrate their Jewish identity with their sexual identity. The Jewish face in the mirror can become a reflection of Jewish pride and self-respect, and an empowering link between generations of Jewish women.

REFERENCES

Balka, C. & Rose, A. (Eds.) (1989). *Twice blessed: On being lesbian, gay, and Jewish.* Boston: Beacon.

Beck, E.T. (Ed.). (1989). *Nice Jewish girls: A lesbian anthology*. Boston: Beacon.

Beck, E.T. (1991). Therapy's double dilemma: Anti-Semitism and misogyny. In R.J. Siegel, & E. Cole (Eds.), *Jewish women in therapy: Seen but not heard.* New York: Harrington Park Press.

Davidman, L. (1986). Sex and the modern Jewish woman: An overview. In J.S. Brewer (Ed.), *Sex and the modern Jewish woman: An annotated bibliography.* New York: Biblio Press.

Genesis, 1.

Gilman, S. (1991). *The Jew's body*. London: Routledge.

Greenberg, B. (1981). *On women and Judaism: A view from tradition.* Philadelphia: Jewish Publication Society.

Heschel, S. (1991). Jewish feminism and women's identity. In R.J. Siegel & E. Cole (Eds.), *Jewish women in therapy: Seen but not heard.* New York: Harrington Park Press.

Kaye/Kantrowitz, M. (1990). *My Jewish face and other stories.* San Francisco: Spinsters/Aunt Lute.

Kaufman, D.R. (1991). *Rachel's daughters: Newly orthodox Jewish women.* New Brunswick, CT.: Rutgers University Press.

Schneider, S.W. (1984). *Jewish and female: Choices and changes in our lives today*. New York: Simon & Schuster.

Siegel, R.J. (1977). The Jew as a woman. *Jewish Spectator*, *42*(4), 40-42.

Siegel, R.J. (1987). Antisemitism and sexism in stereotypes of Jewish women. In D. Howard (Ed.), *Dynamics of feminist therapy*, New York: Haworth Press.

Siegel, R.J., Choldin, S., & Orost, J.H. (in press). Religious influences on women's identity and development. In J.C. Chrisler, & A.H. Hemstreet, (Eds.), *Variations on a theme: Diversity and the psychology of women.* Albany: SUNY Press.

IMA'S NOT ON THE *BIMA*: PSYCHOLOGICAL BARRIERS TO WOMEN TAKING LEADERSHIP IN JEWISH RELIGIOUS PRACTICE

NORA GOLD

Over the past two decades Jewish feminists have challenged the traditional male domination of leadership in the Jewish community, and have demanded a more visible, and viable, role for women in all public aspects of Jewish life. As a result of these efforts, there have been many major achievements. In the area of religious leadership, the emergence of female rabbis and cantors is perhaps the most visible; but equally significant has been the articulation of special and unique possibilities for women's spiritual expression, which have greatly expanded the opportunities for the average Jewish woman (i.e., not only the "professional Jew", such as the female rabbi) to participate fully in the religious life of her community.

This expansion of opportunities, however, has not necessarily resulted in increased participation by women in the leadership of services. At the egalitarian synagogue that I attend (egalitarian here meaning that identical leadership opportunities are available to women and men), out of two hundred and fifty adult members (mostly in their forties), we have only four women who, on any regular basis, lead any aspect of the service. The rest choose, for one reason or another, not to exercise this option, and on any given *Shabbat* (Sabbath) or *yom tov* (holiday), it is an unsubtle male-dominated *bima* (podium) above us. Discussions with Jewish women from all over North America confirm that this situation is typical. It appears that, contrary to what many Jewish feminists might like to believe, the "revolution" is far from underway for the great majority of Jewish women; and in fact (to twist the title of a children's book by Portnoy), *ima* (mom) is *not* on the *bima*.

There are a number of reasons why Jewish feminists should be concerned about this. (1) What happens at *shul* (synagogue) is psychologically significant, even for Jews who seldom attend. It is the place (especially for infrequent attendees) where Jewish girls and boys learn communal norms regarding their place as females and males in Judaism, and in this sense it is critical to their gender identity formation. (2) History is replete with examples of opportunities revoked due to lack of utilization. Jewish women are now at a crossroad, a crucial historical moment with unique opportunities and possibilities. These cannot be taken for granted; they will not wait around for us, unused, until we feel ready. What we do not embrace and make our own may be lost to us. (3) Most Jewish feminists, like other feminists and activists, have focused their energy on expanding opportunities for Jewish women, on the assumption that these opportunities would lead to change. Clearly the relationship between opportunity and action, between structural change and personal revolution, is far more complicated than this. An exploration of this relationship is essential if there is to be real change for the majority of Jewish women.

A research study was therefore undertaken to examine Jewish feminists' lack of participation in prayer leadership, how these women understand their lack of participation, what (if anything) they feel is holding them back, and some possible solutions. "Prayer leadership" here refers to the public leading of religious services (i.e., in the presence of a *minyan*: a congregation gathered for prayer, requiring a minimal quorum of ten adults) and it includes both the prayers (*shacharit, mincha, ma'ariv,* and *musaf*: those for the morning, afternoon and evening, and the additional prayers for *Shabbat*), and the chanting of the *haftorah* (readings from the prophets) and the *Torah* portion (the weekly reading from the Pentateuch).

Although there is no previous research or writing bearing directly on this topic, obviously its conceptualization has been informed by feminist psychology, by Jewish feminist writing (in particular on the dual oppression and silence around being Jewish and female, and learning to celebrate Jewish women). Developmental psychology addresses the power of internalized childhood images of mother and father as norms and authority, and the difficulty of challenging these images even in adulthood.

METHOD

For this study, thirty women were interviewed. Subjects were recruited through the newsletter of an egalitarian synagogue in Toronto, which invited interested women to contact the researcher directly. Those who did so were also asked if they knew of any other women who might be interested in taking part. Participating women had to be over 30 years of age and members of an egalitarian congregation in the Toronto area.

The final sample was a group of women from three different egalitarian synagogues who were, for the most part, university graduates, employed in paid work outside the home (many as professionals), and who had received a typical Jewish education for women of their generation. All were heterosexual and of *Ashkenazi* (Eastern European) origin. The women in this sample were eminently representative of the population I wanted to study in that they identified strongly with egalitarianism, and clearly valued the right to lead services at their *shul* if they wanted to. Over two-thirds had actually joined the *shul* they went to because it was egalitarian, and four spontaneously mentioned their daughters as a major factor in this decision. For example: "Though I would have been able to tolerate a lack of egalitarianism at the *shul* for myself, I could not tolerate it for my daughter. I wanted her to start off in a way I didn't start off, feeling a full participant, an equal." Yet none of the thirty had ever made use of the opportunity to lead the prayers.

RESULTS

Perceptions of the status of women and women's work at shul

The fact that these women did not embrace the possibilities for prayer leadership does not mean that they did not contribute in numerous other ways to their communities. Ninety per cent of the women in this study contributed time, energy and some form of work to their *shuls*. In addition to serving on the board or on committees, women did tasks like landscaping the area around the *shul*, producing the newsletter, and making the *kiddish* (the light meal following *Shabbat* services).

One woman washed all the *kiddish* tablecloths for a year, and she commented: "This is hard work because you have to pick out all the toothpicks."

These contributions fit theoretically into recent feminist discussions about women and work (Finch & Groves, 1983), and the non-recognition and/or devaluation of the kind of work women often do, such as providing emotional and physical nurturance to others and creating and maintaining social networks. In this study, women provided for the physical needs of the community through caring for the physical building (the "sanctuary") and organizing the food, and they also nurtured the fabric of the community socially, emotionally and aesthetically; yet, they perceived these contributions as relatively trivial and insignificant. Of course, it is still germane to ask, without in any way diminishing the value of these contributions, why so many women at *shul* are cleaning up and making the *kiddish*, and not leading the prayers.

Regarding the overall status of women at *shul*, subjects were asked how many of the important leadership positions at the *shul* they thought were filled by women. All respondents distinguished between two kinds of leadership: prayer leadership and organizational leadership (board or committee work).

In terms of prayer leadership, four women said, "That's mainly men." There was consensus among the rest of the subjects that women led the prayers about 30% of the time, although a few saw it as even less. This estimate, in fact, greatly exceeded the "real" percentage, which was closer to 15%, and this may be explained at least in part in terms of the relationship between perception and expectation.

Regarding board and committee work, almost everyone said that women held about 50% of the leadership roles. (In one of the *shuls*, the president is currently a woman, and this was cited with pride by many of the women from there.) One woman, however, pointed out that at her *shul* there is a significant, and predictable, breakdown by gender in terms of who heads the various *shul* committees. Women chair the child care, education and *kiddish* committees, and take responsibility for secretarial tasks and the newsletter; only men head the building committee, or the ritual committee, seen as the most powerful and important committee at the *shul*, since it deals with liturgical change, primarily (and ironically) the issue of feminizing the liturgy.

Relationship of background variables to the non-leadership of prayers

An obvious question of this research was whether any of the demographic or background variables correlated with women's non-leadership. In this study, none of the variables investigated (including religious background, extent of Jewish or secular education, feminist identification or having a mother who was an active leader in her *shul*) correlated with any of the following: male vs. female leadership imagery, degree of current involvement in prayer leadership, or the desire to take a more active role in the future.

Subjects' initial explanations of their non-leadership

Early in the interviews, women were asked to give reasons for not performing prayer leadership roles at the *shul.* Their reasons divided into three general categories. (1) Eighteen cited some kind of inadequacy, either educational or personal, such as insufficient Jewish belief, background or knowledge; not a good enough ear or good enough voice; or the fear of doing a less than perfect job. (2) Two women expressed doubt about women's right to be doing this, and (3) ten said it would demand a lot of effort and that this was not a priority for them. This last point, which involved diminishing the importance of the task, clearly conflicts with subjects' initial statements about the importance to them of egalitarianism and female leadership in the *shul*, and may be linked to the other two in that one tends to diminish the importance of "impossible", very threatening, or conflict-laden goals.

Subjects were then asked which of the leadership roles at the *shul* they could see themselves conceivably filling at some point in the future (as opposed to what they had done to date). With reference to board and committee work, some women were able to conceive of taking on increased responsibility and leadership in the future. However, in terms of prayer leadership, the women in this study could only see doing in the future more or less what they were already doing. Furthermore, a full one-third said that even if they were offered the ideal resources and supports, they still could not see themselves participating in prayer leadership. This confirmed the researcher's hypothesis that for many Jewish women there is a profound resistance to prayer leadership, something which will not be loosened up simply by a little encouragement or the presence of opportunities at *shul*, as has often been assumed.

Images and associations

In order to probe this resistance a little more deeply, subjects were invited to engage in some word association. They were asked to say the first thoughts or memories that came to mind when they heard each of the following phrases. After each response, subjects were asked if the image or person they had identified was pleasant, unpleasant or neutral.

A Jewish woman:

In all but one response to this question, subjects' associations with "a Jewish woman" were pleasant. Eleven of the women thought of their mothers, five thought of Golda Meir (her image recurs throughout this study), five responded with women who were admired from the *shul* or the community, and three mentioned their grandmothers. One woman said: "The Jewish woman is the backbone of humanity, the salt of the earth, and not to be compromised; throughout history Jewish women have held their families together through adversity."

Three mentioned two superimposed images, both pleasant: a traditional woman of her mother's generation who stayed at home, and a Jewish woman of her own generation. One woman put it as "the mother in Tevye vs. a lecturer I heard talking about a feminist *haggadah*" (the story of the Jews' deliverance from slavery read at the Passover meal). These latter comments suggest some conflict, or at least the sense that for some, the image and reality of the Jewish woman is in a state of transition.

A Jewish woman leading services:

All subjects but one had pleasant associations with women leading services. In all cases, specific women were named, underlining their importance to the women interviewed and their significance as role models.

A Jewish woman wearing a tallis (prayer shawl):

Half the women had either pleasant or very pleasant associations with women wearing *tallesim*, such as: "beautiful feelings, gorgeous feelings," "very warm and protected," and "power." One woman commented that "women's *tallesim* are more personal because we make our own," and another said, "When I wear a *tallis* I feel enveloped in

Judaism, like a cocoon in the middle of the *shul*: it doesn't feel then like it belongs to men any more."

About one-quarter thought a woman wearing a *tallis* was okay (e.g.,"initially strange but now it's a fact of life, that's what women do at our *shul*"). Five women expressed unpleasant feelings about women wearing *tallesim*, such as, "Intellectually, I think it's okay, but I have trouble with it emotionally," or "I don't find it necessary, it's not a positive feeling." One woman said, "I felt like I was masquerading as a male."

Being a Jewish girl around the age of 12:

Here, less than half the subjects (43%) expressed pleasant associations. Those who did mentioned going to *shul* as a family, feeling proud of being Jewish, or preparing for their *bat mitzvah* (a rite of passage ceremony for girls, supposedly parallel to the *bar mitzvah* for boys, but often treated as less significant). Five women said Judaism didn't play a significant role in their lives at the time. Three had unpleasant associations, specifically related to having a *bat mitzvah*. One woman was not allowed to have one, which she found very upsetting. Two others found the process of deciding whether or not to have a *bat mitzvah* very stressful because of peer pressure, and both ultimately decided against it.

Someone leading services:

Women responded to this question with predominantly male images, mainly rabbis from childhood, and a few *chazzanim* (cantors). Either a pleasant or a neutral image of a male constituted two-thirds of the responses, and there were also three unpleasant male images. For the four subjects who pictured a woman leading services, these images were only pleasant.

A Jewish leader:

In this question, men figured in sixteen out of twenty-six responses, thirteen pleasant and three neutral. The men identified were predominantly rabbis and Israeli politicians. One subject did not name a specific male, but responded: "It's not a woman, I say this with a pang." Two subjects identified both a male leader and a female leader, and eight identified only a woman. It is significant, however, that seven out of the ten subjects who associated a woman with Jewish leadership identified the leader as Golda Meir. In this study, subjects reflected a very limited awareness of Jewish women leaders, either past or present. This dearth of role models, in contrast to the numerous and various men identified, seems of some psychological significance.

A Jew to be admired:

Fourteen responses to this question identified a Jewish man, ten identified a Jewish woman, and six identified a "type of person" with no reference to gender, e.g., "a person who gives *tzedakah* (charity) anonymously." The only woman mentioned more than once was Golda Meir, again, and she was chosen six times out of the ten.

In this sample, then, it appears that Jewish women are associated with some beautiful and loving images, both generally and in specific relation to religious practice (e.g., leading services, wearing a *tallis*). However, subjects' images of prayer leadership emerge clearly as male. The question about "someone leading services" elicited overwhelmingly male imagery, and this finding is very likely related to the difficulty the women in this study have in seeing themselves in prayer leadership, either currently or in the future.

Subjects' final explanations of their non-leadership

At the end of the interview, subjects' limited involvement with prayer leadership was contrasted with their initial comments about the importance of women taking leadership roles at *shul*, and they were asked: "How do you understand this discrepancy?" Many of the answers were thematically consistent with those of the earlier question regarding the leadership roles women could not see themselves fulfilling. However, this final question elicited more thoughtful, lengthy and intense responses, enabling women to pull together their ideas from the whole interview and probe a little more deeply into themselves.

Many women used metaphor to describe their fears of taking an active role in prayer leadership, and the impact on them of early socialization. One woman referred to "a block in my psyche" and another to "that unseen hand holding me back." Others made use of the powerful symbols of *tallis* (as the garment of power) and *bima* (the place of power):

"Last time I had an *aliyah* (was called up to the *bima*), I borrowed my husband's *tallis*, and I tripped on it."

"I was on the *bima* only once, to *bentsh gomel* (offer a prayer of gratitude for narrowly escaping danger), and I thought I'd be struck down by lightning. I thought I was being watched from the sky by my childhood rabbi."

Women spoke eloquently about the effects of family conditioning and community socialization processes:

"In terms of religious leadership, I've had it hammered into me that this is not allowed, it's not for me. I think that's true for so many women, especially those of us who have had the 'advantage' of stronger Jewish educational background. Basically, the stronger your traditional network, the harder this is going to be."

"When I was 12 and preparing for my *bat mitzvah*, the cantor said, 'This is usually the week when I teach the boys the notes, but since you never again in your life will have occasion to use it, I'll just teach you your *parsha*' (the weekly reading). I never learned the notes to be able to move and generalize to other *haftorahs*. So I've had a *bat mitzvah*, and I can do a *haftorah*, but I can't do *haftorahs*."

Some spoke about the impact of these influences on their self-confidence or self-image:

"I think the problem is early conditioning, early and later. In some way I've internalized the patriarchal message that we get, even though consciously I'm very assertive and feminist in my attitudes. There's a lack of confidence—at my *bat mitzvah*, I did *haftorah* but I never got to do the *davening* (prayers). So while I'm extremely comfortable going to *shul*, I know the *niggunim* (tunes) and *davening*, I didn't have the experience of *leading* the service. Also I'm not that musical. But the ironic thing is I can sight-read *haftorah trop*" (the musical score, in this case for chanting *haftorah*).

"I'm not that much of an outgoing person—you have to have a lot of confidence to lead prayers and I have none of that. I don't have the confidence. Also, for real, at the back of my mind, I think: women don't do that. I love the egalitarian thing but sometimes it's a little hard, not to accept, but to get involved in."

"Because of how we were raised, in an Orthodox male-dominated family, it's not in my core to play that role. It's in my core as an adult now but my Judaism comes from my childhood family. My now family doesn't have much Judaism in it, I have to make it. In Judaism, my inside reverts back to my childhood core."

This raises the crucial point about where in the psyche things Jewish reside. For many of the women in this study, Jewish experiences were, and still are, an intimate part of the experience of childhood, and intricately connected with family roles and family love. Some may even look to Judaism as a way to return to, or recapture, one's childhood, or some aspect of it. One woman from an Orthodox background articulated in these terms the flavor of the Judaism/family connection. She associated "a woman leading prayers" with "a total breakdown of traditional Judaism, of *comfort Judaism*, there is no comfort." (emphasis author's) This, of course, has enormous implications in terms of trying to encourage women to practice Judaism differently from the way it was done in their parents' homes.

Time and time again in this research, women referred to the importance of the role models that were available (and unavailable) to them as they were growing up. For example:

"The rabbi's wife didn't mean to do something negative, there was just no other role model, nothing to contradict her. There were no positive role models. She taught us more than anything, that women don't do that [lead prayers]. You believe what your teacher tells you. And it's even worse when a woman inculcates these things."

"I could never imagine walking around holding the *Torah*, or putting on a *tallis*, or going up there to the *bima*. I have difficulty, being brought up with traditional Judaism. These things jar with me because I never saw women doing them."

This, too, has obvious relevance for the process of helping women explore new roles and behaviors related to prayer leadership.

DISCUSSION

Two crucial themes emerged from the results of this study: (1) the impact of early socialization on these women's capacity to take an active role in prayer leadership, and (2) the importance of role models in providing them (and the future generation) with alternative religious roles, both in childhood and later.

Early socialization and its effects

It is hardly surprising that early socialization had a deep and powerful influence on subjects' ideas about religious observance. These ideas spring from, and are inextricably intertwined with, our most intimate relationships, with our love for and images of our parents, as well as our extended families and communities. Because of this, examining our beliefs, our discomforts, our "intuitions" about what is "right" Jewishly, means questioning, even confronting, our mothers and our fathers, or more accurately, our images of them.

Naomi Goldenberg, in *Changing of the Gods* (1979), posits a psychological connection between (1) challenging patriarchal religious traditions, (2) fearing the death of one's father, and (3) overcoming the Oedipal (or Electra) complex and achieving psychological independence. I would agree that for many women, getting up on the *bima* has the flavor of father-negation, father-death, or even father-murder, in it. When we talk about feminist reconceptualizations of Judaism and of women leading prayers, we are talking at another level about killing or shattering (graven) images of an all-powerful father; God-as-father. Of course this also implies challenging and destroying our converse feelings of safety, as little girls who can (as one woman in the study put it) "come to *shul* to rest and have no obligations", while the men take charge.

As if this psychological dynamic were not sufficient, anxiety about sexuality may also accompany this process for heterosexual women. Although in this research, women's feelings in this area were not systematically investigated, several women spoke spontaneously about the *tallis* (read "role") in terms of "masquerading like a man," or "wearing the male uniform, and feeling like I'm a man, or trying to be a man". Because gender roles are constructed so early in life and within the family, and because it was impossible to picture, for example, a "female rabbi" as most of us were growing up (this seemed like a contradiction in terms), some women in this research seemed to be wondering, "Am I trying to be a man?" "Will I be seen as unfeminine?" "Will men view me differently?" and so on. One woman in this study expressed this confusion through her association with the image of female leadership when she said she admired Golda Meir "because she had balls". For both these reasons (the association with father-murder and with definitions of sexuality), both highly anxiety provoking, Jewish women may fear the anger of their fathers for entering, uninvited, into the inner sanctuary, both literally and metaphorically.

Unfortunately, these fears are reinforced, rather than diminished, by women's encounters with men in "the real world." Women have a history to draw on of men's anger in response to women's challenge: in the corporate world, in academia, in all fields of endeavor, and of course in the Jewish community. To fear anger, rejection, expulsion and ridicule, either from real men (husbands, lovers, friends, fathers, sons, co-worshippers) or from internalized male figures (dead, remembered, or symbolic fathers, rabbis, Hebrew school teachers, and of course God, whom we were taught to think of as male), and to long for the acceptance of these figures, is reasonable and natural.

When juxtaposed against the vividness of these images, the idea of our mothers neglected, or our daughters limited or unexpressed, may seem relatively pale. When a woman considers taking on a leadership role in prayer, this may mean to her, in terms of her father images, a sin of commission (doing something forbidden). On the other hand, when she considers retaining a relatively passive role, the sin (toward her mother images) is "only" a sin of omission (not doing something she ought to). Furthermore, for many women, their mothers (real or internalized) would agree with, and support, traditional attitudes, and would not necessarily want to be "liberated," or "honored." It seems, then, that the images of our mothers are weaker than those of our fathers, at least in terms of shaping our behavior in religious leadership, and we are bowing to the stronger, more fear-inspiring image when we do not fully realize ourselves.

The assumption that sins of omission (towards our mothers, daughters and ourselves) are somehow less "serious" morally than sins of commission (against fathers) appears to be essential to the dynamic which underlies Jewish women, like the ones in this study, not taking on the opportunities and responsibilities of prayer leadership. However, we do know both rationally and intuitively that sins of omission are every bit as significant as sins of commission. On *Yom Kippur* (the Day of Atonement, the holiest day of the Jewish year), we are held accountable for both. We atone for lying and stealing and for not resisting evil and for not using our power (Harlow, 1987). But somehow we delude ourselves that if we just "carry on" passively, leaving it to others to change things, it is less of a sin. At least no one will be angry at us, attack us, call us names, or say we're "unfeminine" or worse.

Role models

The problem, of course, is our daughters—both our real flesh-and-blood offspring, and the woman-future that they symbolize. The recurring theme of some of the women in this study, of "I didn't get this, I want my daughter to" is sobering, in light of the clear indication in the data that these women are not providing any role modeling for their daughters different from the kind they themselves received as girls from their mothers. Joining an egalitarian *shul* is a good first step, of course, but by itself it is something of a half-solution. These women are providing their daughters with alternative ideas and images through Jewish women other than themselves, who carry the responsibility of providing role models for their daughters. We all know, of course, that our children follow what we do, not what we say. The daughters at our *shul*, although having had the benefit of four or five women role models on the *bima*, are getting clear messages from their mothers: clear "mixed messages", that is. What they are learning from their mothers goes something like this: "Dear daughter, I intellectually value women taking on leadership roles in Judaism, and I want you to have these opportunities in a way that I did not. So I have brought you here to this place. But while we're here, don't look at me, instead emulate and learn from those women up on the *bima*. I'm too afraid, it's too hard. You, and your generation, work it out."

The power and significance of role modeling are well documented, not only in learning theory and moral education, but also in the data in this research. The difficulty women in the study had in identifying a Jewish woman leader other than Golda Meir cannot be irrelevant to their difficulties seeing themselves as Jewish women leaders. However, these same women, instead of providing such positive role modeling for their daughters, are now modeling fearfulness and passivity for them. At the one *shul* where I have spoken to and observed these girls, they seem so far to be following very closely in their mothers' footsteps, having already internalized tremendous ambivalence by *bat mitzvah* age. There is reason to be very concerned about our daughters, as individuals and collectively. They will not automatically be different, nor will future generations, unless something (i.e., the number of women leading) changes now.

Strategies for change

Where do we go from here? First of all, it is crucial not to "blame the victim." Women are not responsible for the structural forces which have shaped us, nor for the impact of internalizing these structures (and the roles they imply) on our psychological responses. Nor are women responsible for the real conditions and social attitudes which make it necessary to have unusual courage, commitment and assertiveness, if a woman wants to take a leadership role in Jewish prayer.

On the other hand, the stakes are enormous, and only we can do anything to change things. The first step must be taken by each of us alone. This involves getting in touch with some of our internalized images and assumptions, and beginning to question these. It means affirming deeply our right to question and to dissent, and asking what we really believe is "okay." It means questioning what we think God really wants of us and how we think about God. And it means examining who we are and what is real to us.

The second step has to be taken collectively, and this work involves talking to, and supporting, each other. Many women, when encouraged to reflect on it, locate their feelings of discomfort about prayer leadership around very specific images. In some cases, this is as obvious as the image of a woman on the *bima*. Some are prevented from stepping up on the *bima* to lead, because they can't "see themselves" there. It is an axiom of imagery theory and therapy that one rarely does things which one cannot first envision (Lazarus, 1977).

It is on this level that we must struggle, and for this we need each other. Although intellectually many women in this research supported egalitarianism and full participation for women, and could be quite outspoken about this, emotionally they felt uneasy, and could not "do anything different" (i.e., from their family of origin) until they felt totally certain it was right. Such a woman is aware of the inconsistency in her position, but feels she is struggling with it, and will move forward in her own time. So she attends an egalitarian *shul* but lets other women take the lead, while she tries to figure it out. This woman may have been in this place for a short time, or for ten to twenty years. What the results of this study indicate is that, in fact, women in this place do not move forward just with the passage of time. They remain "stuck" because the underlying dynamics and resistance are so profound and threatening. A specific kind of process needs to be engaged in to loosen this up and help women move forward to assume leadership roles.

One woman suggested starting where women have particular blocks in imagery. "For me, the *tallis* is such a basic image, I feel it's my father or my partner, not me. Maybe a desensitizing is needed here for me, and elsewhere for other women who have similar blocks in other places." It is only as Jewish women talk together about our blocks, and where they come from, that we can overcome them. We must validate each other in the right to be doing this, help each other discover what we want and need, and offer each other the moral support necessary to build our collective strength.

We also need to educate ourselves. When the women in this study were asked what kind of aid or support (practical or emotional) would help them to be more active in leadership roles, the overwhelming response was a request for more education. Twelve (two-fifths of the women) thought they would be helped by classes teaching them to lead services, and these included specific skills, like learning Hebrew, or *trop*. One woman preferred to study with an individual teacher, another wanted to learn with a study partner like herself, and three wanted to learn alone with tapes.

The differences in format mentioned (for example, classes vs. having an individual tutor) may reflect both differences in learning style and personality factors (for example, being too shy to practice singing in a group at the initial stages). But what was clear was that women were concerned with their own education (or re-education) in the broadest possible sense, i.e., not only in terms of learning skills, but also in terms of empowering themselves and each other. They were very aware of not wanting to repeat the negative "knowledge + attitude" package they had been given as girls (i.e., getting *haftorah* skills along with the message that women shouldn't be doing this), as well as needing a safe place to explore this together. Several women referred to the process of this education, with four women suggesting a study group "for women only": "Maybe there need to be groups for women just to do it alone to gain the skills, without resident experts, men, around. We could learn alone and then come forward more publicly." The comments reflect these women's feelings of vulnerability and inadequacy in the area of Jewish religious leadership, and the importance of providing this education in an environment that is strongly supportive and builds self-confidence. One woman thought a group *bat mitzvah* for women, as a kind of "graduating ceremony", would be wonderful for the women involved and also an important public statement to the community.

In brief, the process of empowering ourselves involves a reversal of the traditional injunction, *"na'aseh v'nishma"* (do and then hear) from Exodus 24:7. We must first hear ourselves and each other and then we must do (*nishma v'na'aseh*). At one level, what is described is immense. But it is no more immense than what so many before us have done, as women or as Jews, in the Jewish community and in the secular world, in the struggle against oppression, stereotypes and limitations. Furthermore, "it is not upon us to finish the work, it is only upon us not to desist from it" (*Pirke Avot*). "Not having to finish the work" does not mean leaving it to others to do (our friends at *shul*, or our daughters), but it also does not mean we are doing it all alone. We are in it together, all Jewish women, past, present, and in the generations to come. May we, whose turn it is now, be strong and of good courage.

Table 1. Demographic Characteristics of Subjects

Age (Mean Age = 41)	
30-39	10
40-49	17
50+	3
Marital status	
Married	21
Divorced or Separated	6
Unmarried	3
Employed in paid work	
Yes	23 (18 professionals)
No	7 (3 Ph.D. or postdoctoral students)
Secular education (Highest level attained)	
High school	3
Bachelors' degrees (1 in law)	14
Masters' degrees	9
A.B.D.	3
Ph.D.	1
Jewish background	
Orthodox	10
Conservative	11
Reform	3
Secular or Unaffiliated	3
Converted, Christian Home	3

Jewish education	
Afternoon school, Sunday school, or private lessons	16
University studies	4
Day school	2

Was either parent an active leader in your *shul* as you grew up?	
No	15
Yes (Father)	6
Yes (Mother)	5
	(4 as President or V-P of a sisterhood)

Table 2. Subjects' Responses to Selected Questions

Do you consider yourself a feminist?	
Yes	26
Unsure	3
No	1

How important is it to you that women play a central leadership role in the *shul*?	
Extremely important	7
Very important	14
Moderately important	8
Somewhat important	0
Not important	1

Reason for joining this *shul*	
Egalitarian	22
Felt comfortable	6
For my daughter	4
Small, intimate	3
Close by	3

Frequency of *shul* attendance	
Once every week or two	11
Once a month	10
Two or three times/year	9

Number of *aliyot* to date	
1-5	11
More than 5	19

REFERENCES

Beck, E. T. (1991). Therapy's double dilemma: Anti-semitism and misogyny. In R. J. Siegel & E. Cole (Eds.), *Jewish women in therapy: Seen but not heard* (pp. 19-30). New York: Harrington Park Press.

Beck, E. T. (1982). *Nice Jewish girls: A lesbian anthology.* Boston: Beacon Press.

Berger, K. S. (1988). *The developing person through the life span.* New York: Worth Publishers.

Berkovits, E. (1990). *Jewish women in time and Torah.* New Jersey: Ktav.

Bridges: A Journal for Jewish Feminists and our Friends. New York: New Jewish Agenda.

Cantor, A. (1987). *The Jewish woman 1900-1985: A bibliography.* Fresh Meadows, New York: Biblio Press.

Cantor, A. (1983). The Lilith question. In S. Heschel (Ed.), *On being a Jewish feminist* (pp. 40-50). New York: Schocken.

Cantor, A. (1978). The sheltered workshop, *Lilith, 5,* 19-20.

Cantor, A. Z. (1973). The oppression of the Jewish woman. *Response, 7*(2), 47-54.

Caplan, P. J. (1985). *The myth of women's masochism.* New York: E.P. Dutton.

Finch, J. & Groves, D. (Eds.). (1983). *A labour of love: Women, work and caring.* London: Routledge & Kegan Paul.

Gilligan, C. (1982). *In a different voice.* Cambridge, MA.: Harvard University Press.

Goldenberg, N. (1979). *Changing of the gods.* Boston: Beacon Press.

Greenberg, B. (1981). *On women and Judaism.* Philadelphia: Jewish Publication Society.

Greenspan, M. (1983). *A new approach to women and therapy.* New York: McGraw Hill.

Grossman, S. & Haut, R. (1992). *Daughters of the king: Women and the synagogue.* Philadelphia: Jewish Publication Society.

Harlow, J. (Ed.). (1987). *Mahzor for Rosh Hashanah and Yom Kippur.* New York: Rabbinical Assembly.

Henry, S. & Taitz, E. (1990). *Written out of history: Our Jewish foremothers.* New York: Biblio Press.

Hyman, P.E. (1973). The other half: Women in the Jewish tradition. *Response, 7*(2), 67-75.

Kaye/Kantrowitz, M. (1992). *The issue is power.* San Francisco: Spinsters/Aunt Lute.

Kaye/Kantrowitz, M. (1991). The issue is power: Some notes on Jewish women and therapy. In R. J. Siegel & E. Cole (Eds.), *Jewish women in therapy: Seen but not heard* (pp. 7-18). New York: Harrington Park Press.

Kaye/Kantrowitz, M. (1988). To be a radical Jew in the late twentieth century. In C. McEwen & S. O'Sullivan (Eds.), *Out the other side* (pp. 243-268). London: Vivago.

Kaye/Kantrowitz, M. & Klepfisz, I. (1986). *The tribe of Dina: A Jewish women's anthology.* Montpelier, VT.: Sinister Wisdom.

Lazarus, A. (1977). *In the mind's eye.* New York: Rawson Associates.

Levine, H. (1982). The personal is political: Feminism and the helping professions. In A. Miles & G. Finn (Eds.), *Feminism in Canada: From pressure to politics* (pp. 175-209). Montreal: Black Rose.

Lilith. New York: Lilith Publications, Inc.

Ozick, C. (1983). Notes toward finding the right question. In S. Heschel (Ed.), *On being a Jewish feminist* (pp. 120-151). New York: Schocken.

Penfold, P.S. & Walker, G.A. (1983). *Women and the psychiatric paradox.* Montreal: Eden Press.

Pirke Avot, Talmud.

Plaskow, J. (1990). *Standing again at Sinai: Judaism from a feminist perspective.* San Francisco: Harper and Row.

Plaskow, J. (1983). The right question is theological. In S. Heschel (Ed.), *On being a Jewish feminist* (pp. 223-233). New York: Schocken.

Pogrebin, L. C. (1991). *Deborah, Golda, and me: Being Jewish and female in America.* Toronto: Doubleday.

Portnoy, M. A. (1986). *Ima on the bima.* Rockville, MD: Karben.

Reinharz, S. (1992). *Feminist methods in social research.* New York: Oxford University Press.

Schneider, S. W. (1984). *Jewish and female.* New York: Simon and Schuster.

Siegel, R. J. & Cole, E. (Eds.). (1991). *Jewish women in therapy: Seen but not heard.* New York: Harrington Park Press.

Umansky, E. M. & Ashton, D. (1992). *Four centuries of Jewish women's spirituality.* Boston: Beacon Press.

Weiss, A. (1990). *Women at prayer: A halakhic analysis of women's prayer groups.* New Jersey: Ktav.

Wine, J. (1982). Gynocentric values and feminist psychology. In A. Miles & G. Finn (Eds.), *Feminism in Canada: From pressure to politics* (pp. 67-87). Montreal: Black Rose.

ACKNOWLEDGMENTS

This chapter and the research that preceded it is in honor of my two grandmothers: Leah (Laka) Stein Gold and Terry Leibovit Lubin.

THERAPEUTIC ENCOUNTERS

Robin B. Zeiger
Sara R. Horowitz
tova
Yonah Klem
Melissa Schwartz
Barbara Eve Breitman

REFLECTIONS ON INFERTILITY

ROBIN B. ZEIGER

MEDITATION ON THE *SUKKAH*
For seven days we dwell
Under the sun and stars in this fragile hut
Sheltered only by branches once rooted in the ground.
We leave the solid fortress of our houses
Where we are lulled into false security, closed in,
Where we need not look at the vastness of the world and God.
Here, open under the sky, faith is the only shelter.
Remember the Israelites wandering in the desert.
We, too, wander in deserts,
Lonely, through drifting sands of passing time,
Searching the heavens for living waters and shady resting
places,
A place within ourselves to call home.
Miriam Lippel Blum, 1990

At the height of my painful encounter with infertility, after numerous problems becoming pregnant, three miscarriages and a difficult decision to pursue foreign adoption, I happened upon this poem. The words echoed my personal grief, longing and struggle with God. Further, they symbolize the quest of the religious woman and man throughout their search for faith and inner peace.

This quest for faith and inner peace is often a difficult journey for the religious Jew faced with infertility. Judaism as a culture and a religion places an extremely high value on children. Celebrations center around family. In an attempt to carry on tradition, fight assimilation and counter the ugly realities of the Holocaust, we are a nation that is often obsessed with passing on the family name and tradition.

In addition to cultural norms, childbearing is virtually required for the traditionally observant Jew. The religious Jew is taught from an early age the Biblical mandate for having children: "And God blessed them, and God said unto them, 'Be fruitful and multiply and replenish the earth and subdue it...'" (Genesis, 1:28).

This passage is the first *mitzvah* or commandment given to humankind. From time immemorial the Jew has viewed procreation with the highest respect, love and awe. To women and men with a strong belief that they are created in the image of God, pregnancy and childbearing represent an important aspect of godliness.

This paper attempts to identify some of the common experiences, reactions and spiritual crises of the Orthodox Jew faced with infertility. In addition, implications for counseling are briefly discussed. Finally, it offers some thoughts on the need for ritual to help heal the pain; in this regard, I offer some personal reflections on my own healing process.

A DEFINITION OF INFERTILITY

According to one of the foremost authorities on the subject, "Infertility is defined as the inability to conceive a pregnancy after a year or more of regular sexual relations without contraception, or the inability to carry pregnancies to a live birth. It is estimated that 15 percent of the population of childbearing age in America is infertile at any given time. This amounts to 1 in every 6 couples of childbearing age—more than 10 million people in this country alone. Infertility is further classified as either primary, when there is no previous history of pregnancy, or secondary, when it occurs after one or more successful pregnancies." (Menning, 1988, p. 4).

THE MILIEU

In an attempt to develop a framework and understand the everyday experiences of the Orthodox Jewish couple faced with infertility, let us follow the first few years of marriage for two hypothetical Orthodox couples; one of a modern Orthodox orientation and one couple who is more fundamentalist.

Couple One

Miriam Misel and Daniel Schwartz meet at a college Hillel event. They are 24 and 26 respectively. Daniel is finishing law school, while Miriam is studying architecture. They both grew up in Orthodox homes, attending day school and participating in Jewish youth groups. Both consider themselves modern Orthodox. For them, this means a commitment to *halacha* (Jewish law), while at the same time maintaining a strong connection to a secular society.

After several months of dating, Miriam and Daniel begin to talk seriously about marriage. Among many other topics, they discuss their goals for a family. Both would like to wait a year or two before having children. They wish to establish themselves professionally and buy a house. However, they agree they would like three or four children.

Miriam and Daniel marry shortly thereafter. The first two years of marriage are relatively blissful, although tiring due to their new careers. After buying and moving into a house, they begin to long for a baby and set about realizing this goal. They spend the next several months trying to become pregnant.

At first they are nonchalant when Miriam gets her period each month. After the sixth month, they become anxious and buy a book on how to get pregnant. What follows are several months of temperature charts, ovulation predictor kits and carefully timed intercourse. Yet, they still have no luck.

Meanwhile friends and family begin to nudge the couple, "You are settled professionally. You have a beautiful house. So *nu*, what are you waiting for? When are you going to have a baby? You aren't getting any younger." Miriam's mother pleads, "I want to be a grandmother before I die."

Miriam and Daniel try valiantly to remain calm and ward off unwanted comments. They don't feel comfortable sharing their frustrations with others. Yet, as people nudge, they become more upset, anxious and depressed.

After a year, Miriam, now 28, decides to consult her gynecologist. An initial work-up does not reveal any problems. Many sleepless nights later, Daniel and Miriam make the difficult decision to consult an infertility specialist.

This fated step leads to a stressful year of tests and treatments. After several months, Miriam discovers she is pregnant. Yet delight quickly turns to despair, as she miscarries. The doctors can't seem to offer any real solutions. Gradually Miriam and Daniel become more depressed and anxious. They find themselves preoccupied with treatment.

Meanwhile the nudging goes on. It gets to the point where they don't feel like attending synagogue on *Shabbat* (Sabbath). They seem to be surrounded by pregnant women, baby naming and *brit* (circumcision) ceremonies. Holidays are particularly painful in that they are often so family-oriented.

One day Miriam wears a T-shirt dress to synagogue. A couple of people whisper. Someone she hardly knows is bold enough to ask if she is pregnant. Miriam quickly answers that she is not and walks away on the verge of tears. She decides to go home early. After that experience, she finds herself spending less and less time at synagogue and other community events. Daniel and Miriam find themselves drifting away from married friends, because they all seem to have children. They begin to feel isolated and in deep despair. They wonder if they will ever be blessed with children.

Couple Two

Shmuel Cohen and Faige Segal meet through a *shiduch* (matchmaker) at the ages of 19 and 18 respectively. They date six times under the watchful eyes of their families and *rebbe* (rabbi). From the beginning, they both discuss their religious backgrounds and goals for marriage.

Both grew up in *Yeshivah* (school of higher Jewish learning) families, in which Judaic learning was a top priority. Shmuel plans to study full-time for a year in *kollel* (full-time learning program in a *Yeshivah*). After that, he would like to work part-time in the family business and study part-time. They both hope to live totally immersed in a *Torah* (religious) life. This includes living in a religious neighborhood in New York. It also includes a lifestyle without a television and other secular distractions.

They hope to raise a large family; at least seven children would be a wonderful blessing from God. Faige would be willing to help out in the family business if needed. However, she sees her primary role as wife and mother. She looks forward to household tasks, entertaining, raising children and performing charitable functions for the community.

After determining their goals are similar and that they really like one another, Shmuel and Faige decide to get married. They have a relatively short engagement. Five months after meeting one another, they are married and ready to start a family. Faige looks forward with anticipation to becoming pregnant, as many of her schoolmates already have one or two children. Thus, she is disappointed each month when she gets her period.

Shmuel is somewhat less preoccupied. He is enjoying his year in *kollel* and is very happy to be married to such a special woman. However, as the end of their first year of marriage approaches, he too becomes somewhat anxious. One *Shabbat*, they both find themselves having a serious discussion about their desire for children. Shmuel quotes some thoughts from a recent *Talmudic* (part of Jewish oral law) lesson on the subject. They resolve to begin praying more earnestly for children.

Another six months pass. Faige finds herself somewhat anxious and unhappy. She has begun to help Shmuel in the family business, yet she finds this role unfulfilling. Family members have begun to hint to Shmuel and Faige about having children. Little is talked about directly. While Faige has considered asking some friends for advice, she fears it may not be reflective of *stzenut* or modesty. A few friends have offhandedly suggested asking famous *rebbes* for a blessing.

Gradually Faige finds herself becoming more and more depressed. She resolves to become an even better wife, involving herself more fully in household chores and acts of *chesed* (charity and kindness). She is always the first to volunteer to cook for a new mother or to house an out-of-town guest. The *Shabbat* table is always full with company from all parts of the community. She begins to volunteer at a nearby pre-school once a week. Suddenly there never seems to be enough hours in the day. Faige often goes to bed after midnight. Yet, she still has trouble sleeping. She spends many an hour lying in bed reviewing her *midot* (characteristics). Faige becomes convinced that she must do more *teshuvah* (repentance) to bear a child. She feels God must be punishing her for some flaw in her religiosity.

Shmuel is also quite upset. However, he rarely shares his feelings, even with Faige. Instead, he immerses himself in his learning. He often spends long hours at the *beit midrash* (study hall). His understanding of a difficult piece of *Talmud* appears to help him tremendously with his frustrations.

Faige becomes particularly depressed one day when her best friend announces she is pregnant with her third child. That Friday night when praying for a child, she becomes extremely tearful and sullen. Shmuel notices her change in behavior and attempts to talk with her. They finally decide to consult their *rebbe*.

The following week, they sit down with their *rebbe* and attempt to tell him of their longing for a child. He listens sympathetically. He offers a good deal of advice and support, reminding them of the struggles of the *emahot* (foremothers) and *avot* (forefathers) for children. The *rebbe* suggests a few *tehillim* (psalms) to recite on a daily basis. He tells them about a famous *rebbe* who will be visiting next month and urges them to ask for his blessing. He suggests that Shmuel review with him the laws of *taharat ha'mispacha* (family purity and use of the *mikvah* or ritual bath). Maybe there is something they are forgetting. Perhaps more meticulous observance of these laws will help them. Finally, he suggests trying all of this for another six months. If they have no success, he recommends a *frum* (Orthodox) doctor with whom to consult.

Shmuel and Faige return home feeling better. They embark with fervor on the course suggested by the *rebbe*. However, six months pass without any success. Once again they are faced with an important decision; should they consult with the doctor?

Both couples are clearly struggling with infertility on a day-to-day basis. They have many things in common with the average infertile individual and the infertile Jew. Yet, these two scenarios attempt to identify some of the unique struggles of the Orthodox couple struggling with infertility. The following section will detail more clearly some of these struggles. In addition, treatment implications will be offered for the psychotherapist, rabbi or spiritual counselor involved with infertile individuals.

THE PROBLEMS—IMPLICATIONS FOR COUNSELING

First and foremost, the religious Jewish community is centered around the family. From an early age, one is preparing for marriage and parenthood. Having children is regarded as a very important *mitzvah* for the married couple. It is almost unthinkable to choose child-free living.

As a result, Orthodox couples tend to have at least three or four children. It is typically expected that the newly wed couple will soon begin to have children. Some couples, like Daniel and Miriam, are more likely to wait awhile before beginning a family. Establishing a career, developing marital closeness, and becoming more comfortable financially are often considered acceptable reasons to postpone children for a year or more. Certain forms of birth control are utilized and considered acceptable according to *halacha* in such circumstances by some modern Orthodox rabbis and couples. However, as more and more individuals are marrying at a later age, there is the added pressure of the biological time clock. For the couple committed to having several children, there is less time to begin a family. For the infertile couple, this biological time clock ticks very loudly as they face the many treatment options.

Faige and Shmuel represent the other side of the spectrum. For couples like them, *Yiddishkite* (Judaic commitment), *mitzvot* and building a Jewish home are number one on the priority list. Postponing a family for career, a house, or more money is almost unthinkable. Birth control is frowned upon except in the most difficult of circumstances (e.g., danger to the mother's life). The question is more likely to be, "Why wait? Let *Hashem* (God) decide when and how many children to bless us with. He will provide." Thus, it is not uncommon to become pregnant within the first year of marriage. Furthermore, like Faige and Shmuel, couples struggling with infertility in this community often are faced with peers who have five, six or seven children. Thus, their lives seem worlds apart from that of their friends.

It is important for the therapist to communicate empathy and understanding of the milieu of which the couple is a part. This includes religious mandates about children, as well as self-imposed and community pressures. The first phase of psychotherapeutic treatment might be best devoted to exploring with the client(s) the meaning of, and reaction to, infertility. The therapist unfamiliar with traditional Judaism can develop a better understanding by consulting with a colleague or reading about the subject. Two books of particular relevance are, *And Hanna Wept* (1988) by Rabbi Michael Gold and *How Long the Night?* (1991) by Mindy Gross. It is certainly also appropriate to ask the client to share and explain the relevance of their religious practice to infertility.

Additionally, religious couples like the Schwartzs and Cohens typically spend a good deal of time with the community. There are numerous reminders of their childlessness. Synagogue attendance alone may make one feel bombarded by pregnant women, babies and children. Community celebrations often center around children. There are the numerous baby naming, circumcision ceremonies and *b'nai mitzvah* (plural - coming-of-age ceremony) to deal with, often on a weekly basis. These celebrations frequently evoke feelings of sadness, loneliness, longing and envy. Many infertile couples have confessed to me, somewhat shamefully, that they find themselves avoiding such participation. This can lead to further isolation and guilt.

The Jewish holidays are replete with references to, and rituals for, children. The Passover *seder* (ritual) centers around the four sons. The story is meant to be told to the children. What happens when one's *seder* is without children? *Chanukah* has *dreidels* (spinning toys) and presents for children. *Purim* has costumes and carnivals. The average family *sukkah* (temporary shelter of the holiday) is decorated with the drawings by the children. The list goes on and on. For the infertile religious couple, the holidays are often tainted with a bittersweet happiness and longing for a complete family.

In a close-knit community, there are also friends, families, rabbis and others with whom one must contend. Well-meaning individuals may begin to press the couple about their childlessness. There are those people who begin to look for signs of pregnancy, noticing any change in weight or dress. Woe to the woman who gains weight due to infertility drugs. She is a particular target for rumors and comments.

The "nudgers" are often not close friends, making it even harder to know how to respond. Does one make a joke (e.g., "I'm just getting fat.")? Does one tell them off? Or perhaps one launches into all the personal and clinical details of infertility treatment and hopes they are so turned off that they never ask again. The deeply religious couple, such as Faige and Shmuel, may have a particularly difficult time knowing how to respond. They may feel compelled to show a nice, happy face, even when deeply offended or uncomfortable.

When members of the community are aware of infertility problems, the couple may become the target of unsolicited and often unwelcome advice. In addition to all of the typical comments (e.g., just relax and take a vacation), there are numerous uniquely religious tidbits. Mindy Gross in her recently released book, *How Long the Night?* (1991), does an excellent job of identifying the myriad of religious solutions. They range from the more common such as seeking blessings from famous *rebbes*, leaving a note in the *kotel* or Western Wall, and praying harder, to the less common, such as drinking holy water or wearing a tie from a *Torah* (Bible) scroll. While these customs may provide comfort and assistance to some, they are not useful when unsolicited. In addition to meddling, this type of advice smacks of blaming the victim (e.g., you are not religious enough; it is not your destiny to have children).

Therapy can help the couple or individual manage the pressures of community. At times, it is easy for the religious individuals, concerned with community *mitzvot* or obligations, to overextend themselves and become tied up in "shoulds". Their own needs take a back seat to the needs of others. These individuals may need "permission" to withdraw a bit from community for awhile and revitalize themselves.

Others may find themselves becoming too isolated from friends and community because they don't know how to handle comments and painful feelings. These individuals may need assistance to talk with fertile friends and others. For example, it may not even occur to them that it is okay to share feelings of envy with a close friend who is pregnant. Principles of assertiveness training may be particularly useful here.

When faced with infertility, it is generally difficult for individuals to decide what to say to whom and how to say it. Telling too much can feel like an invasion of much needed privacy and may lead to extreme vulnerability. On the other hand, hiding such painful feelings can lead to exacerbation of loneliness and grief, as well as the development of an "as if" or falsely cheerful persona.

Because the Orthodox community is typically small and intimate, confidentiality can pose numerous challenges. Telling one person may sometimes feel akin to putting an ad in the local Jewish newspaper. Moreover, the traditionally observant Jew may feel isolated from others who do not share the infertility experience. Due to hesitancy over self-disclosure, the couple may not come into contact with others who are infertile. In contrast to the more centrist or modern Orthodox individual, the more fundamentalist Orthodox Jew is highly unlikely to seek out friendship and advice outside of the community. This further narrows their support network. Interestingly, my husband and I have noticed that when we have traveled around the country on various occasions, fellow Orthodox Jews have given us detailed infertility histories. We have speculated that it is often easier to talk with a relative stranger who is passing through town and seems to have similar values and experiences.

Often the infertile individual or couple enters mental health treatment having disclosed little about the diagnosis and/or medical treatment involved. The therapy may be one of the first places that s/he discloses the pain and vulnerability. Thus, it is important that the therapy room become an extremely safe place to practice this disclosure. Once the client becomes comfortable enough to share in therapy, s/he may decide to tell others of the struggles. The therapist can then help the patient decide what s/he wishes to share with whom.

The therapist or rabbi may also help the client to develop a support system. For example, the therapist may put the client in touch with other resources. For some religious individuals, this may include secular resources (e.g., RESOLVE, a national, grass-roots infertility organization for infertile individuals). For others, it may include helping to network Orthodox couples through workshops, lectures and support groups. Over the past several years, there has been a major increase in time devoted to this difficult issue in religious circles. Unfortunately, the Orthodox infertile Jew is more likely to find such support only in large Jewish centers such as New York, Los Angeles and Chicago. Thus, it can be a much more isolating experience for the average infertile Orthodox Jew in a smaller city.

These aforementioned problems have focused more heavily on behavior vis-à-vis the community experience. Yet, the religious infertile individual is often faced with an even more difficult area, that of crises of faith—internal struggles with self and in relation to God. In another paper, I have dealt at length with these crises of faith (Zeiger, 1993). Here I will briefly outline some of the difficulties.

For the average individual, infertility poses more questions than answers. Individuals may experience anger, depression, confusion and a whole myriad of negative emotions. The religious individual often looks to God for strength and answers. This may include questioning her or his relationship to God and to religion. S/he may even become angry with the Divine Creator, who withholds the longed for child. Sometimes, when faced with such challenges, individuals may begin to believe that God is an uninvolved deity or does not exist. While these feelings are normal and expected in such circumstances, the typical religious individual is often totally unprepared for such an existential crisis. At times, religious education discourages or downplays questions of faith. People do not easily admit to doubt and/or anger at God. Thus, the individual of faith may attempt to downplay, repress or deny such feelings.

The flip side of this crisis of faith is anger, depression and blame directed at self. The religious individual may wonder, "Why me? What did I do to deserve this?" S/he may conclude that s/he is being punished for some unforgivable sin. We see the beginnings of these struggles for Faige. This type of attribution, when taken to extreme, can lead to a vicious cycle of depression and self-blame.

At the other extreme, infertility has the potential to promote spiritual growth. Many of our esteemed foremothers and forefathers in the Bible struggled with infertility. Individuals such as Sarah and Abraham, Rachel and Jacob, and Hannah and Elkanah emerged from their struggles with an incredible amount of strength and commitment to God and Jewish values. Both psychology and religion have long recognized that personal crises and struggles can lead to renewed strength and transformation.

For the couple struggling with infertility, it is important to recognize that these crises of faith are normal and to be expected. This is where the counselor and/or rabbi becomes very important. The privacy, safety and confidentiality of the counseling setting is an ideal place to help the infertile individual acknowledge shameful, painful and scary thoughts. The counselor can help normalize the crises by reassuring the couple that other religious individuals also struggle with these thoughts. The rabbi, as well as the counselor familiar with religious sources, can provide the couple with references legitimizing doubt in the quest for faith.

This acceptance of doubt can hopefully free the individual from incapacitating guilt. Ultimately, it is hoped that acknowledging doubt, crises, anger and other such difficult emotions will aid in the healing process and promote spiritual growth.

For the Jew committed to a *Torah* lifestyle, *halacha* has something to say about all aspects of daily existence. The myriad of laws, combined with a complex philosophical system, provides a framework for such decisions as what to eat, how to dress, how to speak and in which way to approach the miracles of modern science. Some laws, such as whether to drive a car on *Shabbat*, are generally clear-cut. It is either acceptable or not acceptable. However many important life situations are characterized by gray areas, in which the *halachic* response is not always clear. Many times, it depends upon the specific circumstances of the individual as well as the particular understanding and approach of the rabbi. Thus, the woman and man of faith usually consult with their own personal *rav* (rabbi) for a specific answer.

Jewish medical ethics is replete with such gray areas. For example, a rabbi may be consulted on questions about organ transplants and/or how far to go in employing heroic measures to keep one alive (e.g., use of a respirator for terminally ill patients). In such cases, the rabbi typically consults with the medical authority to understand the specifics of the science. He then applies his understanding of the applicable Judaic principles, while at all times keeping in mind the specific needs of the person involved. Thus, the same rabbi may render two very different decisions for the same *halachic* questions when it involves two different people.

Infertility diagnosis and treatment is characterized by a host of *halachic* laws, principles and gray areas. It is well beyond the scope of this paper to attempt an outline of these issues. However, several brief examples will be provided.

One important overriding principle throughout the entire infertility *responsa* (rabbinic literature containing questions and answers to noted Jewish scholars about modern-day problems of Jewish law) is the biblical mandate to be fruitful and multiply. Thus *halacha* tends to favor utilizing most scientific advances in infertility. While prayer, *teshuvah* and general religious commitment are important and legitimate approaches to infertility, couples are also typically encouraged to seek out the best possible medical treatment. Some couples, such as Faige and Shmuel, may wait longer to seek out medical intervention. However, most religious couples who are not successful in childbearing will eventually consult a doctor.

An example of a diagnostic procedure that is problematic is sperm collection. It is a *Torah* mandate not to waste sperm. Masturbation, in and of itself, is prohibited according to *halacha*. Thus, in general, sperm are to be intentionally released only within the framework of intercourse between husband and wife. Many rabbinic sources state that sperm should only be tested when deemed absolutely necessary. Among the rabbinic *responsa*, one can find a hierarchy of acceptable ways to collect sperm for infertility treatment. For example, a post-coital test is among the least problematic. Coitus interruptus and use of special condoms for sperm collection are other less problematic alternatives. Many sources allow masturbation if it is the only viable medical option. However, a special vibrator is preferable to actual manual stimulation for procuring the sperm.

What about the actual infertility treatment and *halacha*? Many of the commonly used procedures are generally acceptable to *halacha*. For example, use of fertility drugs and male or female surgery to repair damaged organs are among the least problematic. Artificial insemination with a husband's sperm is usually fine, as is IVF (in-vitro fertilization), GIFT (Gamete Intrafallopian Transfer), and ZIFT (Zygote Intrafallopian Transfer).

Major concerns arise in the *responsa* with some of the newer technology. For example the rabbis generally frown upon artificial insemination by donor and surrogacy vis-à-vis donor ovum or a donor uterus. Questions of maternity, paternity, incest and symbolic adultery arise. It is also important to recognize that in general, Orthodox couples vary in their approach to the application of *halacha* to science. Couples like Faige and Shmuel are almost always likely to consult their personal *rav* every step of the way. For them, it is unthinkable to take such a delicate matter into their own hands without *halachic* guidance. They would also be more likely to prefer dealing with a *frum* doctor. Along these lines, many major Orthodox Jewish centers such as cities in Israel, New York and Los Angeles, now boast of physicians and/or hospital programs with a sensitivity to *halacha*. For example, Laniado hospital in Netanya, Israel is specially known for this commitment.

Other Orthodox couples are more variant in their approach to rabbinic counsel and concern with *halacha* in their infertility treatment. Some may not want to know what the *halachot* (specific laws) are, hoping to avoid difficult decisions and/or residual guilt. Others may initially rely on their own knowledge of the laws based on learning opportunities. Nowadays, there are some excellent English and Hebrew sources to serve as guidelines. Many eventually choose to consult with a *rav* when faced with a clear *halachic*/ethical dilemma; for example, when the only viable option the doctor presents them with is artificial insemination via donor sperm.

A note about the importance of the rabbinic counseling and the role of rabbinic authority is important here. To the individual unfamiliar with the notion of rabbinic permission, it may seem strange or even repulsive to rely on this authority in such an all encompassing way. Yet this role is an important part of religious life. Hopefully, the *rav* helps to relieve the couple of the pressure of sole decision making in such crucial areas of life. In the ideal situation, the *rav* is able to act as a spiritual advisor and counselor.

The sensitive and empathic rabbi is also often called upon to engage in pastoral counseling. Prior to any contact with a psychotherapist, many couples may approach a rabbi ostensibly with a *halachic* question. Yet consciously or unconsciously they may have a hidden agenda. They may really need support, permission to vent feelings and/or spiritual and psychological guidance.

The rabbi and, at times, the Orthodox Jewish therapist, may find him/herself walking a difficult role. All too often, I have heard infertile religious couples complain about their interactions with rabbis. They feel talked down to, misunderstood or trivialized. At times, the rabbi or religious therapist may fall into a didactic or teaching role, attempting to impart moral lessons and reassure the couple that all will be fine; that God will provide. In fact, what the couple may most need at times of spiritual crisis is a supportive ear and a shoulder on which to cry. Once the pain is somewhat diminished, issues of faith can continue to be discussed. It is akin to the mourning process. Immediately after the death of a loved one is not the ideal time to tell someone all will be fine or to discuss complex religious dilemmas.

At times, the rabbi may also be called upon to deal with more serious psychological problems. For example, the crises of infertility may highlight psychopathology in one's life, or more commonly, precipitate a marital crisis. Hopefully, the rabbi can serve as an initial contact. However, at times, his role may be to refer the more troubled individual or couple for professional psychotherapy or further medical advice.

Psychotherapists familiar with infertility can also serve as resources to rabbis, both as consultants and educators on the common and not-so-common reactions of infertility. In addition, rabbis can serve as consultants to psychotherapists vis-à-vis spiritual and religious issues. It is important to note that rabbis, like all professionals, have various areas of expertise. There are several rabbis nationwide that are noted for their expertise with medical *halacha*. Thus, a therapist who specializes in infertility would be wise to familiarize her/himself with these individuals.

While rabbis are often helpful and an important part of a religious individual's life, some clients may allow the rabbi to take on exaggerated importance in the counselor's office. The resistant client may consciously or unconsciously attempt to play the therapist against the rabbi. For example, any time the therapist offers a suggestion, the client may state that it is against *halacha.* They may state that their rabbi would never allow it. The rabbi then becomes an absent third-party who is symbolically allowed to impede any progress. Thus, at times it may become appropriate, with proper releases, to either consult with the rabbi or bring him into a session.

Psychotherapy among the Orthodox community, while gradually becoming more common and more acceptable, continues to bear more of a stigma than in the community at large. Couples like Miriam and Daniel are more likely to see this as an option. Faige and Shmuel are less likely to consult a therapist, but even among their community, it is not unheard of. It is also important to recognize that some Orthodox Jews are only comfortable with a *frum* psychotherapist and/or a *frum* support group. At times, particularly in smaller Orthodox communities, this can be quite limiting. RESOLVE, a national infertility organization, has over 50 chapters nationwide. They offer many types of services, such as support groups and informational lectures on infertility. Many infertile individuals receive inexpensive and/or free advice, counseling and/or assistance through this organization. Couples like Miriam and Daniel are more likely to seek out such assistance. As individuals involved in a secular society, they are more comfortable relating to non-religious Jews and non-Jews. Thus, an infertility support group could serve their needs. In contrast, it is hard to imagine Faige and Shmuel attending a group with non-*frum* Jews. The double bind is they may be fearful of attending a lecture on infertility in their community, due to their hesitancy about confidentiality. Thus, they are likely to have many fewer options than the average infertile couple.

THE NEED FOR RITUAL

Judaism is a religion of action and deed. While we ascribe to an important and all-inclusive belief system, the sages have been quick to point out the overriding importance of *mitzvot* or commandments based on action. To the Orthodox Jew in particular, the concept of a Jew at heart is difficult, if not impossible, to understand. Instead, they state one must demonstrate commitment with one's head, feet and mouth.

Ritual plays a crucial role in traditional observance. Ideally the doing helps bring one closer to belief in God and spirituality. Everyday objects have the potential to bring one closer to God. Thus, the religious ritual helps transform the *chol* (mundane) into the *kodesh* (holy).

The average observant Jew is provided with daily rituals and blessings such as prayer. There are weekly *Shabbat* rituals (e.g., candle lighting, *kiddish* or prayer over the wine). There are holiday rituals, such as the *lulav* and *etrog* (ritual objects of the holiday) on *Sukkot*. The life cycle rituals are particularly symbolic. There are methods to sanctify birth (baby naming, circumcision), adulthood (*bat* and *bar mitzvah*), marriage and death (burial, *shiva*). Yet, there are other seemingly important events that do not boast clear-cut rituals, such as the woman who receives her Ph.D. or the man who retires after 40 years at work.

The religious individual is left with at least three options on these occasions. One can utilize secular rituals (e.g., graduation party, retirement party). One can ignore the event. One can attempt to apply religious principles to add a spiritual dimension. Many people sponsor a *kiddish* on *Shabbat*, give *tzedakah* (charity) and/or prepare a *d'var Torah* (short talk on a *Torah* subject) for significant life events.

Infertility is an important life event without set religious rituals. At times, this lack can become quite painful. Among the many strong reactions, couples often report feelings akin to loss and mourning. Each month with the onset of menses, many face a mini-death experience. Couples begin to lose hope in their fantasy of a family. Some infertile couples have to struggle with more tangible losses, such as miscarriages and/or a stillbirth.

There are few, if any, guidelines for infertility rituals. Some may choose to utilize already existing customs for difficult life situations. As mentioned previously, prayer is very important in this regard. Tradition states that many of our foremothers and forefathers prayed to God for children. Channa (Samuel I), is the foremother par excellence in this regard. She prayed fervently for a child and was answered with the birth of a prophet, Shmuel. This portion is considered so important that we read it as a *haftorah* (addition to the *Torah* reading) on *Rosh Hashannah*, a day dedicated to introspection and *teshuvah*. Infertile women have developed a custom of reciting Channa's prayer after lighting *Shabbat* candles on Friday night.

Mikvah is another important monthly ritual that infertile women can choose to focus on to help heal the pain. In traditional Jewish law, married women are considered *tameh* from the onset of menstruation for about 12-14 days. *Tameh* is a Hebrew word without a good English translation. It is a state of ritual impurity that can occur through various means for both men and women. In the time of the Temple, men and women who were *tameh* could not enter the Temple or eat from the sacrifices. In addition, married, observant, Orthodox women who are *tameh* due to menstruation observe various laws in regards to physical contact with their husbands.

At the end of this time, they immerse themselves in a *mikvah* or natural collection of waters. These laws and rituals have their basis in the *Torah*. There are many excellent psychological, philosophical and mystical explanations for these laws. One of these is that blood is often associated with death and loss. The menstrual blood symbolizes loss of potential life. In contrast, *mikvah* or natural waters are symbolic of life, hope and rebirth. Thus, each month, the woman is spiritually transformed. She symbolically experiences another birth experience.

For the couple struggling with infertility, it is easy to imagine the connection to this symbolism. The time of *tameh* or menstrual blood indeed symbolizes another month of loss. The potential life did not flourish. It can coincide with depression, anger at self or God and a true spiritual low. In contrast, immersion in the *mikvah* marks the potential for hope, rejuvenation and rebirth. Once again the woman's body is prepared for potential life. She can secretly hope, "Maybe it will all work out this month."

It is extremely important to realize the meaning of ritual for one individual may not be the meaning of ritual for another. This is the beauty of spirituality. We are taught that the *Torah* has 70 facets. Ritual is but a potential. The action is offered to the individual as an opportunity for spiritual growth. Some may not relate at all. Further, what is meaningful in one month or one moment is not necessarily inspirational in the next. Along these lines, I have heard religious infertile women confess to me that going to the *mikvah* is very hard. For them, it serves as a constant reminder that they are not pregnant.

Some infertile individuals do not find existing ritual helpful. Others do not experience any motivation to focus on infertility rituals at all. Others utilize existing rituals and practices. Faige and Shmuel are a couple likely to utilize existing customs, such as prayer, consulting famous *rebbes*, and becoming even more scrupulous in observing the laws of *taharat ha'mispachah*. Still others feel the need to create their own rituals. In this vein, I would like to end with some reflections on my own personal healing journey.

PERSONAL RECOLLECTIONS—MY HEALING JOURNEY

In October of 1990, my husband and I learned for the third time that I was pregnant. We were convinced that this pregnancy would bear fruit, that after three years of longing for a child, we would hold our treasured infant in our arms. Because of the infertility treatment we had gone through, we knew for certain that this baby had been conceived on the Jewish holiday of *Sukkot* (or *Sukkos*). *Sukkot* to me is the holiday that symbolizes God's protection. It represents the Jew's faith in God to provide security in our everyday existence. Interestingly, when I was praying in the *Sukkah* one morning during the holiday, I was aware of some physical symptoms that convinced me an embryo was implanting in my womb. At that moment, I experienced what seemed to be a numinous event. I knew I was pregnant, and my prayers became filled with hope and further connection to God.

The last day of the nine-day festival was the holiday of *Simhat Torah* (happiness in the *Torah*) in which Jews rejoice over our *Torah*. I have looked forward with great anticipation to this experience each year. As a traditionally observant Jewish woman who participates in Orthodox prayer services, I typically do not have the opportunity to hold the *Torah* scroll during the year. *Simhat Torah* was the one time of year that I was afforded this experience. As I embraced the *Torah*, the Book of my people, and was surrounded by a community of females dancing with joy, I experienced a sense of spirituality that I was unable to adequately portray through words. Through the embracing of the *Torah*, I encountered an intense intimacy with tradition and with God.

That *Simhat Torah*, as I danced with the *Torah*, I was blessed with what seemed to be another numinous experience; once again, I had a feeling I was pregnant. I thought of how beautiful it was to rest a *Torah* scroll on my stomach, the protector of my baby-to-be. The *Torah*, representative of God's protection, was united in that moment with my hope and love for the future. This moment represented a sense of completion, peace and hope.

Thus, you can imagine my delight and validation of my internal voice upon learning that I was pregnant shortly after the holiday. The six weeks that my husband and I knew I was pregnant were special ones. All of the tests were much more positive than those in the past. We hoped and prayed and believed. We affectionately patted my stomach and named our creation the "*Sukkos* Baby."

Likewise, you can imagine our disbelief, despair and anger when I began to miscarry once again. How could God give us this special gift only to take it away? How could we lose our "*Sukkos* Baby?" What was the purpose of it all?

In retrospect, after this miscarriage I felt a need for a special healing process. Through readings and participation in an infertility support group, my husband and I had learned that many people who suffer miscarriages feel the need for a ritual to mourn the loss. Modern Western society doesn't appear to pay enough attention to this painful life event. Other cultures are much more aware of the need for a healing ritual (see *Mothers of Thyme: Customs and Rituals of Infertility and Miscarriage*, Sha, 1990).

I was drawn into a healing journey that lasted several months and led to many internal transformations. It began with an attraction to art. I participated in an arts and crafts class in which I painted preformed plaster figures. Participants were not required to sign up or make any type of commitment. Thus, I was afforded anonymity. The teacher did not even know my name. This allowed me greater freedom to dispense with my persona and concentrate on my internal needs.

As I worked on each figure, I contemplated the symbolism of the images I chose. One piece I painted was of a woman with long hair sitting on the ground holding a jug. I decided to paint her one color, an earth tone of rust, with turquoise for trim. In some ways, she looked Native American, very primitive and in touch with the earth. Yet my choice of one color felt as though my attraction to this lady came from a very important place. I reflected upon her archetypal significance. She began to look like a wise woman—the wise woman in me who knew where to go, how to make decisions, how to heal myself. For another piece, I dared to do something I had flirted with for some time. I painted a figure of a woman and her baby. This action appeared to represent a readiness on my part to come closer to the pain of miscarriage and the longing for a baby.

It was shortly after beginning my art projects that my healing journey led my husband and me to a very different place. We decided to develop a ritual for our "*Sukkos* Baby." In Jewish tradition, still-born babies, as well as amputated parts of the body are buried. After consulting with our rabbi, who was very supportive, we decided to utilize this tradition and bury our "*Sukkos* Baby." Next to a stream, symbolic of life and rebirth in Jewish tradition, we buried our "*Sukkos* Baby." I then recited Channa's prayer (Samuel I, 2). We took pictures to mark the occasion. This ritual turned out to be a very moving and healing moment for both my husband and me.

After being involved in the crafts class for several months, I decided I wanted to create from scratch. A woman whom I know and admire began a short-term class entitled, *Painting as Prayer and Meditation.* In this class we were encouraged to utilize meditation images to create through drawing or painting. Our teacher stressed the spiritual qualities involved in art and in meditation. This was just what I was looking for.

As a final art piece in this segment of my healing journey, I completed a drawing. This piece appeared to emerge out of a meditation experience. My picture was of a mountain scene with question marks in the sky. I have always been very attracted to mountains. They symbolize beauty, majesty and a journey onward and upward. Climbing a mountain represents struggling with and reaching a lofty goal. But even more important to me, the mountains reach up into the heavens and help bring us closer to God. Thus, the mountains symbolized my journey onward and upward, and the questions represented my current life situation that was entrusted to God on high.

What was most amazing to me was my teacher's comment about this picture. She looked at the mountains and said that they looked like part of a woman's body, specifically the stomach and legs. When she said that, I experienced an "ah hah" reaction. Earlier in the evening I had admired some figure drawings of female bodies on the wall. I had an urge to sketch one, yet I did not feel capable of this yet. It appeared that out of the depths of my unconscious I had drawn a woman; in fact, I drew the most important parts of a woman for me at that moment in time—the stomach, womb and legs. I was recreating the seat of the birthing process. My mountains, my questions, my healing journey and my upward struggle had centered around this birthing process. What a wonderful revelation to me.

Almost five cycles of holidays have passed since "*Sukkos* Baby." Yet, I suspect that *Sukkot* will never be the same. Today my art projects enjoy a place of prominence in our home. They serve as gentle reminders of the struggles. At the same time, our home is finally blessed with the special laughter and joy of a daughter and a son. Like my creations, my relations to self, community and God have been colored and transformed forever.

IN CONCLUSION

Infertility presents difficult life challenges. To the Jew, committed to family, community and God, the diagnosis of infertility is particularly crushing. To the Orthodox Jew, faced with *halacha* and tradition, infertility poses many unique struggles and challenges. The infertile Orthodox couple is often surrounded by community. Friends, family, community and professionals, such as psychotherapists and rabbis, can help or hinder the healing process. This paper has attempted to outline some of the more specific struggles of an Orthodox population in an attempt to aid the healing.

The struggles of infertility and life crisis are often long and arduous. They present many challenges to the individual and couple. Yet the healing can occur from many places: from a supportive friend, a helpful rabbi, a sensitive psychotherapist and ultimately from self and God.

REFERENCES

Genesis, 1.

Gold, M. (1988). *And Hannah wept: Infertility, adoption, and the Jewish couple.* Philadelphia: Jewish Publication Society.

Gross, M. (1991). *How long the night? A triumph of healing and self-discovery.* Southfield, MI: Targum/Feldheim.

Menning, B. E. (1988). *Infertility: A guide for the childless couple* (2nd ed.). New York: Prentice Hall.

Samuel I, 2.

Sha, J. L. (1990). *Mothers of thyme: Customs and rituals of infertility and miscarriage.* Minneapolis, MN: Lida Rose.

Zeiger, R. B. (1993). *Infertility and spirituality: A test of faith.* Unpublished manuscript presented at a workshop at The Association of Orthodox Jewish Scientists, New York, N.Y. and at a workshop at Lincoln Square Synagogue, New York, N.Y.

ACKNOWLEDGEMENTS

I would like to offer recognition to my art teacher and friend, Judith Margolis of Los Angeles, California for her encouragement of my creative endeavors; to Rabbi Levi Meier, Ph.D., Clinical Psychologist and Chaplain at Cedars-Sinai Hospital in Los Angeles, California for special support; and Sydney Fleischer, L.C.S.W., Assistant Director, Jewish Family Services, Richmond, Virginia for her comments on the manuscript. I would like to recognize with special gratitude the help of Rabbi Abner Weiss, Ph.D. of Beth Jacob Congregation, Beverly Hills, California, who offered spiritual counsel, support and a shoulder to cry on when needed. Finally, I am forever indebted to my husband and soulmate, Jonathan Ben-Ezra, M.D., for his never-ending love and support, as well as for his helpful criticisms of my professional writings.

OPENING A GATE AT THE CLOSING OF THE GATE: TOWARDS A NEW RITUAL AT THE GETTING OF THE *GET*

SARA R. HOROWITZ

This exploration of a woman's experience in traditional Jewish divorce—the getting of the *get*—is not scholarly in the conventional sense. It is not, in other words, the product of research or objective analysis. The kernel of the presentation is a personal account, a meditation I wrote the day after my own Jewish divorce to remember and to work through my experience. In it, I look at *get* as a ritual of separation, grief and renewal. In the present context, I will set this personal story within a double framework. The inner frame describes the function my writing served, several years after its composition, in the divorce ceremony of another woman. The outer frame considers some of the issues raised by the personal story: the need for a woman's ritual connected with divorce, possibilities for that ritual, and the use of storytelling as ritual.

THE OUTER FRAME

Is there anything feminist in what is, after all, an account of a traditional, *halakhic* (Jewish law) divorce? I think so. First, it brings the personal into the realm of the scholarly, by blurring the line that separates the "outsider" who watches and analyzes "objectively" from the "insider" who experiences, recounts, but often does not get the last, authoritative word. Second, a feminist way of knowing begins with and always returns to (and takes as its measure) a woman's experience in the world, her situatedness. Both my account and the frames "read" (that is, observe and interpret) the ritual of divorce, the getting of the *get*. In them, I explore the tension between the generality of ritual, which must speak for everyone, and the particularity of personal experience, which ritual can never adequately contain. At the same time, my discussion examines the way individuals may inscribe themselves and their experiences onto ritual, making it personally meaningful. Third, the presentation considers the possibilities for developing women's rituals connected to the enactment of traditional Jewish divorce.

I know that *halakhic* divorce is a locus of anger for many Jewish women. Women feel silenced or effaced by the male-centered ritual, and frequently must make outrageous concessions to obtain a *get*; other women are left in ritual limbo by husbands who play out marital dynamics by denying a *get*. Called *agunot* (literally, "anchored"), these women are considered married under Jewish law, even though they may be divorced under civil law and marital relations may have been severed for decades. For some women, these considerations so taint the procedure that they want nothing to do with Jewish divorce, and choose not to obtain one. However, many Jewish feminists do want *gittin* (pl. of *get*). Many women, that is, want to reclaim and perhaps change the *get* into a meaningful and powerful ritual, much as they (we) reclaim, reinterpret and recontextualize *mikveh* (ritual bath).

THE INNER FRAME

Before acquiring my *get*, I searched for writing which would describe to me what women felt as they divorced Jewishly. There was precious little available beyond the legalistic.

The day after my Jewish divorce, I sat at my word processor and typed what came to mind. I titled and saved the file "*get*" and forgot about it. The piece had served the function that writing always serves for me: sorting and owning my experience.

Several years later, a woman I'd known for many years talked to me about her own impending Jewish divorce. I recollected my own search for a woman's narrative. I remembered having written something, I no longer could recall just what, and offered to show it to her. What follows, with minimal editing, is what I gave to her.

THE GETTING OF THE *GET*

One week before our appointment to transact a Jewish divorce—a *get*—my husband calls to ask me if I will drive him to the Rabbi's house, where the *get* will be written and delivered, since I have a car and he does not. I agree, but warn him that I will not drive him home. He agrees to this, adding that I can drop him off at the subway. I consider, and realize I do not want to drive him any place after the *get*. I do not want to share with him the small, contained space of my car. I speak to him twice after that conversation, reiterating each time that I will not take him home (or part way home), that he will be on his own after the *get*. Each time, he says he understands and that he respects my feelings. The second time, he sounds annoyed and tells me I need not repeat myself.

On the day of the *get*, he calls me, as agreed, several minutes before leaving his house. He sounds awkward on the telephone. I sound businesslike. It occurs to me that he does not really wish to divorce, but cannot admit this to himself. Never mind about that, I think. Let's get it done.

On my way out, I remember that we had agreed to exchange photo albums. I was to give him the wedding album, he would give me the other photos, so that we could each select the mementos we wished to keep. I scoop up the album and take with me also the *ketubah*, the marriage contract, as the Rabbi had asked. When he buzzes I go downstairs laden with the wedding album and the *ketubah* in its massive purple frame. I see that he has forgotten to bring his photos.

We ride together. He fusses over my new car. He asks me whether I know about transportation to the center of the city from the Rabbi's house. I tell him there is a subway, I have taken it, and that he will have to take a bus to reach the subway. I do not know which bus and suggest he ask the Rabbi.

We find the Rabbi's house and ring the doorbell. A bearded man opens the door and asks us to wait outside for a few minutes. Soon, a couple exits. Newly parted, I think. I am sad for them and for myself.

I sit in the Rabbi's study thinking, this is not the saddest day of my life. This is not the most difficult. I try to place it on the continuum of grief and grieving.

The role that a woman plays in getting a *get* is minimal. I sit in this room, the Rabbi's study, with the Rabbi and two other young rabbis—together they form the *beit din*, the Rabbinical court. Also here, two witnesses, men I have never seen before, and a scribe. The scribe has a name, but the Rabbi calls him by his function. "*Sofer*!" he calls out, whenever he wishes to address him.

There is something comfortingly impersonal about the proceedings. Husband and Rabbi conduct a type of catechism, questions which Rabbi reads, and answers which Husband reads. Then instructions to *Sofer* and witnesses, verbal confirmation of what shall transpire, what has transpired. All this occurs in formulaic language which never varies.

But first, the names: Rabbi must know our exact names, all the names we go by, so that anyone reading the *get* will know that it is indeed we who have been divorced. Husband is simple: one name, given at birth, the same in English and in Hebrew, no nicknames. But Wife's name is more complicated. My name given at birth, in Hebrew: *Sara Rivka*. Called by Husband (and others) simply *Sara*, in Hebrew, which is pronounced differently from Sara, which I am called in English by most people who know me. And then, there are those who call me Sara Reva. "How many call you Sara Reva?" Rabbi asks. "Five people? Ten? How often do they call you Sara Reva? Once a year? Ten times a year? Twenty? A dozen? Once a month, then?" This is very important, because for Wife, the touchstone of naming is not valid in this Orthodox context: they ask by what name Husband is called up to the *Torah*, but they will not think of asking that of me.

Finally, Rabbi decides that all variations of my name must appear on the *get*, just in case. I am "*Sara Rivka, miskareh* (called) *Sara, mekhuneh* (known as) Sara, *mekhuneh* Sara Reva, daughter of *Moshe mekhuneh* Morris." This is the longest name in Rabbi's experience. He worries whether *Sofer* can fit it all in the *get*. The *get* must be twelve lines exactly and each line must have at least one letter which extends upward beyond the line and one letter which extends downwards. *Sofer*, a dark haired, dark bearded man in his late twenties, proud of his craft, assures Rabbi he can do it.

Thus begins the ritual, the ritualized dialogue. Does Husband give this *get* of his own free will? Yes, he gives it of his own free will. Has he made a vow that would invalidate the *get*? No, he has not made a vow that would invalidate the *get*. Had he done so, would he like to be released from it? Yes, in case he has done so, he would like to be released from it.

Sofer makes a gift to Husband of his craftly tools—quills, parchment, inks. Husband accepts, lifting them above his head to indicate ownership. Husband asks *Sofer* to use his tools to write on his behalf a *get*, to divorce—*le garesh*, to chase away—"*Sara Rivka, miskareh Sara, mekhuneh* Sara, *mekhuneh* Sara Reva, daughter of *Moshe mekhuneh* Morris." *Sofer* accepts the charge and says he will write on Husband's behalf a *get*, to divorce "*Sara Rivka, miskareh Sara, mekhuneh* Sara, *mekhuneh* Sara Reva, daughter of *Moshe mekhuneh* Morris." Husband then charges each of the witnesses to witness the writing and delivery of the *get* to "*Sara Rivka, miskareh Sara, mekhuneh* Sara, *mekhuneh* Sara Reva, daughter of *Moshe mekhuneh* Morris." They each accept the charge. And so it goes. My name, in all its variations, is called on again and again. It is a mouthful, I think. They give me no role, but they must give my name its due, must repeat each of its variants, each syllable of each of its variants, over and over. I am silenced, but they must speak in my name. With each command, my name is in Husband's mouth. It is in Rabbi's mouth, in *Sofer*'s, in the mouth of each of the witnesses. My name stands in for me where I have no place to stand.

Again and again I hear my names called: "*Sara Rivka, miskareh Sara, mekhuneh* Sara, *mekhuneh* Sara Reva, daughter of *Moshe mekhuneh* Morris." Finally, the "*miskareh*" begins to sound to me like "miscarry." I think, a miscarried marriage, not borne to term. Marriage miscarriage, miscarried dreams, hopes, possibilities; aborted potential. I don't think about babies.

Scribe begins his work. I wait. Women's work, but here we all must wait, myself together with the six men—Rabbi, Husband, two witnesses, and two young rabbis who form the *beit din.* Waiting brings the demons, but I have brought with me my talismans: a book of poetry by Rachel Korn, Kathryn's inscription, Nancy's card. These resonate with the well wishes of other women, their blessings to me during these past difficult months—my aunts, my colleagues, my friends. The memory of my mother who birthed me and died—a talisman against grief; the image of the mother who raised me and lives—a talisman for life ahead and joy and strength. A nexus of woman's sorrow, womanloss and womanhealing. A healing ring to replace the wedding ring.

I begin to read Rachel Korn's poetry. I select the section on grieving. I follow her across generations, merging with Korn's nostalgia for her dead mother and for the lost scents of childhood. I sit in this room full of men, this room where the ties of love are severed, and I think of every woman who has loved me and whom I love. In this room of men, I fill up my space with strong and caring women. I feel their presence and their love for me, their wishes for me, womanblessings, and this centers me.

Husband walks around the room, inspecting the books, chatting with Rabbi and witnesses. He chats about where he has studied, his knowledge of *Talmud* (oral law). He wants their friendship (he does not have a healing circle of women). Rabbi expresses wonderment that Husband seems so friendly, so happy at such a moment.

Rabbi asks me for the *ketubah*, the marriage contract. He asks to keep it, since the marriage to which it bears witness will soon be undone. He adds that if I want to keep it, he can invalidate it for me. I do not want it. I do not know what I would do with it. Husband cannot bear to let it go. He points out to them the lovely lettering, the design. He wants to keep the *ketubah*, it is so lovely. For me, this loveliness is now hollow, lifeless. Husband asks them to look for what he added to the *ketubah*. They read the *ketubah* through and cannot find anything added. They think he means he has composed and added on a word, a phrase to the traditional text. He means, can they find the letter he has filled in, thus fulfilling the requirement that a husband must write his own *ketubah*, his lettering which completed the writing of the *ketubah* and made it his own. Of course, it is the *aleph* (first letter of the Hebrew alphabet), the same as in every *ketubah*: *aleph*, the beginning.

Finally *Sofer* is done. He reads the *get* aloud. Again, the names. The witnesses each read it aloud. Again and again, the names. Rabbi reads it aloud.

I begin to feel weak-kneed and light-headed. I know I must stand up soon to accept the *get* and I wonder if I will faint. I think back to the first time I fainted, at sixteen, when I walked into my father's hospital room and saw him laced through with tubes. I woke up to the harsh lights and strange faces in the emergency room. I thought of how I fainted when Uncle Lou pierced my ears in my bedroom, falling from my chair onto the floor. I awoke on my bed, with Lou's worried face peering down at me. How that small, frail man, by then in his sixties, must have struggled to lift me up from the floor and onto the bed. Who will pick me up here if I faint? I think of the seven men in black hats and earlocks, who will not touch a woman. What will they do if I stand up, begin to sway back and forth, and finally buckle and hit the ground? I picture them standing around my crumpled body, astonished, confused, undecided. Will they help me up, prop a pillow under my head, give me air?

It is Husband and not I, though, who stands and sways. Rabbi folds the *get* into a neat, small packet. Husband and Wife stand facing one another. Rabbi tells Husband to hold *get* above Wife's outstretched palms, to prepare to drop *get* in her hands, and to repeat the divorce formula. Husband begins. He stops. He cannot speak. He begins to sway. He still cannot speak. Finally, his voice breaks with a sob, and he finishes. He cannot let go of the *get*. Instead of letting it drop into my palms—a clear sign of his willingness and willfulness in granting the *get*—his hands move downwards and he presses the *get* into my hands. Drop it, drop it, Rabbi calls to him. Perhaps the witnesses will think I took the *get*, I wrested it from him and will not be able to attest to his willfulness. No, she did not take it, they all agree; he gave it and she accepted it. The transaction is valid, is kosher. In a breath, in an instant, Husband has become Exhusband. Rabbi tells me to take the *get* and walk away, walk out of the room with it, indicating that it is in my possession, is my property. I walk out, tears coursing down my face. When I return, Rabbi takes the *get*, *Sofer* slashes it with a blade so no one else can use it.

The giving and accepting of the *get* ritually undoes the binding of the *chuppah*, the marriage canopy. The wedding, a public ceremony, takes place under the open sky; all those who know and love you come to witness and celebrate. The *get*, a private ritual, takes place in the cloistered privacy of a rabbi's study, in the presence only of those who have a role to play and perhaps one friend for support. At the wedding, a document—the *ketubah*—is completed. Bride, wearing no other jewelry, accepts the wedding ring, encircles Husband, receives *ketubah*, and becomes Wife. At the *get*, Wife removes wedding ring, receives *get*, and becomes Exwife. She steps away. The stepping away undoes the encircling of the wedding ceremony. Wife leaves the *chuppah* wearing a ring and in possession of the *ketubah*, full-handed and full-hearted; empty-handed, Exwife leaves the *get* in the trusteeship of the Rabbi and no longer wears her ring. From the *chuppah*, Husband and Wife leave together, entering the privacy of *yichud*, a special room into which they retreat briefly between the ceremony and reception. In that private space, the two become one (*yachid*). From the *get*, Exhusband and Exwife go their separate ways. The one has become two, each a *yachid*, a separate individual.

I may not marry a Cohen, a priest, Rabbi tells me. I may not marry for 92 days. This brings my first chuckle of the day. I am not planning on a wedding that soon, I tell him.

Exhusband shakes hands with Rabbi and witnesses. They wish him luck. I know they will not shake my hand. I wish they would wish me luck. One of the witnesses—the older of the two—catches my eye and nods. I thank Rabbi and leave.

I think to myself, something is missing. Later, it occurs to me: a benediction. Judaism has a benediction for every act and every ritual. After a marriage, for example, come the seven blessings for joy. Even after a funeral, comforters offer up a benediction on behalf of the mourners, asking the Divine Presence to comfort them along with all the other mourners of Zion. But for a *get*, no benediction. This is what I am waiting for, this is what I feel lacking. Bless me, Rabbi. Let the black hatted men form two lines, let me walk between them and let them utter words of comfort. Wish me a full life, a new beginning, surcease of sorrow. Let them wish me a husband, a lover, a child. Wish me the richness of life and the fullness of seasons. Wish me a new life, new as the new moon. Bless me with the blessing of the new moon. Merge my cycles with her cycles, mingle with her also my waxes and wanes.

Later still, I recite to myself the blessings of the new moon and take this as my blessing. For this is *Rosh Hodesh Av* (new moon of *Av*)—beginning of *Av*, month of mourning and comfort; like each new moon, it promises renewal.

Be it Your will
O Creator our God
and God of our ancestors
to renew for us this new moon
with goodness and with blessing.
Grant us long life,
a peaceful life
a good life

a blessed life
a life of sustenance
a life of vigor,
a life of faith and of moral strength
a life free of shame and of reproach
a life of wealth and of dignity
a life of Torah *and mindfulness of heaven*
a life which fulfills (only in a good way) our heart's desires

And let us say
Amen.

But we leave Rabbi's home, Exhusband and I, without that blessing. Exhusband offers to carry the empty *ketubah* frame to my car. I refuse his help. He walks me to the car anyway. We reach the car. As I open my door, he asks me if I would be passing by the kosher restaurant.

I look at him. "You want a lift," I say flatly.

He shrugs. "It's raining."

So after all, here he is, asking for a lift. Not home, of course. He sticks to the technical bargain. Too drained to fight, I open the car door for him. The restaurant is half a mile down the road and does not put me out of my way. Aside from asking him which way to turn, I do not speak. I drop him off in front of the restaurant.

"*Shalom,*" he says.

Shalom.

I drive off, with ocean salt tears in my eyes and the prayer for the new moon on my lips.

May the holy one
the blessed one
renew this new moon
for all of us
for life and for shalom
for happiness and rejoicing
for salvation and consolation
And let us say
Amen.

THE INNER FRAME

My friend brought the account I've just read into the place where she transacted her *get*. Its words became for her, she told me, the comforting presence that other women's words had been for me. Women's voices fortify other women and help them to own their experience.

THE OUTER FRAME

In reflecting on what I had written, I noticed two things. First, while the traditional *get* ritual can work to silence and humiliate women, women need not feel humiliated. The support of friends and our own interpretive capacities enable us to choose how we experience and contextualize this and other events. Second, insofar as divorce, like marriage, is not only a contract but a ritual, it is woefully incomplete. Without thinking it through, I found a ritual suggesting itself to me, which had three components: death (mourning), birth (celebration), and *hagadah* (telling). My imagery drew first on Jewish burial rituals, during which mourners walk between two rows of comforters who utter words of compassion. Divorce involves loss and grief, for a dream lost, a relationship ended, and a part of self undone. At the same time, divorce also marks the beginning of new dreams, new possibilities. I connected this with *Rosh Hodesh* imagery—central to feminist Jewish renewal—and with the hope of the new moon and the cyclical promise that loss need not be final. Thus, I draw my title for this article from a verse in the *Ne'ilah* service, the final section of *Yom Kippur* liturgy: "Open for us a gate at the closing of the gate, for the day is ending." The verse suggests that as a gate closes behind you, a gate opens before you. Finally, the telling itself becomes incorporated into the ritual. As at the Passover *seder*, *hagadah* creates an enchainment of memories linking the woman's married self to her divorced self and to the stories and experiences of other women.

Since writing this meditation, I have come across a number of other articles addressing *get* rituals. A particularly moving one by Rabbi Dianne Cohen appears in *Conservative Judaism*. Cohen's ceremony utilizes traditional funeral and mourning rituals. It leaves intact the traditional Conservative divorce and is enacted afterwards at the woman's home. Other divorce ceremonies might do something different. They might shift, rewrite, or even replace the divorce itself. For example, Rabbi Vicki Hollander supplemented the text and symbols of the traditional divorce ceremony to create a new, gender-equal ritual. Still other ceremonies mark the dissolving of relationships other than traditional marriage.

Like new covenant ceremonies for baby girls, and menarche and menopause rituals, the divorce ritual is in an early developmental stage. Debra Cantor and Rebecca Jacobs (1992-93) use existing covenant ceremonies, often written by parents for their baby daughters, to develop a modular ceremony, published in *Kerem*. The "Covenant Ceremony for Daughters" can serve as a resource or a basis for future ceremonies. As Cantor and Jacobs remind us in their recent discussion of the ceremonies, we should not look "to canonize or calcify" (p. 46) these rituals; the women who use and develop them "are partners in their creation" (p. 43). *Get* rituals for women, developed by divorcing women and their friends, can serve similarly as resources and models as we seek to inscribe ourselves in Jewish practices.

REFERENCES

Cantor, D. & Jacobs, R. (1992). Brit banot: Covenant ceremonies for daughters. *Kerem: Creative Explorations in Judaism, 1*, 45-55.

Cohen, D. (1992). The divorced woman: Toward a new ritual. *Conservative Judaism, 44*(4), 62-68.

Hollander, V. (1994). Weathering the passage: Jewish divorce. In D. Orenstein (Ed.) *Lifecycles: Jewish women on life passages and personal milestones: Vol. 1.* Vermont: Jewish Lights.

does it hurt?

tova

I.

how does your shoulder feel today? let's check its range of motion. how does your back feel today? can you walk, can you bend, can you? how does your neck feel today? how does it feel today? where do you feel it? is the pain sharp, long or short, how long did it last, was it a day, an hour, is it pins and needles or is it needles and pins? can you move it this direction or that direction? is it better, worse, or the same as it was at your last appointment? which days was it the same? which days was it worse? which days was it better? how does your body feel?

> think. think quick, think hard, when was it worse? was it worse yesterday or the same? or was that a few days ago? did i feel it at all? how can i know how it felt? how can i know what real pain is? what pain is? i don't know how my body feels. ok, then make something up, say its the same, try to know which hour it was or make up an hour.

yes, it was worse at 12:35 p.m., yes, i'm sure it was 12:35 p.m., i'm sure that's when it hurt the most.

II.

we only gave you a little slap on the wrist, a slap on the wrist.

it was more than a slap on the wrist, i have scars.

well, you...
you, you
you were uncontrollable,
we had to do something.

look, here is the scar from the wrench.

no...
no, no
that scar isn't from when your father hit you with a wrench,
that scar is from when i threw a glass at you.

a glass, what glass? i don't remember a glass.

you,
you, you
you're always making things up,
that scar isn't from the wrench,
it's from the glass.

and my nieces and my nephews...

why, why are you yelling about your brother-in-law now, he's only like your father. your brother-in-law is just like your father, that's all, he just doesn't realize how strong he is, he doesn't mean to be so heavy handed, he's just like your father.

III.

duck,
he's got the wrench in his hand,

he's picking up his hand with the wrench in it.

duck,
she's going to throw the glass right at me.

duck,
she's chasing me, she's hitting me with the heel of her shoe, she has those really pointed spiked heels, she doesn't want to hurt her hand, she's afraid her bursitis will hurt so she uses the shoe.

pick up the wrench, hit the child,
pick up the glass, hit the child,
pick up the shoe, hit the child.

gramma, gramma, see what he did, my arms are all swollen and red...

oh he's just a jerk, that's all, he's stupid, just pay him no mind.

run to the bathroom.
run, grab a chocolate bar and run
run, to the bathroom and lock the door.

you'll be laughing on the other side of your face once i get you.

IV.

what do you mean you never hit me,
i have scars on my body
i have scars...

you're making it up,
you're a liar,
it wasn't that bad,
you're always making things up.

and my nieces and my nephews...

oh, no, no,
you exaggerate,
you are always exaggerating,
your brother-in-law is just like your father,
that's all,
he's just like your father.

V.

how does your shoulder feel today? can you move it better or worse or the same? how does your back feel today? can you bend? how does your neck feel today? can you move it better or worse or the same? how does it feel in your body? does it hurt, where does it hurt?

i don't know.

did it hurt at six p.m., did it hurt for days, which day was worse?

think fast,
do you know how it feels?
do you know when it hurt?
do you understand real pain?
just make up a story, say something,
say anything,
anything at all,
make up a story of when it hurt.
maybe it doesn't hurt at all,
maybe i just make it all up.

what does it feel like in your body? sharp pain or dull, pins and needles or needles and pins?

what does my body feel like?
well, i don't know.
i don't feel my body.

where does it hurt?

maybe there's nothing wrong at all.

does it hurt, does it really hurt,
or maybe

maybe i'm making it up.

repeat the facts:

i was on my bicycle, i got hit by a car, i have injuries, the doctors say so, there are witnesses, i must believe the doctors, i must look at the facts, look, i have scar tissue, look
i have scars.

VI.

i'm losing control again. i notice everything. i'm sitting on the floor shaking. i notice everything.

there's a knife, there's a scissors, there are the books, heavy books, good to bang myself with, hit my head against the wall. harder,
harder,

pull my hair, pull on my hair,
yes, hit my head,
that's comforting, that feels better.

why does it feel better?

i don't know, it just does.

please stop banging your head. does it hurt when you bang your head like that?

i don't know.

does it hurt when you hit yourself like that? doesn't that hurt? it looks like it does.

i don't know.
i'm not sure,
it just feels better, i think
i don't know

i'm losing control again, i notice everything. look over the knives, pick up the knife, place the cool metal gently across your hot palm. ok,
wait,
wait,

think, think,

don't cut yourself,
don't bang your head,
don't hurt yourself.

VII.

how does your shoulder feel today? what's your range of motion? how does your back feel today? how much can you walk? how much can you move? how does your neck feel today? are you in pain? are you in pain now, were you in pain yesterday, when were you in pain?

when was i in pain?
when was i not?

what's your body feel like today?

i want to feel my body

when did it hurt most?

i don't know,

it hurt at 12:35 p.m., i'm sure of it, it was worse at exactly 12:35 p.m., i think

does it hurt now? did it hurt in the past?

pick up the wrench, hit the child,
pick up the glass, hit the child,
pick up the shoe, hit the child.

i have scars on my body

does it hurt?

look,
my arms are swollen and red,
run,
run to the bathroom,
don't feel your body,
i need to hit my head against the wall,
does that hurt?
i don't know,
maybe i make it all up,
pick up the knife, pick up the scissors,
it's real if i have a scar,
i have scars,
and my nieces and my nephews,

your brother-in-law is just like your father,
that's all,
he's just like your

father,
he's got the wrench,

not from the wrench, from the glass,
you're making it up,

maybe i do make it up,
maybe i should make *something* up,

does it hurt?

pick up the knife, pick up the scissors,
cut your hand, bang your head,
pick up the wrench, hit the child,
pick up the glass, hit the child,
pick up the shoe, hit the child

how does it feel today, how does your body feel?

i have scars, i have scar tissue, i have scars.

it hurts.

does it hurt?—
this is not an explanation

when i am thinking about publishing "does it hurt?", i have this fear. how can i do this? how can i write a piece about the abuse i grew up around, the abuse that is still existent in my family? this is not something that happens in jewish families, in jewish communities, in jewish life. this is not something you let other people know about; and if by some possibility it does happen in jewish homes, it has nothing to do with being jewish.

i want to write some explanation; i want to figure out something, some disclaimer, some way to explain it really wasn't *that* bad, they had their reasons, it really doesn't have anything at all to do with me being a jew, it's just i'm jewish and writing about it. the problem is, though, there is no explanation. it happened. i cannot separate my past from my jewishness or from my abuse. and while being abused didn't happen *because* i am jewish, it also did not happen *despite* being jewish. as much as part of me might want to write an essay that could be an explanation of the abuse that occurred, that could explain it away, make it logical somehow, i will never be able to adequately explain it, because it cannot be explained away. so this essay will not be an explanation.

how is it i can feel so much contempt for the world i grew up around and yet have such a deep abiding respect, love, need for its tenets? how do i heal the contradictions of learning in so many ways and on so many levels what i was taught every day: being told the jewish community were the only people i could trust in a world that killed millions of jews and would again at any opportunity, and the foundation of that community was rooted in the family; and realizing these were people i could not trust, who instead of respect and love, beat me out of their own frustration, told me again and again that i was a liar, that i was stupid, and then that i was perfect and was going to save them from their terrible fate in the world, that i was their only and every hope?

how can i understand the contradictions of growing up in a family, a culture, a community, that instilled in me such a strong respect for ethics, for other people struggling, for not letting people walk over you, with being physically or verbally or emotionally abused? how do i understand this abuse in light of the love i saw in my family and my community when dancing the *hora* at a *bar mitzvah*, when wailing at a funeral, when lost in prayer or meditation on *yom kippor*, when teaching me of the importance of unions and of not crossing picket lines, of feeling the magic of burning *khumets* on the street before *pesakh*, of the importance of making the right and ethical choices?

i think about my family and repression. i think about all the stories i never heard, all the ways people around me when i was growing up didn't talk about the war. i think about the small apartment in the tenement i grew up in, the lack of privacy and quiet, the lack of money, the level of frustration, the confusion about wanting to maintain their own culture in a hostile world, and wanting desperately to assimilate—"we speak english now, we are in america," a frequent statement followed by much animated discussion in yiddish. i think about what those around me went through. i cringe when someone calls me a "survivor." how can you call me a survivor, when the people i know who were and are called survivors, survived concentration camps, the warsaw ghetto, the american sweat shops and more? what i survived is nothing compared to that, i tell them. do not use that word with me, that sacred word for special people. but while that word, survivor, brings up many different issues for me, i also know that i too lived, "survived" if you must, through some other types of horrors, horrors that were real, horrors that are no less horrible because of what my family and the jewish community survived. their survival, pain, nightmares are not an excuse for what happened to me: reasons, perhaps, but not excuses.

but the sifting, how do i do all this sifting through these entangled ways of life? i feel i am still very much in a stage of accepting and rejecting—accepting that what happened to me really was bad, really was abuse (a word that still does not slip easily off my tongue), and rejecting those values, those ways of being, that taught me i am a terrible person, that i must do everything perfectly and i never will do anything well enough, that tempers cannot be controlled, anger cannot be anything but a cruel lashing out at others, that there is always a crisis... and at the same time, i have come to a place of realizing the importance of my jewishness and my working class background, of embracing them in a deeper way.

as more and more of my family members die, i feel a deep sadness, not only for each individual and my particular relationship with them, but for a culture that is dying, for a way in which i feel more and more orphaned living in a world and a community so radically different than the working-class jewish eastern european immigrant one i grew up around. but it was also a culture and a world that almost destroyed me at times to the point of "madness" and suicide.

to heal from my abuse, i've had to separate myself some from my family and their immediate community. my friends are often amazed at how connected i am with my family, while for my family it's an outrageous distance. for me it is a mixture of relief and guilt and sadness. to live sanely, i must have some separation, but i cannot and will not totally sever ties from a culture that is so absent from my daily life that i feel distant and alien from the world i live in today.

as i sit here trying to come to conclusions i have not yet figured out in my head, let alone in my heart, i think about my afternoon. tomorrow is the first night of passover. i spend a good deal of today cooking for *seder*—as usual making too much *kharoses* and miso matzoh ball soup. as i cook i listen to my grandmother's old album of *sing along with yiddish, fiddler on the roof,* some contemporary klezmer music. i melt into emotion, confusion, and contradiction.

i miss my grandmother severely and the talks and licking the bowls over the kitchen table before *yom tov.* i miss all the family joking about whose *kneydlakh* was light enough to fly and whose was heavy as lead. i miss my child-self excitement at getting to stay up late for this sacred event. and i miss the daily *matzo brey.* but in there too, is the franticness and the screaming and fighting and tension and ensuing fear that each holiday would hold.

i think again about how my day is going. yes, i spend the day cooking for *pesakh*, but i go to a potluck and do not drive myself to hysteria with responsibility; yes i make *kneydlakh* and worry if they will be light enough, but i make miso soup, not chicken soup, and the vegetables are organic and the scraps go in the compost, not the garbage; and yes, the streets are not filled with jews i know scurrying before *pesakh*, the stores are not lined with *pesakh* products, and i have to explain at work why i refuse to work on a jewish holiday. and while not everyone i know is at *seder*, there are many lesbian *seders* happening this week. and the one i go to is only two blocks from my home.

and while i feel alien in some ways from my present community, missing what is no longer possible from my past one, i try to take with me and share what is possible. and i try, at least, to be the hope my family and my community placed on me. to keep alive as much as possible the wonder and the magic of judaism that i loved so deeply, and to learn from and leave behind the horror that became so intimately connected to it. my life and my relationship to my family and my past community are not the way they wish, as my life here in the community i live in is not always what i wish. but perhaps my balancing attempts are a deeper way to keep that hope alive, keep the survival of my culture and my family alive by telling the *full* story. perhaps trying to maintain a jewish life and perspective while changing the abusive patterns is living that ethical life they taught me after all. and while i'm generally not a very optimistic person, i try to listen to that voice singing on the record: to life, to life, *l'chaim.*

NO ORDINARY BATH: THE USE OF THE *MIKVAH* IN HEALING FROM INCEST

YONAH KLEM

INTRODUCTION

I heard a story recently, whose details may not be quite accurate by this telling, but the essence of it is probably true. A rabbi was invited to be a guest lecturer at a small New England college. One of his talks was about violence in the Jewish family. After the lecture, a Jewish student who heard it went home and told her father, a major financial contributor of the lecture series. The father promptly withdrew his financial backing. As I recall the tale, the reasons the father gave were twofold: First of all, we Jews must never give our enemies ammunition with which to persecute us; and, second, he asserted that there is no violence in Jewish homes. The message here is "it doesn't happen with us, and don't talk about it." The truth is, it does happen with us, and almost no one is willing to talk about it.

While the subject of incest does occur in many books on Judaism, it is almost invariably presented in terms of the Biblical prohibitions against it. At the time this paper was being researched there were very few references in books (Bass & Davis, 1988; Umansky & Ashton, 1992) to childhood sexual abuse perpetrated by Jewish parents or relatives upon Jewish children. There was nothing at all on the use of the *mikvah* (ritual bath) in healing from incest. My search of various periodical indices uncovered many articles about childhood sexual abuse, incest and adult survivors, but little about these issues in the context of the Jewish family. My purpose will be to address the broader issue of Jewish family incest, and to describe how a uniquely Jewish resource can be of help in the healing process.

BACKGROUND

While there may not be published statistics on the prevalence of incest and childhood sexual abuse in the Jewish community, the problem is hardly unknown. When I spoke to the director of the Orthodox Jewish shelter for battered women in the Chicago area and said there must be incest survivors among their clientele, she readily agreed. Every counselor and psychotherapist I know who works with Jewish clients knows of Jewish incest survivors (all of whom were women in this very informal survey). Without making any attempt at a scientific survey I spoke to Reform, Reconstructionist and Orthodox rabbis who know Jewish survivors in their congregations or communities. The studies may not have been done, but the abuse and its legacy of distress is evident to anyone who looks for it.

Incest and childhood sexual abuse, like all other kinds of sexual abuse and assault, are about the perpetrator imposing his or her power and control over the child. The severity of the consequences depend on a number of factors including the frequency and severity of the trauma, the age of the child and the support she has if and when she complains. (Throughout this paper, the survivor will be referred to as female because most, although not all, are.) Because of these factors, adult survivors of childhood sexual abuse and incest may manifest a large number and variety of symptoms. Some of them, such as a sense of shame and guilt, anger and anxiety, may be remnants from the days when the abuse was taking place. There may be symptoms of Post Traumatic Stress Disorder such as flashbacks, nightmares and unnecessary hyperalertness. Secondary symptoms, such as addictions, sexual acting out and self-injury, may actually be outgrowths of the original, untreated symptoms.

Many survivors repress or dissociate their memories, especially of events that were psychologically and physically too overwhelming to manage with the resources available at the time. When the memories return, in a situation where the adult incest survivor has support and validation for the significance and reality of her experience, she is likely to re-experience the feelings she was trying to avoid: feelings of betrayal, shame, dirtiness, guilt, denial, rage and grief. Her relative ability (or lack of it) to manage these feelings may create more distress. Remembering can feel like re-experiencing the original abuse.

Recovery from the destructive aftermath of childhood sexual abuse involves a number of fairly predictable stages, although the process generally involves going back and forth between them, rather than a linear progression. The first is remembering and owning the knowledge that one is an incest survivor. Then, the unexpressed feelings, especially of anger and grief, need to be acknowledged and expressed in a healthy way.

Perhaps one of the most difficult challenges of the recovery process is dealing with the pervasive sense of shame and victimhood that so many survivors feel. They must come to believe that they are entitled to the same benefits of a full life that people who were not victimized as children can enjoy. In my observation of many survivors it seems that the shift from victimhood to simple personhood is not just a shift in thought process and attitude. It is a paradigm shift, a fundamental alteration in the way the survivor understands herself in relation to the world. This is a spiritual as well as cognitive shift because ultimately it is an act of faith.

THE RITUAL OF THE *MIKVAH*

The cleansing ritual of the *mikvah* may have something very important to add to the spiritual aspect of recovering from incest. Currently, the *mikvah* pool and ritual immersion are used primarily by married, Orthodox women seven days after the end of their menstrual cycle and before the resumption of sexual relations. The non-Orthodox Jewish community has thought of the rituals of the *mikvah* (if it has thought of the *mikvah* at all) as vaguely punitive, specifically anti-feminist, and somewhat superstitious relics of antiquity, having no place in present times. Orthodox women who use and claim to enjoy their monthly ritual are seen, by some of their less observant sisters, as brainwashed by a patriarchal *halakah* (law) into a distinctly second class status.

As befits any practice that has endured over at least several millennia, there is considerably more to the ritual of *mikvah* than most Jews outside the Orthodox community know. It is no ordinary bath. The purpose is not the cleansing of the body. Cleansing can and does take place just fine in the properly equipped bathroom. The purpose of the *mikvah* is spiritual cleansing or purification. Even more, the ritual was meant, from earliest times, to make a person ritually pure, or suitable to enter the Temple in Jerusalem.

In the days of the Temple, a person was considered ritually defiled (*tomah*) because of contact with or involvement with death and human imperfection. Immersion in the gathered waters of the *mikvah* not only cleansed a person of these defilements, but in doing so changed the person's status to ritually clean (*tahor*). The change of status is much like a rebirth: "When a person submerges himself [or herself] in a *mikvah*, he [or she] momentarily enters the realm of the non-living [because one cannot sustain life without breath, fully underwater], so that when he [or she] emerges, he [or she] is like one reborn." (Kaplan, 1982, p.14).

The idea of the cleansing waters washing away the defilement of human imperfection is to be found in the image of the great River flowing from the Garden of Eden. If the Temple was considered a miniature Garden of Eden, then immersion in the flowing waters of the Garden's River (represented by the natural waters of the *mikvah*) could properly prepare one for re-entering the state of perfection that existed in the Garden.

These aspects of the *mikvah* ritual, the association with spiritual defilement through contact with death and human imperfection, and the idea of a rebirth or major change of status, are important for incest survivors. Survivors often talk about feeling dirty. This is the deep sense of defilement that only shame can produce. The shame can be the result of many factors and is generally impervious to both strong soap and strong argument. It is rooted in the victim paradigm that somehow the child deserved what abuse she got, or caused it, or asked for it, and she does not deserve anything else. The change of status from victim to thriving survivor is an important goal of the recovery process.

The incest experience is a kind of death. To a degree the child must stifle her urge to protest, to say no, to fight back in order to prevent the potentially more extreme dangers of abandonment by a caretaker upon whom she is still dependent. Sometimes attempts to protest are met with violence and death threats. After the experience itself is over, she must continue deadening herself in order not to be overwhelmed with feelings she cannot manage or express, and to keep secret what was done to her and by whom. Children who are repeatedly abused, especially if they are threatened and tortured, become expert at living half-dead lives. This requires a kind of change of status, from one who is emotionally and perhaps spiritually dead, to one who is more fully alive.

In the contemporary world, the *mikvah* is used most often by observant women for well established and traditional reasons. The *mikvah* can also be used by custom or design, rather than commandment, at other times for self-renewal and rebirth. For example, some observant men use the *mikvah* before major holidays or *Shabbat* (Sabbath). At least one person (Levitt & Wasserman, 1989) has reported using the *mikvah* in recovering from an adult rape experience. Canadian Reform Rabbi Elyse M. Goldstein has written about expanding the use of the *mikvah* to non-traditional, but valuable rituals for less observant Jewish women. Some women, like the client I will describe next, have quietly taken it upon themselves to seek out the spiritual "cleansing" of the *mikvah* ritual when nothing else seemed adequate.

A CASE STUDY: LEAH M.

Leah M. (a pseudonym) is a professional woman in her mid-40's living in the northern suburbs of Chicago. She has a solid, twenty-three year marriage to a chemist. Together they raised two sons and two daughters, who were in various stages of their college careers, when I met her. Leah had been in therapy twice before, successfully addressing the issues she had presented. She returned to deal with a persistent low grade depression and occasional strong urges to suicide even though, as she put it, everything was going right in her life. We worked together for several years during which I had a developing sense (which I did not share with her) that she had been sexually abused as a child. For a long time this was more evident from her symptoms than memories, of which there were very little.

The breakthrough occurred during one session, which was interrupted briefly by an emergency phone call. When I returned, Leah was curled up on the floor, and in a childlike voice began to tell me in detail about an assault by her uncle, who lived nearby. This memory, which emerged fully in the course of several sessions, was accompanied by shock and amazement, shame, fear, and, as she put it, "an incredible sense of dirtiness" which did not change no matter how much she bathed. It was that sense of dirtiness that led her to thinking about the *mikvah* when the initial shock wore off. Although I had no experience with the *mikvah* myself, I supported the idea completely.

Leah is a Reform Jew who knew a little about the *mikvah* from magazine and newspaper articles. Except for two members of her congregation whom she knew had converted to Judaism, she did not know anyone who had ever gone to a *mikvah*. When she decided to explore the possibility she found that even her Rabbi could only give her a phone number that might lead to other phone numbers. The main Chicago area *mikvah* is not at all hard to find if you know where it is; otherwise it keeps a most modest profile.

After a number of phone calls Leah finally reached one of the *mikvah* contact people. A long call ensued in which Leah eventually said exactly why she wanted to come. The contact person was an observant Jew, and regular user of the *mikvah*. She was also well trained to thoughtfully and gently answer questions. She made it clear that even a non-observant middle-aged woman, who had no interest in using the *mikvah* in the more traditional ways, would be welcome. With Leah's consent, she arranged for someone to be there to greet her and personally help her in whatever ways she needed on the night she decided to go.

The contact person explained the rules about how to get ready to go to the *mikvah*, and advised Leah to follow them as much as she could. If the rule felt too uncomfortable Leah looked to the intent of the rule and tried to follow the intent in a way that was manageable for her. Throughout, her husband was very supportive.

Leah went to the *mikvah* the first and subsequent times without friends or relatives. She had not prepared any particular prayers for the occasion, but recited the standard blessing. What she did do was cry a lot, which had previously been difficult for her. She said that nothing profound or miraculous seemed to happen, yet she emerged feeling clean at a deep level, open and more whole. She went through the process slowly, as she had been advised, and, in the process, learned things about herself and her body she had not known before. Her experiences created intense outpourings of feeling, that were both cleansing and nourishing. Leah discovered that for her the *mikvah* experience was not a quick cure, but a very useful part of the healing process.

CONCLUDING OBSERVATIONS

Questions emerged for me about what elements of the ritual made the experience so valuable, and how to present them so that other non-observant Jewish women (and men, too) might feel more comfortable about availing themselves of this addition to recovery. I also wondered how this experience might be extended for non-Jewish incest survivors who would not be able to go to a *mikvah*.

What seems most important about the *mikvah* ritual is precisely that it is a ritual and not an ordinary bath. What makes the process a ritual begins with setting the intent that the experience be out of the ordinary. It is more than just thinking, "I want this experience to be out of the ordinary." Setting the intent begins with noticing the onset of menstruation and choosing to cease all sexual activity at that point until after the immersion in the natural waters of the ritual bath. It continues with the maintenance of sexual abstinence throughout the menstrual period and the careful counting of the seven days after the menstrual flow has completely stopped, therefore heightening both awareness of the waiting, and building a sense of anticipation that something important and meaningful is going to take place.

When the day finally comes (starting well after sunset in the Jewish fashion) the woman goes to a place that is different, not only in location, but also in the structure and content of the bath. At home, the bathroom is familiar and the water, the same that usually comes out of the tap. Leaving the ease and familiarity of home to bathe in a different bathroom, and then to go further to immerse in the natural waters in a pool that has no counterparts anywhere else, also builds expectation and intent.

The preparatory bath is also probably different for most women. Few people put as much time and attention to their daily bath or shower as they do getting ready for the ritual immersion. This bath involves hair washing, nail clipping, make-up removal, jewelry removal, ear cleaning, tooth brushing and even a belly button check. The body must be thoroughly clean and thoroughly bare, with nothing foreign on it.

As Rabbi Elyse M. Goldstein (1986) points out, more and more non-Orthodox women are reclaiming the *mikvah* to use for their own life cycle purposes. A valid purpose is to help cleanse the incest survivor of the sense of spiritual as well as physical defilement that often accompanies the recovery and healing from childhood sexual abuse.

The fundamental elements of the ritual of immersion in the *mikvah* can be of use also for Jewish women or men who choose not to go to the *mikvah*, and for non-Jews as well. What is crucial to the process is a decision to create an event that will be meaningful. Planning the behavior, preparing and waiting with intent all seem important. The use of special water, or perhaps soap that was purchased specifically for the occasion, is useful. For example, the non-Jewish mother of a young woman who had been raped thoroughly scrubbed down the bathroom her daughter was to use for her cleansing ritual. The mother also adorned the room with candles and fresh flowers, and provided a tape of music put together for this event.

Laura Levitt and Rabbi Sue Ann Wasserman (1989) describe the service they created for a ceremony of healing at the *mikvah* following Laura's rape in November of 1989. Their service included things they wrote, poetry they borrowed and traditional prayers. This process could be used by anyone. Non-Jews may wish to use prayer from their own religious traditions or elsewhere.

The question of whether other people should actively participate in the ceremony can be considered. Leah got support from her male Rabbi, her husband, a few very close friends and me, but no one there was aware of her purpose. Laura Levitt was joined by her mother and Rabbi Wasserman, who was also her friend.

There is obviously almost no precedent for the use of the *mikvah* for healing from incest and sexual abuse. This leaves the door open for creativity. Women who use the *mikvah* regularly speak of a sense of wholeness and a spiritual connection that they are fortunate enough to reclaim at least once a month. Non-observant Jewish incest survivors who need the healing qualities that the *mikvah* can provide can have them, too. Non-Jewish survivors can extract some essence of the original and create cleansing rituals of their own.

The use of natural waters in the ritual pool reminds us of the waters of Eden, from whence comes all the waters of the earth, with their nourishing and cleansing properties. For a short while the Jewish survivor of childhood sexual abuse and incest can be reconnected to that powerful image of perfection and peace, to be nourished and rejuvenated so she can continue her ongoing process of recovery.

REFERENCES

Bass, E. & Davis, L. (1988). *The courage to heal.* New York: Harper & Row.

Blume, E. S. (1990). *Secret survivors.* New York: Wiley.

Briere, J. N. (1992). *Child abuse trauma: Theory and treatment of the lasting effects.* Newbury Park, CA: SAGE Publications.

Courtois, C. A. (1988). *Healing the incest wound.* New York: W. W. Norton.

Fredrickson, R. (personal communication, March 22, 1991). *Advanced clinical skills in the treatment of sexual abuse.*

Goldstein, E. M. (1986). Taking back the waters: A feminist re-appropriation of the Mikvah. *Lilith 15*, 15-16.

Kaplan, A. (1982). *Waters of Eden.* National Conference of Synagogue Youth/Union of Orthodox Jewish Congregations of America: New York, N.Y.

Levitt, L. & Wasserman, S. A. (1989). *Mikvah* ceremony for Laura. In E. M. Umansky and D. Ashton (Eds.). *Four centuries of Jewish women's spirituality* (pp. 321-326). Boston: Beacon Press.

Umansky, E. M. & Ashton, D. (Eds.). (1992). *Four centuries of Jewish women's spirituality.* Boston: Beacon Press.

TRUTH BENEATH THE SYMPTOMS: ISSUES OF JEWISH WOMEN IN THERAPY

MELISSA SCHWARTZ

Anger and tenderness: the spider's genius
to spin and weave in the same action
from her own body, anywhere—
even from a broken web.
—Adrienne Rich, "Integrity"

As is generally the case with unconscious material, issues particular to Jewish women do not necessarily reveal themselves directly in therapy. They oftentimes come through in subtle ways, overshadowed by content which might seem to have no relevance to the woman's Jewish history or identity. As it is vital for clinicians to recognize the effects of oppression in our clients, it is equally important for us to be able to recognize clues to such issues in our Jewish clients. A clinician who possesses a working knowledge of the relationship between symptoms and socio-cultural position will then be able to skillfully guide her client into finding the deeper connection to her oppression. In this way, the client can move from pathologizing her pain into politicizing or externalizing her pain, which can facilitate a shift in her self image (Caplan, 1985; Lerner, 1983; Sue & Sue, 1990; White, 1989). In this paper, I will examine issues of Jewish women in therapy, and the often veiled ways in which these issues manifest.

UNDERLYING ISSUES

In my work as a psychotherapist I have learned that four core areas of painful and confusing emotion underlie many of the issues which Jewish women bring to therapy. These areas can be seen as: 1) the internalization of anti-Semitism; 2) chronic terror; 3) grief and loss; 4) pressures to assimilate into the gentile world.

By the internalization of anti-Semitism, I am referring to a subtle and insidious process by which Jews come to believe negative stereotypes about themselves promulgated by the majority culture. Numerous theorists have written about the phenomena of internalized oppression with different minority groups (Bulkin, Pratt, & Smith, 1984; Cliff, 1985; Deming, 1984; Memmi, 1962, 1965, 1968), and certainly much has been written about women's internalization of sexism and the resulting negative beliefs we then have about ourselves (Caplan, 1985; Eichenbaum & Orbach, 1983; Friedan, 1963, 1981; Greenspan, 1983; Johnson, 1988; Miller, 1976).

Jewish women are subject to this same process, but like members of other groups, we are not necessarily aware of messages we have swallowed, much less that we have swallowed anything at all. Some of the more common of these toxic, racist messages about our personalities are: that we are too pushy, too nosy, too aggressive, too self-centered, too loud, too whiny, too negative, too powerful, too money-hungry and too materialistic. On the level of appearance, many of us carry painful feelings of self-hate as well, believing that we are too fat, that our breasts, hips and bellies are too large, that our noses are too large, that our faces are too large, that we have too much body hair, that our hair color and skin color are too dark, and that our hair is too curly or frizzy (Beck, 1988, 1991; Kaye/Kantrowitz, 1991; Schneider, 1984; Siegel, 1986). Like women of color, we are comparing ourselves against the image of the perfect gentile woman, the "Breck girl," and come up feeling generally too large, too dark and too unrefined.

My use of the terms "chronic terror" and "grief and loss," refer to the psychological effects of a history of diaspora and genocide. We are a people who, until recently with the formation of the state of Israel, have never had a home. Our history is of a people who have fled or were driven out of every homeland we had, due to anti-Semitic persecution (Davidowicz, 1977; Weinberg, 1988). My use of the term "gentile" refers to the non-Jewish majority culture of white Christians. For many Jews the image of the gentile carries a strong connotation of a people who are the alien "other", at varying times seeming better than or worse than the Jew, depending on the context.

There are two general ways of viewing the psychological effects of this history on the psyche of the modern-day Jew. A Jungian or transpersonal view would suggest that these thousands of years of persecution are lodged in the collective unconscious of the Jew, while a psychodynamic orientation would focus on the personal history and family dynamics of this same individual, who was either affected directly or indirectly by anti-Semitic persecution.

We Jews have a history of trauma, whether seen and experienced directly, passed down through family stories, or inherited through pathological family interaction. Much like the survivor of trauma, we too, are terrified of what we have seen and heard, frightened that it may happen again, and vigilant about protecting ourselves from that possibility. Like the survivor of trauma, we are horrified and grief-stricken by the loss of loved ones whom we have actually known or perhaps only heard about through family stories. I have seen many Jews in therapy come to the realization that they grew up with a vague awareness of family members who have been lost for generations back. Far more common though, is the sense that the family "just started" with one's parents or grandparents; the great majority of Jews I have worked with in therapy do not have information about their ancestors. As with families who have survived trauma, many of our families were loath to consciously look at and give speech to the images they carried. Instead, many of us learned to bury these affects in anxious efforts aimed at boosting our own survival, such as through compulsive efforts to succeed.

The pressure for a minority group to assimilate into the majority culture on both physical and psychological levels has been written about extensively (Cliff, 1985; McGoldrick, 1982; Memmi, 1965; Sue & Sue, 1990). While general assimilation patterns of North American Jews do not differ from other groups (Howe, 1990; Howe & Libo, 1979), one feature of our experience does alter our psychological adjustment significantly. Because we are mostly Caucasian, we are often categorized as being part of the gentile world and thus our differences not only go unseen by others, but potentially by ourselves as well. While, for example, the black woman living among whites may have a constant reminder of her difference through the subtle or blatant prejudiced behavior of others, the Jewish woman, who can and most frequently does "pass," is spared this kind of discrimination. I am suggesting here that our relationship to our ability to pass is a mixed one. On the level of both physical survival and day to day comfort, it is indeed a privilege to look like the privileged majority. On the level of psychological identity, the white-skinned Jew, assumed to be gentile by others, can all too easily collude with the messages of the culture because of her own internalized self-hate, and forget who she is.

SYMPTOMS AND THEIR RELATIONSHIP TO UNDERLYING ISSUES

Various kinds of symptoms can originate or become exacerbated from each of these areas of core distress. One of the primary tasks of insight oriented therapy is to unravel or deconstruct the seemingly irrational, dystonic aspects of a symptom to reveal its underlying truth about the person's earlier and/or current life circumstances. I have seen many Jewish women in therapy break down issues they have felt mired in, by connecting to their pain and conflict of being Jewish and female in our culture. They have emerged from this process psychically lighter and more flexible with a vastly increased sense of pride and dignity. The power in understanding the sanity behind a seemingly irrational symptom is great indeed.

Internalized Anti-Semitism

It is wise to wonder if your client's low self-esteem or lack of self-acceptance might relate to the core issue of internalized anti-Semitism. Specifically, I have seen four different symptoms repeatedly spring from this area.

First, a number of Jewish women speak of feelings that their bodies are dirty, without any corresponding memories of sexual molestation or psychological sexualization (Westkott, 1986). I have learned to not necessarily see this as an indicator of repressed memories of sexual abuse, but instead to wonder if this might be a concrete expression of her self-hate as a Jewish woman. I will want to know how she feels toward Jewish women's bodies, and I'll want to ask of the images, cultural messages and life experiences she has about Jewish women's bodies. What kinds of stereotypes, for example, does she carry about Jewish women and their bodies? Does she mention the caricatured image of the Jewish American Princess and/or the Jewish Mother? If so, I'll want to ask her, "What do their bodies look like? Feel like, from the inside? Smell like?"

Similarly, if a woman struggles with an eating disorder, especially anorexia, bulimia or bulimarexia, it is important to wonder if there is any relationship to possible self-hate as a Jewish female. With eating disorders which involve struggles to be thin, I'll wonder about her images of gentile women's bodies, of Jewish women's bodies and of Jewish women's bodies that she has loved. The struggle to be thin might represent a casting-off of deeply held images of the *zaftig* (full-figured) Jewish woman's body. She might be influenced by a complex and subtle hate against the women in her childhood whom she loved and who loved her. She has possibly grown to hate the very bodies that loved her, that held her, that nourished and nurtured her, partly as a result of growing up Jewish and female in American culture. Her image of bodily perfection—long, lean and small-breasted—may result from growing up female in America and from her eagerness to reject the Jewish woman's body and thereby embrace the image of the gentile female body.

Additionally, many Jewish women engage in continuing, rather frantic efforts for self-improvement. It can be important to question such efforts, but it is first important to distinguish these from our legacy as Jews to value education and lifelong learning. By "frantic efforts" I am referring to a certain quest for learning which has less of a sense of joy in assimilating new skills and information, and more of a sense of anxious activities for a make-over.

In working with the Jewish woman who is taking ballet lessons, language class, a second Master's degree, T'ai Chi and the EST training, I'll want to understand the meaning behind all of these learning efforts. If she doesn't keep striving to improve herself, is she then not enough? Are there some basic aspects of herself that she is trying to change, and if so, are they integral to her sense of what being Jewish means? Is she unconsciously trying to hide her Jewishness or re-make herself into her image of a gentile woman? Is she trying to be more conventional or more normal, either of which, perhaps, really means more gentile? This process is similar to the psychological underpinnings of the eating disorder issues described above, but here the body does not serve as the battleground for the make-over. Instead, the transformation is of a more global nature.

Internalized anti-Semitism can also be traced to the Jewish woman's feelings and relations with other Jewish women. Some women in therapy continually speak of anger and dislike toward other women. Before I wonder about internalized sexism, I will first want to listen closely to whether there are any patterns in the ethnic identities of the women about whom she speaks, i.e., is there a preponderance of Jewish women? If so, I will want to point this out and specifically ask her how she feels toward Jewish women.

This same issue can come up in relation to the ethnic identities of her friends. If she doesn't have any Jewish women friends (and she lives in an area where there is a sufficiently large enough Jewish population for her to be able to have some) I will take note of this fact and will want to explore this with her. What does it mean to her that she has few or no friends who might be deeply linked to her own sense of self? Does this lack shed any light on how she might feel toward herself, in that she has no friends who can mirror back some basic aspects of where she comes from, of who she is? Given that she may be quite comfortable with her friendship network, the goal here is not to problematize her, but rather to use her situation to illuminate images and feelings she may have about herself.

Chronic Terror and Grief

The deep, pervasive terror that many of us live with, the legacy of many generations of persecution and danger that have come before us, can manifest in a variety of conventional anxiety symptoms. Some of the more common of these symptoms are: 1) anxiety disorders, generalized anxiety in particular, as well as obsessive and/or compulsive disorders or tendencies; 2) facial tics, (after first ruling out those tics which have an organic component such as Tourette's disorder); 3) low sexual desire (as it's very difficult to want sex when one is chronically scared and may not even be aware of it); 4) self-mutilating behaviors which contain an anxiety component, such as nail-biting, trichotillomania (chronic hair pulling), and chronic joint popping, such as cracking knuckles; 5) features of paranoid personality, including repetitive suspicion, distrust and paranoia.

There are additional possible signs of chronic anxiety which can appear in less obvious form. For example, some women have adapted rigid features of a counterphobic personality style, where the woman defends her overwhelming need to be protected by assuming various postures of strength, toughness, arrogance, superiority and/or competitiveness. Underneath this stance can be a terrified little girl who may have learned to hide her fear and weakness because of particular family dynamics and the unconscious edict of "I must be strong."

Secondly, compulsive overeating is the eating disorder that I have seen to be most closely associated with fear. Oftentimes a woman will report that food binging is her way of relaxing herself, of self-medicating from an ongoing sense of urgency or hypervigilance. I'll want to know if this woman also uses alcohol or other substances to soothe her anxiety, though I have repeatedly seen a tendency in both gentile and Jewish female compulsive eaters to avoid any substance other than food for tranquilizing. The woman who eats compulsively will speak of this avoidance as a need to "stay on the physical plane," to remain in the here-and-now; she fears that drugs or alcohol will make her lose control in a way that feels risky. Here, I'll want to know what she is soothing with the excessive food as well as what her apparent vigilance is about. Exactly what is she guarding against; what are the dangers from which she needs to be so hypervigilant?

Another indicator of deep terror can be a Jewish woman's feeling of being driven to succeed in her career. As with most anxiety states, it is often very difficult for the client to realize that this state of being to which she is so accustomed is not necessarily a measure of objective reality but instead is a psychological mind set. The state of mind associated with being frantically driven to "make it," which can feel especially syntonic to the Jewish woman, can have at its core, deep fears about safety and survival.

Many of us whose ancestors hearken back to the eastern European *shtetl* (Jewish ghetto community) carry a dominating image of the strong Jewish woman who alone has to take care of hearth, home and the business of making a living while coddling a rabbinic type husband who cannot be relied on to help with the family's survival (Weinberg, 1988). In this image, the woman alone has to provide for her family in a hostile, gentile society where financial survival can be a tremendous challenge, as Jews were frequently denied access to a variety of trades and professions which involved having real power (Meyerhoff, 1978; Zborowski & Herzog, 1952).

Though this image may seem far-fetched or sentimental, for some of us it is palpable in its reality. Women who were raised on stories of the "old country" at their *bubba's* (grandmother's) knees, heard tales of survival in a very harsh world, where one had to depend on her own cunning, shrewdness and moxie in order to survive. For myself, the *bubba* stories take on special meaning when I compare the stories of my grandparents, which I eagerly absorbed as a child, with those of my close gentile friends. While I was raised on stories of poverty, orphanages, hunger and violence, my gentile women friends by comparison have images of their grandmothers in gardens raising flowers, loving the earth, childhoods in one-room rural schoolhouses, etc. We have vastly different images which people our psychic landscape, and the power of these early images cannot be underestimated.

Finally, I have noticed that many of us tend to put ourselves down, more so the more public the context. Several Jewish women with whom I have worked have reported patterns of compulsively apologizing and belittling themselves in front of others, especially so in situations which present increased opportunities to feel successful and powerful. The paradox is that the subjective experience of themselves can be far more favorable than how they portray themselves to feel. Upon closer inspection, this de-selfing tactic (Lerner, 1983), can be understood to be a ruse, a way of fending off the enemy, by knocking one's self down before others will want to do so. As we unravel this symptom, we see that the message underlying the behavior can be something like: "I shouldn't look too good, take too much attention, be too visible or too powerful... If I do they'll envy me and then hate me and then I'll be killed."

While these behaviors are not limited to Jewish women, their particular etiology is unique both to Jews and Jewish women. In fact, I believe that it would be unique to be a Jew in this day and age and not have some fear around getting killed, whether conscious or unconscious, given that the Holocaust happened only fifty years ago. In the words of Evelyn Torton Beck (1991):

> "In varying degrees and in different ways, the Holocaust has marked the psyche of every Jew the world over. *I believe that most Jews, even the most assimilated, walk around with a subliminal fear of anti-semitism the way most women walk around with a subliminal fear of rape*" (p. 22).

It can be very useful to ask your client how much of her family was killed in the Holocaust. If she says something like, "No one was killed, we were all here in America, the Holocaust never affected me in any significant way," it may be useful for her to interview her family to make sure of this assumption. The task for many Jewish families in post-World War II North America was to put the recent genocide behind them, in part by not talking about it. Consequently many of us have feelings of terror and dread that we cannot explain, that do not seem to fit our safe, suburban childhood memories. The opportunity for your client to find out about various relatives, some of whom may have been killed in the Holocaust, whom she never met and will never know, can be a tremendous relief. Finally her lifelong feelings of dread and fear can now seem sane within what was an invisible context. That context, too overwhelming for the family to speak of, thought best to shield the children from, can now become visible.

Understanding this context may also explain long term feelings of depression. The grief which many of us carry can be very complex. At its most concrete, some of us carry the unshed tears of our grandparents and parents, who did not know of, or have the safety, to embrace their sadness: "...given the pain... with which being Jewish has usually bathed our families, our Jewishness is often buried under oceans of tears." (Kaye/Kantrowitz, 1991, p. 11). At its most complex, some of us may carry the grief of generations of oppression. We have come to carry it in the form of depression, muscular aches and chronic, deep despair.

Another source of grief becomes activated when an assimilated Jewish woman is actively trying to reconnect with her Jewish identity. For a woman who has left the Jewish culture as an adult, much of her early, familiar images of home are nowhere to be seen in her adult world. Perhaps she hasn't smelled deeply familiar foods in years (because she's now a vegetarian); perhaps she hasn't heard Yiddish in years; perhaps she hasn't been in temple for years, yet she spent hours of her childhood in Hebrew school. When a client comes to you in therapy she has not necessarily touched this grief, yet there can be many unshed tears over what she feels has been lost. The world of her childhood feels in some ways like the Holocaust survivor's European childhood: it is gone forever. Conversely, unconscious fears of touching this grief can prevent some Jewish women from leaving home, both literally but more typically, figuratively. Separating from one's family of origin can be too painful to bear, as leaving the family can feel like leaving the Jewish culture, especially if one has not made ties with the wider Jewish community.

Assimilation

"But assimilated, identified, or... somewhere in between, she will grapple with her Jewishness or she will be *split from herself...* Don't assume Jewish identity is unimportant... Understand that what appears to be a client's casual attitude towards her own Jewishness may... mask a loss of which the client is not yet aware, or may protect a tenderness the client feels around her Jewishness because of the common assumption of insignificance. *Don't assume you know how assimilated a Jewish woman client is; the woman you know as a radical lesbian carpenter may have spent hours of her childhood in Hebrew school*" (Kaye/Kantrowitz, 1991, p. 9-10). (italics mine)

The psychological effects of assimilation can be especially subtle. The wound of unconscious assimilation can lead to the feeling that one is divided or lost from one's self. This deep phenomena can be incorrectly diagnosed with as serious a label as depersonalization disorder.

It is important to pay especially close attention when a Jewish client makes statements like, "Sometimes I feel like I don't exist," or, "I feel shadowy, like I'm not all here." The task for the therapist is to help the client explore who the "I" is that she speaks of, asking her to examine if any part of that "I" has been left out or lost somewhere in the journey of growing up. Which contexts, for example, previously helped her to feel more whole, more comfortable with herself? Do any of those contexts still exist in her life? Chances are they do not.

I have found that playing Yiddish music in session on a cassette recorder can be very powerful; the musical *Fiddler on the Roof* can be especially evocative in bringing up longings for one's Jewish past, for the lost sense of comfort and home. After your client has begun to reconnect with her tears of homesickness, you might ask her a possible key question: In the process of joining the Christian world, has she not only lost her outer symbols of home but her inner symbols as well, a core part of her sense of self?

Similarly, the woman may report long term feelings of isolation. This sensation can manifest in a few ways. She might have difficulty with trusting people. Or she might struggle with a continual feeling of being "alone in a crowd," even though she has several friendships. Here, the woman may be describing the sensation of being cut off from parts of her buried self. She may be describing a sensation which would make more sense to her if she knew that many of us, at bottom, feel that we are visitors in a Christian world (Kaschak, 1992).

Additionally, a woman may have excessive fear of being rejected by others, thus appearing to have features of an avoidant personality. Have her examine who she is afraid will reject her, and for what reasons. The Jewish woman's obvious fear and alienation of the gentile world can go unseen by the therapist who has not yet been sensitized to the psychology of the Jewish woman.

TREATMENT ISSUES

At the countertransference level, there are three potentially charged areas for the Jewish woman therapist to be aware of when working with a Jewish female client. First, it is important to stay aware of your own internalized anti-Semitism, which may "bubble up" in the far edges of your mind, as you sit with a Jewish woman. The task here is not to push such thoughts and feelings aside, but rather to allow them into consciousness and address them. This is the best insurance against the thoughts and feelings inadvertently coming through in your unconscious behavior.

Second, understand that many of us have a hard time with collecting money from clients, Jewish or non-Jewish. Issues resulting from being female and battling internalized sexism may lead us to feel that we don't deserve the money that we are charging, that we don't really know what we're doing, and that we have no business charging a professional fee for these fraudulent services! These feelings get even more complicated when we add in the twist of being female *and* Jewish.

As Jews, we may carry a fear of being seen as money-grubbing, materialistic and/or power hungry. We may then try to compensate, or to protect ourselves from the feared anti-Semitic responses of others by acting as if money doesn't matter. We can do this by allowing a client to accumulate a balance, by not encouraging her to examine the meaning of running up a balance or by sliding our fees down too low to an amount we eventually resent. While none of this unconscious behavior on our part is in the client's interest, (we are potentially robbing her of the experience of looking at her own difficulties with money), my focus here is more on the well being, pride and personal satisfaction of the therapist. I think it is very important to work with a practice consultant who is aware of the possibility that issues around fee collection may be connected to the therapist's experience of being Jewish and female. To miss this obvious connection is parallel to the therapist missing such connections with her own Jewish women clients.

Finally, as Jews many of us are sensitive to "group think" and cult process, resulting from our painful awareness of Hitler's Germany. This sensitivity can make us somewhat uncomfortable with our clients' transference processes, especially that of positive transference. Positive transference can be unnerving because it can feel like the client is in an idealizing, trance-like state which makes her vulnerable to making you into some kind of guru. Negative transferences from clients can be less charged and easier to tolerate, because these relationships do not feel like the client has lost her powers of critical discrimination, her ability to think clearly. Some of us thus have difficulty being with and sustaining a positive transference and find ourselves interrupting it through premature self-disclosure. It can be helpful here to bring in the lens of Jewishness and examine our horror of blind hero worship, in terms of difficulties we may be having with the client's transference.

There are several important points to consider in working with a Jewish woman client. First, she often needs more "air time," more room to verbalize her experience than do gentile clients. For Jews and Jewish women, words and the communication of words through speech can feel like a lifeline, a necessity for survival. For a variety of complex reasons we tend to value verbal communication and many of us have deep needs to be heard. Possible reasons for this need are complex, and have been written about by others (McGoldrick, 1982). For our purpose as therapists, it is important to keep in mind that your client may need to spend many hours verbalizing the nuance, contradiction, paradox and ambivalence of her experience to you, before she feels safe and satiated enough to go deeper within her own experience.

We are practicing therapy in an era of both brief and experiential therapies, where a major goal is to cut through the client's need to protect herself through intellectualization. Pushing the Jewish woman to do this too early in the therapy can be a great mistake and disservice. She often needs ample time to be able to speak at length so as to finally feel "seen." The need itself to talk at such length needs to be examined. If her process of disclosing is artificially speeded up, the potential for subtle and significant work can be lost. If her natural unfolding is taken away, she will lose the opportunity to become aware of her process. The work here on the therapist's part is to be patient and to work with your feelings of impatience, which may have some relationship to your own longings to be heard.

Similarly, it is important to restrain your eagerness for her to trust you. One of the key psychological issues for Jews in general is trust; to reassure your client prematurely of your trustworthiness, and of her safety in the relationship with you, can rob her of some difficult but productive work around trust issues. If she complies with your request for her to trust you before she's ready, she may be repeating a process with which she's already very familiar, of ignoring her chronic feelings of distrust and acting as if she's normal (i.e., gentile), in order to get by. She has grown able to ignore this distrust which nags at the back of her mind because she has never had help in becoming aware of it. The relationship with you may be the first time in her life that she is finally safe enough, paradoxically, to admit how unsafe and distrustful she feels with people toward whom she is supposed to feel close. Now she can be encouraged to become aware of the distrust, to be with it openly, and to honor and explore it. There may be some strong resulting countertransference issues for the therapist to explore, in terms of our own discomfort at being the object of another Jewish woman's distrust. Additionally, we might feel resentful at having to once again do what feels like hiding our identities as Jews, in the service of providing her with the blank slate she needs to process her distrust. Sitting still with this can be very uncomfortable!

The Jewish woman tends to comment more than most gentile women about the relationship with the therapist. She may thus appear more psychologically sophisticated because of her awareness of the interpersonal relationship much earlier in the therapy work than most people. Though this can be very engaging for you as the therapist, her tendency is not necessarily an indication of psychological development, but rather symptomatic of her hypervigilant way of being in the world. It may be difficult for this woman to feel connected to herself when she is in the presence of other people. Instead, she needs to be engaged in a continual process of examining who she is relating to in any given moment. It is important not to get seduced by this engagement. While it can provide for a more interesting therapy for the clinician, exploring the interpersonal relationship is not necessarily what the woman needs. Her cutting edge may be to look at what is happening within herself, moment by moment, rather than actively engaging in conversation about the nuances of the relationship with you. The traditional stages of therapy need to be kept in mind: usually the client first explores her own issues and only gradually comes to recognize the centrality of the relationship with the therapist. The Jewish woman who skips over the first stage and moves prematurely into the second stage is also likely skipping over parts of herself.

For many women, basic aspects of psychological change can feel like a betrayal of their Jewish culture. When a woman gets to a point in her inner work where she wants more for herself emotionally and is ready to challenge some of the basic ways that she suffers, she might feel as though she is severing herself from her people. At the time in her therapy when she begins to struggle to let go of her chronic anxiety, dread, distrust and pessimism, she may be met with waves of guilt feelings that tell her she is trying to act gentile. Many Jews come to realize that they have linked their habitual ways of suffering as fundamental to their sense of Jewish identity when they first come up against this wall of guilt.

In this instance and overall, our task as therapists is the same as with all of the complex, murky and painful material we help our Jewish women clients sort out: to gently support the woman to stay close to her own personal truth underneath and in between the overlay of being Jewish and female. Our work is to help her find out where she starts, and where the messages about who she is, end. It is at this initially hard-to-find place that the exquisite work of liberating the self can take place.

REFERENCES

Beck, E.T. (1988). From "Kike" to "J.A.P". *Sojourner: The women's forum, 14*(1).

Beck, E.T. (1990). Therapy's double dilemma: Anti-semitism and misogyny. In R. Seigel & E. Cole (Eds.), *Jewish women in therapy: Seen but not heard.* New York: Harrington Park Press.

Bulkin, E., Pratt, M. B., & Smith, B. (1984). *Yours in struggle: Three feminist perspectives on anti-semitism and racism.* Ithaca, N.Y.: Firebrand Books.

Caplan, P. (1985). *The myth of women's masochism.* New York: Signet.

Cliff, M. (1985). Claiming an identity they taught me to despise. In *The land of look behind.* Ithaca, N.Y.: Firebrand Books.

Davidowicz, L. (1977). *The Jewish presence.* New York: Holt, Rinehart & Winston.

Deming, B. (1984). Confronting one's own oppression. In J. Meyerding, (Ed.), *We are all part of one another.* Philadelphia: New Society Publishers.

Eichenbaum, L. & Orbach, S. (1983). *Understanding women: A feminist psychoanalytic view.* New York: Basic Books.

Friedan, B. (1963). *The feminist mystique.* New York: Dell.

Friedan, B. (1981). *The second stage.* New York: Summit.

Greenspan, M. (1983). *A new approach to women and therapy.* New York: McGraw-Hill.

Howe, I. & Libo, K., (Eds.). (1979). *How we lived: A documentary history of Jews in America.* New York: New American Library.

Howe, I. & Libo, K., (Eds.). (1990). *The world of our fathers.* New York: Schocken Books.

Johnson, M. (1988). *Strong mothers, weak wives.* Berkeley: UC Press.

Kaschak, E. (October, 1992). First there are the questions. Opening Address given at the *First International Conference on Judaism, Feminism and Psychology,* Seattle, WA.

Kaye/Kantrowitz, M. (1990). The issue is power: Some notes on Jewish women and therapy. In R. Seigel & E. Cole (Eds.), *Jewish women in therapy: Seen but not heard.* New York: Harrington Park Press.

Lerner, H. (1983). Female dependency in context: Some theoretical and technical considerations. *American Journal of Orthopsychiatry, 53*(4).

McGoldrick, M., (Ed.). (1982). *Ethnicity and family therapy.* New York: Guilford Press.

Memmi, A. (1962). *Portrait of a Jew*. New York: Viking Press.

Memmi, A. (1965). *The colonizer and the colonized.* Boston: Beacon Press.

Memmi, A. (1968). *Dominated man*. Boston: Beacon Press.

Meyerhoff, B. (1978). *Number our days*. New York: E.P. Dutton.

Miller, J.B. (1976). *Toward a new psychology of women.* Boston: Beacon Press.

Rich, A. (1981). Integrity. In *A wild patience has taken me this far: Poems 1978-1981.* (p. 9). New York: Norton.

Schneider, S. W. (1984). *Jewish and female: Choices and changes in our lives today.* New York: Simon & Schuster.

Siegel, R. J. (1986). Anti-semitism and sexism in stereotypes of Jewish women. In *Women and therapy: A feminist quarterly, 5*(2/3).

Sue, D. W., & Sue, D. (1990). *Counseling the culturally different: Theory and practice.* New York: Wiley.

Weinberg, S. S. (1988). *The world of our mothers.* New York: Schocken Books.

Westkott, M. (1986). *The feminist legacy of Karen Horney*. New Haven: Yale University Press.

White, M. (1989). *Selected papers.* Adelaide, South Australia: Dulwich Centre Publications.

Zborowski, K. & Herzog, E. (1952). *Life is with people: The culture of the Shtetl.* New York: International Universities Press.

UNTANGLING STRANDS OF IDENTITY: GENDER, CULTURE AND ETHNICITY

BARBARA EVE BREITMAN

Sarah, a 45-year-old, high-powered businesswoman, divorced mother of two children in college, recounts a blow-up with her elderly mother. "I was supposed to meet her at a restaurant and I was 45 minutes late. When I got there, she was gone. I panicked because I know how crazy she gets. I called her at home. I tried to reach my father. No answer. I grabbed a taxi and pressed for the driver to go faster. When I got to my mother's apartment, she was standing there, half naked and crazy, wild looking. She screamed at me. 'How could you do this to me? How could you abandon me like this? Anything could have happened to me on that street corner.'" Sarah recounts getting down on her hands and knees like a child to beg for forgiveness: "Please forgive me, mommy. Don't stop talking to me. Please mommy, please."

Sarah's parents are survivors of the Holocaust. Their families were murdered by the Nazis. Sarah has spent her life enslaved to her mother's terror, caring for a fragile psyche that threatens to fragment whenever her mother experiences separation or loss. Sarah screams about how the Nazis reach through her parents' lives to strangle her own; how the Holocaust turned her mother into a brittle tyrant, strangling her own child with the terror they caused.

Crying, Sarah says: "You know, whenever I tried to talk about my parents and the Holocaust with other therapists, especially non-Jewish ones, I sensed their discomfort. Either they avoided the issue completely by saying my mother was just an extremely over-protective, neurotic woman, or they questioned me like anthropologists and I became their history lesson on the Jewish experience of World War II. What I've needed is for someone to help me mourn the Holocaust that lived on in my family."

Lillian, a working class Jewish lesbian, struggles to find a home as a Jew. Turning 30 and ready to have a child, she suddenly faces questions she never asked before. What kind of mother will I be and who is my community? She laments having felt out of place with the Jewish kids in high school: not having enough money, not feeling smart enough, always being marginal. In community college, she had found a spiritual home, but it was with the nuns and working class Catholic women of the Newman club. There she found the spiritual sisterhood she had never found amongst Jews. Becoming a mother, she wants to raise her child as a Jew. Is it possible, she asks me, to find a spiritual community of Jews where she can be at home as a lesbian mother with limited financial resources?

I struggle with questions about boundaries, knowing that for the present the only Jewish community in our area where she can be fully welcomed and included as a lesbian mother is the one I belong to. Eventually, Lillian finds this out for herself. For months we negotiate the delicate and difficult issues of overlapping relationships in a close-knit Jewish community.

INTRODUCTION

The history of the feminist therapy movement has been one of constantly deepening our understanding of what it means for helping professionals to encounter other human beings fully as subjects. Virtually every person we meet through the therapeutic relationship needs to become the subject of their own life story, after having been a misunderstood, acted-upon or abused object in other peoples' stories. Sometimes that objectification has happened because of gender or sexual orientation, sometimes because of race, ethnicity, religion or class, sometimes because of age or disability. Always that objectification gets inscribed in the most sensitive folds of ourselves and often it enters us and is acted out through the most intimate relationships of our lives. As Sandra Bartky, a feminist philosopher, has vividly articulated, "when we internalize the gaze of the Other and become at once seer and seen, appraiser and thing appraised, the stranger who inhabits our consciousness becomes not really a stranger at all, but ourselves" (Bartky, 1990, p. 38).

At our best, feminist therapists enable people who have never articulated the truth of their lives, to do so, making it possible for them, if they choose, to enter history as subjects. "We must appreciate," Marcia Hill (1990, p. 55) passionately asserts in *On Creating a Theory for Feminist Therapy*, "what a profoundly radical thing it is to fully explicate the inner knowing of those whose reality does not come out of the existing Weltanschauung [total worldview]."

Untangling the social context of personal history enables an individual to develop what Roger Gottlieb, in *History and Subjectivity* (1987), has called "awakened subjectivity." The uniqueness of feminism is that more than any other mass movement, we have created a model of political action that depends on self-knowledge. By reflecting on our own autobiographies, we have developed revolutionary theory. "Feminist self-reflection," says Gottlieb, "is an example of how political resistance grows when an oppressed group comes to know itself in terms of its own experience" (Gottlieb, 1987, p. 148-9). "Feminists," he continues, "have presented a model in which subjective knowledge and the transformation of self are combined with a structural account of social life" (Gottlieb, 1987, p. 151). Inspired by Paulo Freire, bell hooks quotes him as saying: "We cannot enter the struggle as objects in order later to become subjects" (hooks, 1990, p. 15).

For a decade, feminist therapists have been engaging in healing processes with people not only to alleviate emotional suffering, but to awaken the subjectivity of our clients. In the past, we focused primarily on the significance of gender, and on the effects of the social construction of gender to the formation of self. We have explored the social construction of sexuality and the differing realities faced by lesbian and heterosexual women. Recently, however, feminist therapists have stressed how the salience of gender varies with the socio-historic context (Espin & Gawalek, 1992, p. 88-105; Brown & Brodsky, 1992; Brown, 1990). We have become increasingly aware that our work has failed to reflect the true cultural diversity of the United States and has fallen into the same trap as other schools of psychology, being too focused on the experiences of the white middle class. We are now challenging one another to develop models of practice to elucidate the complex entwining of gender and sexual orientation with race, ethnicity, class, dis/ability, culture and religion (Espin & Gawalek, 1992; Brown, 1990). Fine and Gordon (1989) have coined the phrase "braided subjectivities" to conceptualize this formation of identity from the interweaving of many strands of self-experience.

Each of us has multiple identities, forged within a social context and shaped by the power relations within that context to produce "socially and historically constituted subjectivities" (Fine & Gordon, 1989, p. 147). Because these strands of identity are twisted together, they are difficult to disentangle. We can experience ourselves at war with our own parts, in a state of disease. In the most simplistic formulation, for example: our woman self, strongly believing in gender equality, may be at war with our Jewish self, steeped in a tradition of gender inequality; our African-American self, identified with the mass of working class and poor black people, may conflict with our middle-class self and aspirations; our lesbian self may be at war with our Catholic or Jewish self, shaped by a religion that has taught us to hate our sexuality. Untangling the different strands of identity, recognizing stages in the identity development of each strand, and understanding how one line of identity is affected by the others is like unfurling the double helix of personality and culture. Feminist therapists are only beginning to find the language we need to conceptualize this multidimensional hologram of self. As we untangle these strands and declare that we are entitled to live in a society which affirms our right and ability to be fully who we are, we create social revolution.

As a therapist, I am always a woman, a feminist and a Jew. Whatever other knowledge I bring to the therapeutic encounter, I bring a self so profoundly shaped by the social, historical and spiritual experiences of being a contemporary woman and feminist Jew, that whatever healing emerges from the meeting between myself and another, flows somehow from those realities.

As a middle-class, currently able-bodied, white heterosexual woman, I have been shaped by dominant cultural experiences. As a woman and a Jew, I have been shaped by minority group experiences. To some people, I represent the dominant culture. To others, I am the outsider, the marginal one. Inside myself, I've experienced what it is to stand in different relationships to power and authority.

As a spiritual woman and the inheritor of the tradition of a people who have passed down the story of their encounter with the Holy, I am heir to a rich and varied civilization, a complex culture that continues to shape and inform my experience of the sacred. As a contemporary Jewish feminist, I am in the process of transforming that tradition by including the voices of women, as whole Jews, for the first time in our people's history.

In the course of my life, I have moved from a state of psychic fragmentation, spiritual alienation, and communal dislocation (diagnosed in the mental health field as depression) to a life of greater inner harmony, spiritual aliveness and communal connection. I've learned it is not possible to feel whole without untangling the inter-connecting strands of selfhood. I learned it is not possible to experience wholeness without living in community and discovering the presence of something larger than ourselves which dwells in our midst when we pursue justice and seek truth together. Integrating the braids of culture, spirituality, privilege and oppression in a contemporary white, Jewish-American woman's identity has given me a deep appreciation for the intricate ways different strands of identity interweave with one another to form a single distinct personality.

Although there are many Jewish clinicians active in the field of feminist therapy, we have written only sparsely about the influence of the Jewish experience in shaping our perspectives, about the significance of our being Jews to how we practice as therapists, about the spiritual ground Judaism offers for engaging in the work of healing, and about how our being Jews affects the way clients, Jewish and non-Jewish, perceive us. We have written little about the significance of the Jewish experience to the lives of our Jewish clients. Rachel Josefowitz Siegel and Ellen Cole's book *Jewish Women in Therapy* (1991) is the notable exception.

RACIAL/ETHNIC/CULTURAL IDENTITY DEVELOPMENT

Over twenty years ago, a multi-racial team of psychologists developed a model of "minority" identity development (Atkinson, Morten, & Sue, 1979). More recently, psychologist Janet Helms developed a model to describe the process through which members of the dominant culture become aware of the meaning and significance of membership in a privileged group. The significance of these models to our work as therapists is that they provide beginning schemas to conceptualize how to blend ethnic, racial and cultural identity development along with the other developmental schemas we are accustomed to considering in our work with clients. They help us think about how an individual's sense of self reflects the worldview of a particular culture or historical era, and about how an individual might become aware of the effects of culture on identity. Like most developmental schemas, these models are linear, and therefore simplistic. They fail to capture the true vicissitudes of human growth or the way experience can form layers of personality to be accessed or forgotten depending on catalyst or circumstance. The minority identity development model assumes a hostile cultural context and does not explore how minority identity might develop in a nurturing or benign context. However, as an aid to conceptualizing change within an aspect of cultural identity, these models provide a useful beginning.

The minority identity development model charts a progression from a stage of "conformity" during which a person identifies with the culture and values of the dominant group and internalizes the negative attitudes toward the self held by the dominant culture, to a final stage called "synergy" marked by the individual's achievement of positive self-esteem, positive identification with his/her own minority group, and an ability to negotiate the experience of living in more than one culture. During the intervening stages, the individual questions the sources of their negative self-valuation, recognizing the impact of societal oppression on their sense of self. This leads to a stage characterized by anger at the dominant culture, viewing people from the dominant culture as the enemy, combined with immersion in the minority culture to develop an appreciation of the contributions of one's own people to the human enterprise. This is followed by a re-evaluation of the ethnocentric stance and the recognition that there is both good and bad in their own minority group, as well as in the dominant culture. The individual is then able to inhabit diverse cultural milieus with both a strong sense of self and an appreciation for others. Other theorists have developed similar models to illuminate the process of homosexual identity formation (Cass, 1979).

The most well-researched of the models describing the development of consciousness in privileged or culturally dominant groups was done by psychologist Janet Helms who proposes a theory about the evolution of "white racial consciousness" in individuals (Helms, 1990). Her model has been informally adapted to apply to heterosexuals, the able-bodied and men. It could also be applied to Christians vis-à-vis Jews.

Helms' model begins with the "contact" stage during which the white person believes skin color makes no difference. We may claim not even to "see" skin color at this stage, to assert that "people are just people." This results in the unconscious support of institutional racism. A transitional stage occurs when the individual becomes aware of the existence of discrimination based on skin color and is jolted into acknowledging that color makes a big difference in how people are treated. This realization occasions much anxiety and guilt, and a desire to make sense of the reality of racial discrimination. People cannot remain for long in such a place of confusion. Therefore we usually internalize/accept/adopt the racism of the dominant culture to justify the discrimination we've observed, and engage, overtly or covertly, in stereotyping members of the minority group, believing in the superiority of the dominant group. White people then become fearful of losing entitlements and associate mainly with people of our own racial group.

The last three stages involve the abandonment of racism and the development of a positive white racial identity. First is a "pseudo-independent" stage characterized by intensified guilt and discomfort about racial injustice, an idealization and romanticizing of the "oppressed victim" blended with a beginning desire to find ways to combat racism. During this stage, the individual seeks out members of the minority group to learn more about racism. Eventually he or she realizes that for white people to develop a non-racist white identity, s/he needs to engage with other white people with a similar interest. The active exploration of friendships with people of color also continues. The final stage is a transcultural stage. The individual accepts her/himself as a white person and no longer idealizes, patronizes or denigrates people based on race; s/he has friendships with people across racial lines, can recognize institutional racism and challenge it, is able to confront mono-racial whites and not judge them harshly.

Most people carry both dominant and minority identities and are shaped by experiences of both privilege and oppression, at different times in their lives and within changing social contexts. Most categories of identity are themselves shifting, changing in cultural meaning within a society at different moments in history. Even the seemingly most essential and immutable categories, like gender and race, are culturally determined; the social meaning and context of being female or male, white or black varies by location and historical moment. We certainly know this as Jews.

These models create a new ideal: the transcultural individual, a person firmly rooted in her/his own cultural identity, who actively seeks opportunities to learn from other cultural groups, and works to eliminate oppression against any group. Jewish feminist therapists who understand the insights of these models can help people become more conscious about the meaning an aspect of their identity has to them, and how it came to have that meaning. People are then freer to choose how to live out a particular identity; how to express an aspect of self.

Because of the structural position of white Jews in Western society, Jewish feminist therapists, conscious about the mixture of privilege and oppression in our own identities, can help clients sort out both dominant and minority identity experiences. We must always be sensitive, however, to how one or the other aspect of our identity will be most salient depending on who is doing the perceiving.

New questions also emerge about the dynamics of the therapeutic relationship. Why did this client choose me as a therapist? Was gender, ethnicity, race, sexual orientation, class or dis/ability an important factor in their choice? If so, why? How aware is the person about that aspect of their choice? At what stage are they in the identity development of the different strands of self that make up their personality and how will that affect transference in the therapeutic relationship? Where am I in the process of development along the many strands of my own identity and how will that affect how I interact with the client?

ADDICTION AS A SYMPTOM OF ETHNO-CULTURAL ALIENATION AND CONFLICT

Maria, a first generation Puerto Rican woman, was referred to me by her medicating psychiatrist when she expressed the desire to see a therapist sensitive to ethnic issues. Maria saw me as "ethnic" rather than "Anglo." My being Jewish and female meant to Maria that I had lived an ethnic experience as a woman. She was more comfortable with me than with an Anglo therapist. On the other hand, Maria's reluctance to see a Latina therapist raised a question about the extent to which she had identified with the dominant culture's negative valuation of her people. My use of self as a consciously identified ethnic woman, able to empathize with the process of minority identity development, has been a crucial variable in helping Maria and me to make sense of her journey.

Maria had recently been discharged from an alcohol rehabilitation center when she was referred to me. She knew that for recovery to continue, she needed to explore the significance of her ethnic background. Reflecting on her childhood in a working class Latino neighborhood, Maria wrote in her journal: "It is important to remember that I wanted to be a part of the American culture because it looked better than my own. I remember living in a place where the walls of the bathroom were cracked; I remember railroad apartments and I remember how pink those other people looked as opposed to my olive skin. Anglo culture ran it all. The men were desirable and the women knew how to dress and attract them. I watched carefully and I assumed the talk, the dress, and manners."

Maria rejected the gender inequality of her culture and sought to escape the economic deprivation of her childhood. Able to "pass" because of her white skin and ability to speak English without an accent, Maria adopted the styles of the dominant culture and gained access to educational institutions of the white middle class.

Like other first generation children of Puerto Ricans who migrated to this country between 1945 and 1965, Maria experienced an accelerated process of cultural transformation (Inclan, 1985). Although she had been successful through work and education in transcending the limiting gender expectations of Puerto Rican culture, Maria's sense of self was overwhelmed in her marriage to a Latino as their home life reproduced the gender inequality of their culture. She became increasingly depressed and eventually divorced. To provide financially for herself and her child, Maria took a position in a white, Anglo-Saxon firm. Here she experienced the greatest sense of alienation. A single parent, a Puerto Rican woman with working class roots attempting to make a place for herself in a hierarchical, upper-class, white male institution, Maria became increasingly unable to function. Her drinking got out of control. She became involved in a series of abusive relationships with men. Eventually, she lost her job.

Reconceptualizing the narrative of her life with a sensitivity to the braiding of gender, class, race and ethnicity, it was possible for

Maria to understand her alcoholism, in part, as the symptom of a woman caught in inexorable conflicts between cultures. As Comas-Diaz (1987) has stated, "Confronted with multi-faceted identities composed of ethnic, gender and racial aspects which are potentially conflictive, (Puerto Rican women) struggle with culturally imposed behaviors, while attempting to develop alternative ones. As women, they cope with gender discrimination and oppression, and as Puerto Ricans they cope with an ethnic identity crisis" (p. 467).

Cross-cultural aspects of the transference have illuminated further how ethnic issues intertwine with gender and other developmental processes. Maria struggled for a long time with disabling feelings of inadequacy and jealousy toward other women. She was troubled by being drawn to male lovers whom she imbued with excessive importance. These feelings were all the more troubling because they conflicted with consciously held beliefs in the need for women's empowerment. Competitive feelings toward other women interfered in Maria's ability to form intimate connections with women.

Sandra Bartky (1990) describes the experience of women who suffer when consciously held feminist or egalitarian values conflict with unconscious passions and longings. Because of "the eroticization of relations of domination, ...(and because) male power is eroticized, and male dominance itself becomes erotically charged, ...a person may experience her sexuality as arbitrary... and alien to the rest of her personality" (Bartky, 1990, p. 51). In Maria's case, the elevation and eroticization of the powerful male and the devaluation of the female merged with the internalization of the ethnic/racial hierarchy.

Maria became romantically involved with an Anglo man who seemingly valued her Puerto Rican heritage, but who devalued her intellectual abilities. Maria could not get angry at this idealized male partner, and was plagued by jealousy toward other women. In her fantasies, she always imagined an Anglo woman "stealing" him away. Maria could become obsessed with feelings of inadequacy and paralyzed by hostile and vengeful feelings toward these women. She felt no threat from other ethnic women.

Because Maria saw me as "ethnic" like herself, she felt free to reveal her fantasies about Anglo women. She remarked that an Anglo therapist would have felt like "the enemy". The transference became more complex when Maria's male friend began spending time professionally with a new colleague, a white Jewish woman. Maria was suddenly faced with the challenge of integrating her positive feelings and identification with me, the "good ethnic woman", with her negative feelings toward the white Jewish woman colleague in her partner's life. As she began to do so, she moved a step forward in gender identification. Instead of being plagued with jealousy and hostility toward women, Maria began to express anger at her male lover. She began asserting herself, pointing out that his devaluation of her intellectual abilities was his problem. A desire to expand relationships with women and to reconnect with Puerto Rican culture also began to emerge.

As Maria became more self-affirming in the relationship with her Anglo lover, she began to understand the origins of a life-long depression. "I made decisions to turn away from my people because my people were subjected. My options if I stayed with them weren't great. But my triumph has only been partial. I have climbed out by disowning them. I have a sense of betrayal. The reason I feel so empty sometimes is because I cut myself off from who I was to make it."

At the stage Maria entered therapy, she probably did not choose a Latina therapist because the similarity to herself was fraught with too much ethnocultural conflict. However, she could not choose an Anglo therapist because she had too much hostility toward members of the dominant culture. As an ethnically identified, white, Jew, I presented a good middle ground.

Obviously, the therapist can never act as the teacher of another's culture. We can only help clients understand what has been in the way of their connecting with their own history and people. However, when we are conscious about our own process of ethnic/racial identity development, engaged in learning about other cultures, we can work with people from other cultures to explore their ethnic identity development. If we are not conscious about the path of our Jewish identity development, we will have difficulty working with ethnic clients around issues of minority identification, especially those that result in self-hatred.

A REFLECTION ON RACE, GENDER, SEXUALITY AND THE PSYCHOLOGY OF JEWISH WOMEN

Many of the Jewish women clients I've worked with in therapy complain of feeling somehow "less feminine" than women of the dominant white Christian culture, and some have admitted, with much distress, to being unable to experience sexual attraction for Jewish partners, particularly Jewish male partners. As I have listened to the relationship histories of several inter-faith couples in marital counseling, it has occurred to me that many Jews partner with non-Jews in order to experience the needed sexual validation and affirmation of self they have been unable to find within themselves or get from other Jews.

Cornel West, the brilliant African-American intellectual of Princeton University, writes in *Race Matters* (1993): "...it is virtually impossible to talk candidly about race without taking about sex... (The) demythologizing of black sexuality is crucial for black America because so much black self-hatred and self-contempt has to do with the refusal of many black Americans to love their own black bodies—especially their black noses, hips, lips, and hair... White supremacist idealogy is based first and foremost on the degradation of black bodies in order to control them... How does one come to accept and affirm a body so despised by one's fellow citizens? ...White fear of black sexuality is a basic ingredient of white racism" (West, 1993, p. 85ff). While African-Americans have been the primary targets of white supremacist hatred in the United States, Jews were the primary targets in Europe. It is my impression that many American Jews of European ancestry have been deeply impacted, particularly in the area of sexuality, by self-hatred that does not seem to go away even though the Jewish body is now under less direct assault than it was in Europe. The wounds that racism inflicts on the sense of self, particularly the sense of self as gendered, sexual and embodied, seem to be deep, long-lasting and tenacious (Breitman, 1988).

Priscilla is a white, Jewish woman in her mid-thirties with a history of involvement in abusive relationships with men. All of her romantic relationships have been with non-Jewish men. Despite Priscilla's expressed cultural preference to marry a Jew, she has never felt sexually attracted to Jewish men, and finally became engaged to a non-Jew. Priscilla presented herself one day in extreme distress, saying she felt "totally destroyed inside" after a blow-up with her fiancé, Sean. The catalyst for the argument was Sean's commenting that Priscilla's front tooth seemed to be turning brown in color and suggesting she see a dentist about it.

As Priscilla and I explored the reasons for her feeling annihilated inside by such a seemingly minor observation about her appearance, she began to talk about the nose job she'd had as a teenager, about the nose she hated, the Jewish nose that felt like it covered her entire face. Priscilla cried as she recalled how much she hated being a

Jew, growing up in a non-Jewish area. She described how she used to ride around with non-Jewish friends who drove cars through a nearby Chassidic neighborhood, throwing things out the windows and screaming racist epithets. "I didn't participate," she sobbed, "but I was too scared to let them know I was a Jew. I couldn't stand up for myself and tell them what they were doing was wrong. I felt totally destroyed inside."

As Priscilla heard herself utter the same words she'd used to describe her feelings after the fight with Sean, she understood why she had felt annihilated by her fiancé's comments; however, she experienced only a little relief. She confessed that she had never told Sean about her nose job. Her sense of shame and fear of rejection were still profound. Priscilla had still not developed enough self-love nor healed wounds to her body image as a Jew to be honest about her nose job. She feared Sean would turn on her with anti-Semitic hostility and reject her as the mother of his children, if he knew his children might be born with ugly, Semitic noses.

INTRA-ETHNIC TRANSFERENCE: WHEN SIMILARITY BLURS THE BOUNDARIES

Working with clients from the same cultural, ethnic or racial minority group as the therapist poses different dilemmas than the cross-cultural dyad. In the cross-cultural dyad, cultural difference at least supports, though it does not ensure, the maintenance of interpersonal boundaries. When the client and therapist belong to the same ethnic, cultural or sexual minority group, and perhaps share communal space, boundaries can more easily be blurred.

Feminist therapists have already acknowledged the danger of using a client's dependence or idealization to reverse the caretaking role. Laura Brown has explored this issue in the lesbian community (Brown, 1988). Marcia Hill (1990) has written about our particular susceptibility to boundary violations because "we are more accessible as people than traditional therapists... because we choose for philosophical and political reasons to be *people* (with human vulnerabilities, pain and needs) as well as therapists with our clients" (p. 58-60). Hill looks at the issue of boundary violations from a therapeutic, rather than a judgmental stance, recognizing that "like all symptoms, boundary violations are an effort at solution" (Hill, 1990, p. 61). She proposes we consider how feminist therapists, as a group, may be at risk of boundary violations because we are women scripted early on to be emotional caretakers, "to get satisfaction from the contact and the power of the helping role" (p. 59), being "trained" to give much but ask for little.

It is easier to deny the inherent therapist-client power imbalance when working with clients who feel, and in some ways are, similar, not only as women but as Jews. As Hannah Lerman and Dorothe Rigby (1990) have discussed in their article in *Feminist ethics in psychotherapy,* in the earliest period of feminist therapy, "we were most impressed with how alike we feminist therapists were to our women clients. We had suffered the same oppression, experienced the same or similar role socialization, and had gone through the same kinds of socially induced traumas. We were aware of how traditional therapies had failed to understand and help us" (p. 51-52). However, we initially failed to recognize the differences in our role and position as therapist in a professional relationship. When clients and therapists are white, female and Jewish, they have often had comparable acculturation experiences and share a common cultural language. When they have suffered similar forms of sexism in the Jewish community, as well as anti-Semitism in the general community, this combination of factors can lead to a tendency to over-identify with clients, causing a therapist to ignore significant differences between herself and her clients.

The complexities of the transference and counter-transference relationship are increased when client and therapist must negotiate overlapping relationships in Jewish, feminist and/or lesbian communities. Other therapists have already written about the difficult boundary issues when therapists live in circumscribed ethnic, rural or activist communities (Sears, 1990; Gates & Speare, 1990; Saks Berman, 1990). Jeanne Adleman and Susan Barrett (1990) have offered feminist therapists guidelines for negotiating these complexities. The ethnic, feminist therapist who cannot rely on cultural difference or social distance to provide boundaries, may feel especially challenged in the process of making ethical and clinical decisions to protect the safety of the therapeutic relationship.

Lillian Comas-Diaz and Frederick Jacobsen (1991) note that a commonly occurring intra-ethnic transference is the idealization of the therapist and the fantasy of reunion with the perfect, all good parent. This is a particularly powerful transference, as the client projects her earliest longings for love and connection onto the therapist. Sometimes, such a transference fulfills the therapist's needs to be special or valuable, and the danger of boundary violations increases. At other times, when a client is extremely needy, idealizing or strongly identifying, she begins to imagine she is or can become like the therapist. The experience of psychic intrusion can be quite uncomfortable for the therapist. Although this type of transference can occur whether or not therapist and client belong to the same ethnic or racial group, a phenomenon well documented in the literature on clients who are diagnosed with borderline personality disorder, the projection can be magnified by ethnic/racial similarity. In my work with Jewish women clients, I have noted a stronger tendency on the part of these clients to identify with or idealize me, and I have sometimes been confused about when the identification is beneficial and when it is interfering with our work. I have noted a stronger tendency for me to feel counter transference feelings of psychic intrusion or invasion than with ethnically different clients.

Susan, a 33-year-old white, Jewish woman, was a member of the same extended Jewish community in which I live. At various times, Susan commented about how similar we were. She saw us as having things in common that differed from my perception of our similarities. She remarked and felt sometimes that she could "become just like me." At those moments, Susan seemed to experience a momentary "high", a transient euphoria, which I understood as the sensation that accompanies psychic merger with an idealized other. Sometimes that euphoria was mixed with erotic attraction.

Susan was painfully aware of her fragile sense of self. At an early stage in therapy she said poignantly: "I don't have a self in my heart. There are boxes, fragments. In one box, rage. In another, fear. If I open the boxes, I'll be totally vulnerable. Like a big hole. It's like my self doesn't live in the center of my body. I feel in touch with myself in my intellect, but not in my heart. I'm not there."

Although she was extremely bright, Susan experienced great difficulty channeling her natural abilities into a stable and financially fruitful career. She had also been unable to sustain an intimate, sexual relationship for more than a few months. Susan used me and other Jewish feminists as role models. The process whereby feminist women function as role models for one another because we have few historic examples to follow, is essential to the expansion of women's visions of possibility. However, as Adleman and Barrett (1990) note, one of the dangers that can arise when a client sees a therapist as a role model in real life is that "rather than confronting her differences from the therapist, she may copy what she sees and fail to explore sufficiently her inner strivings" (p. 89).

An example from Susan's therapy will illustrate. Susan knew of my involvement in a local feminist social work organization and had attended conferences at which I had been a presenter. Seeing me function in an esteemed position in a public forum both magnified Susan's idealization of me and her envy, and strengthened her desire to copy my behavior as a solution to her difficulties deciding on a career path. One day, not long after attending such a conference, Susan looked at me anxiously, but with a glint in her eye: "I've been afraid to tell you this, but I am interested in pursuing a career in social work. I don't want you to be angry at me or think I am trying to become you. I just think I will be good at it."

My instinctive reaction was to feel a flash of rage at the experience of psychic intrusion. Having had several other experiences with Susan during this phase of her therapy when fantasies of merger were predominating, counter transference feelings from my own experiences with boundary intrusions were being restimulated. I felt confused. Susan had previously told me her greatest fear was of being rejected when people found out how empty she was inside. I knew the identification with me was one way of filling up some of that emptiness, acquiring self. Was this a situation in which it would be constructive for Susan to try on, to identify with, an aspect of me she valued as a way of developing her self, or was this a situation in which Susan was trying to copy me as a way of avoiding the more difficult path of self-discovery and the exploration of her own inner striving? Unfortunately, I made, what in retrospect I believe to have been the wrong choice. I replied: "No, I wouldn't be angry. I would think you are identifying with a part of me you value." Susan was visibly relieved. The envy which had accompanied the idealization had not killed me nor caused me to retaliate against her. However, I had unconsciously supported her fantasy of becoming me and had given her permission to pursue a path which would further blur the boundaries between us.

Susan attended other workshops, from which she reported learning a great deal. Our paths did not cross at any of those events. Eventually, Susan stopped talking about becoming a social worker and seemed to have dropped the idea in favor of other options she was pursuing. However, several months later, Susan received an invitation to a weekend mini-conference. One of the events, a rather intimate gathering to discuss difficult cases, was to be hosted by me in my home. There were other more public events scheduled during the weekend: an issue-based forum and a wine and cheese gathering, neither of which were being held in my home.

When Susan received the invitation, she called to ask what I would think of her attending the meeting in my home. I explained I would prefer if she did not attend the meeting in my home, both because I felt a need for privacy and because I thought it would keep our therapeutic work clearer. I stressed that she was free to attend the other weekend events, and therefore this limit should not seriously interfere in her participation in the conference. My drawing this boundary precipitated a crisis in our relationship.

Susan acknowledged I had a right to privacy, but she protested I had no right to sponsor an event to which she might get an invitation but would not be able to attend. Her rage and fear skyrocketed as she experienced me as untrustworthy; she began to feel suicidal. I realized I had unknowingly encouraged Susan's identification with me and fantasies of merger through previous interpretations; that my drawing a limit suddenly felt like a betrayal. Fortunately, the working alliance between us was strong enough to enable a working through of the crisis.

As Susan struggled with the boundary, she confronted the fear she'd been avoiding by focusing on the conference like a life or death issue. She acknowledged that attending the session in my home was symbolic of having access to or being denied intimacy and inclusion in women's community. She spoke of her fear of never finding her niche, of being lonely and isolated her entire life. As equilibrium returned to the therapeutic relationship, Susan's motivation for this type of deeper exploration seemed to be strengthened.

As Adleman and Barrett (1990) conclude: "Overlapping relationships do contain potential hazards for boundary violations and ethical missteps. All of us may err at times, sometimes in being too ironclad, sometimes too fluid" (p. 89). As always, our commitment must be to the exploration of deeper levels of truth.

CONCLUSION

The self is formed in the crucible of culture and always bears the imprint of culture. Both feminist therapists and their clients come to the therapeutic encounter as personalities made up of multiple strands of identity, having been shaped by many cultural experiences in a variety of contexts. Ethnic, racial, class and religious identities are as alive in the transferential aspects of the therapeutic dyad as are gender and sexual orientation, and we need to be conscious about how they affect the therapeutic process.

Until feminists began to do so, psychotherapists in the United States rarely questioned the Western notion of the self as individuated, separate and private. And even as feminists who came to recognize the salience of women's experiences of selfhood as inter-dependent, contiguous with other selves and relational, we continued to be unconscious about the full impact of culture on selfhood by ignoring the profound influences of race, ethnicity, religion and class. When we accept the idea of a simple causal relationship between early childhood experiences in the family and adult psychopathology, we limit the explanation for the causes of suffering to the smallest possible arena, the nuclear family (Watkins, 1992). When our questions probe only the dynamics of family relationships, and our interpretations focus only on those dynamics, we perpetuate the notion of a privatized self and collude unconsciously with the cultural origins of suffering.

As feminist therapist Mary Watkins (1992) has written: "In therapy we listen deeply to that distillation of culture we have labelled 'inner life.' This very labelling, however, has deafened us considerably. What is 'inner' has become the personal, the private; we have lost our ear for the resonances between the personal and the cultural, the private and the collective. Our task is to learn a way of listening, in therapy and in our own lives, to much of what is presented as personal suffering *so that we can hear the culture in it*; hear how personal suffering reflects aspects of suffering in the paradigms of our cultural reality. This kind of listening links the healing of an individual to the healing of a culture and thus fuels the transformation of society in general" (p. 56).

REFERENCES

Adleman, J. & Barrett, S. E. (1990). Overlapping relationships: Importance of the feminist ethical perspective. In H. Lerman & N. Porter, (Ed.), *Feminist ethics in psychotherapy* (pp. 87-91). New York: Springer.

Atkinson, D., Morten, G., & Sue, D. W. (1979). *Counseling American minorities: A cross-cultural perspective*. Iowa: Wm. C. Brown.

Bartky, S. (1990). *Femininity and domination: Studies in the phenomenology of oppression*. New York: Routledge Press.

Baum, C., Hyman, P., & Michel, S., (1976). *The Jewish woman in America*. New York: New American Library.

Breitman, B. (1988). Lifting up the shadow of anti-semitism: Jewish masculinity in a new light. In H. Brod, (Ed.), *A mensch among men: Explorations in Jewish masculinity* (pp. 101-117). California: Crossing Press.

Brown, L., (1990). The meaning of a multi-cultural perspective for theory-building in feminist therapy. In L. Brown & M.P.P. Root (Eds.), *Diversity and complexity in feminist therapy* (pp. 1-21). New York: Harrington.

Brown, L. (1988). Beyond thou shalt not: Thinking about ethics in the lesbian therapy community. *Women & Therapy, 8*(1-2), 13-25.

Brown, L., & Brodsky, A. (1992). The future of feminist therapy. *Psychotherapy, 29*(1), 51-57.

Buber, M. (1967). Healing through meeting. In M. Friedman, (Trans.). *A believing humanism: My testament 1902-1965* (pp. 138-143). New York: Humanities Press International.

Cass, V. C. (1979). Homosexual identity formation: A theoretical model. *Journal of Homosexuality, 4*, 219-235.

Comas-Diaz, L. (1987). Feminist therapy with mainland Puerto Rican women. *Psychology of Women Quarterly, 11*, 461-474.

Comas-Diaz, L. (1992). The future of psychotherapy with ethnic minorities. *Psychotherapy, 29*(1), 88-94.

Comas-Diaz, L. & Jacobsen, F. (1991). Ethnocultural transference and countertransference in the therapeutic dyad. *American Journal of Orthopsychiatry, 61*(3), 392-402.

Espin, O. & Gawalek, M. A. (1992). Women's diversity: Ethnicity, race, class and gender in theories of feminist psychology. In L.S. Brown

& M. Ballou (Eds.), *Personality and psychopathology: Feminist reappraisals* (pp. 88-107). New York: Guilford.

Fine, M. & Gordon, S.M. (1989). Feminist transformations of/despite psychology. In M. Crawford & M. Gentry, (Eds.), *Gender and thought* (pp. 146-174). New York: Springer-Verlag.

Gates, K. & Speare, K. (1990). Overlapping relationships in rural communities. In H. Lerman & N. Porter, (Eds.), *Feminist ethics in psychotherapy* (pp. 97-101). New York: Springer.

Gottlieb, R. (1987). *History and subjectivity: The transformation of Marxist theory*. Philadelphia: Temple University Press.

Helms, J. (1990). *Black and white racial identity*. New York: Greenwood Press.

Hill, M. (1990). On creating a theory of feminist therapy. In L.S. Brown, & M.P.P. Root (Eds.), *Diversity and complexity in feminist therapy* (pp. 53-65). New York: Harrington Park Press.

hooks, b. (1990). *Yearning: Race, gender and cultural politics*. Boston: South End Press.

Inclan, J. (1985). Variations in value orientations in mental health work with Puerto Ricans. *Psychotherapy, 22*(2), 324-334.

Lerman, H. & Rigby, D. (1990). Boundary violations: Misuse of the power of the therapist. In H. Lerman & N. Porter (Eds.), *Feminist ethics in psychother*apy (pp. 51-52). New York: Springer.

Saks Berman J.R. (1990). The problems of overlapping relationships in the political community. In H. Lerman & N. Porter (Eds.), *Feminist ethics in psychotherapy* (pp. 106-110). New York: Springer.

Sears, V. (1990). On being an "only one". In H. Lerman & N. Porter, (Eds.), *Feminist ethics in psychotherapy* (pp. 102-105). New York: Springer.

Siegel, R. J. & Cole, E. (1990). *Jewish women in therapy: Seen but not heard*. New York: Haworth Press.

West, C. (1993). *Race matters*. Boston: Beacon Press.

Watkins, M. (1992). *From Individualism to the Interdependent Self.* Psychological Perspectives, (27). LA: Jung Institute.

CONTEMPORARY TOPICS

Miriam Pollack
Michele Clark
Barbara U. Hammer
Kayla Miriyam Weiner

CIRCUMCISION: A JEWISH FEMINIST PERSPECTIVE

MIRIAM POLLACK

Circumcision is at the heart of gender imbalance in Judaism. For a male Jew, it is a critical mark of identity, an assumed rite of passage, secular or sacred, into the peoplehood and/or faith of Judaism. For a Jewish woman, it may have the same meaning until she is pregnant, with the possibility of bearing a son. It is then that a woman's deepest instincts may arise trembling out of her culturally anesthetized stupor to whisper or plead, "Please, let it be a girl."

Many mothers of Jewish sons, including myself, have confronted this dilemma with shame. We are not only ashamed to object to circumcision, we are ashamed to acknowledge, much less express our feelings. We dare not take them seriously. To do so, we know, is to oppose what our tradition has named holy for hundreds of generations. To do so is to meddle dangerously with Jewish identity and by implication, we are told, with Jewish survival itself. To do so is to risk a potentially damaging confrontation with one's parents, one's in-laws and, possibly, one's spouse. To do so is to trespass upon the exclusive territory of male bonding. And to do so is to assert female, mother-wisdom as a greater power and source of authority than the patriarchal understanding of holiness. The price is too high. We tell ourselves, "If we don't have our baby sons circumcised, they will be rejected by their people. We will be sacrificing their Jewish identity." We capitulate. I did. I did, for all of these reasons, and the screams of my babies remain embedded in my bones and still haunt the edges of my mind.

My goal in writing this chapter is twofold. First, and of paramount importance is to examine what we are doing physically, psychologically and spiritually, when we allow our baby boys to be circumcised. While also taking into consideration the historical contexts, we must look at these questions carefully, one at a time, if we are to be fully responsible for the choices we make on behalf of our sons. Second, my purpose is to challenge Jewish women to reassert our ancient authority to name and celebrate what is holy and what is not holy.

In order to gain some perspective on the practice of circumcision, it is useful to look at its global pattern. Eighty percent of the world's population including Europe, the former U.S.S.R., China and Japan have never engaged in the practice of circumcision. Generally, circumcision has been practiced only within the context of tribal or religious traditions. This is true for Jews, Muslims, most black Africans, non-white Australians and others. The exception is the United States where routine circumcision has gained widespread acceptance since the latter part of the nineteenth century (Wallerstein, 1985).

Several factors have converged to affect the status of circumcision in this country. One was the advent of preventive medicine which included not only the advocacy of vitamins, hygiene and diet, but also surgical removal of potentially troubling body parts (i.e., tonsils, adenoids, breasts, etc.) as legitimate prophylaxis for maintaining optimum health. The foreskin qualified as a site of potential trouble due to the extreme conditions experienced by men at war, a familiar experience for American men during the first half of the twentieth century. Soggy trenches and humid jungles where little possibility for a shower or change of clothing existed were not hospitable environments for maintaining minimal foreskin hygiene. The military soon added its authority to the voices advocating foreskin removal as a health benefit.

Both the medical and military perspectives on circumcision were greatly influenced by echoes of 19th century Victorianism which seeped into the medical literature through the writings of the highly credentialed Dr. P.C. Remondino, who in 1892 published a book entitled, *History of Circumcision from the Earliest Times to the Present: Moral and Physi-*

cal Reasons for its Performance. He stated that circumcision should be implemented to eradicate the widespread and dangerous occurrence of masturbation which could lead to all manner of ills, including insanity. Far from being dismissed for its pseudo-medical and perverse arguments, this point of view was unquestioned for nearly 70 years in the United States as well as in England. The book was reprinted without change in 1974 and was referred to by one physician writing in *Medical Aspects of Human Sexuality* (1974) as a book that was "pertinent and carefully thought out" (Valentine, 1974). Finally, in the 1940's, articles began to appear challenging this point of view. The rate of circumcision in Great Britain has since dropped to about one percent of newborn males, whereas in the United States it is estimated to be fifty-nine percent (Wallerstein, 1985).

The Jewish world was not immune to the Victorian mentality. Even though any hygienic function of circumcision was specifically denied according to medieval and contemporary orthodox Jewish writings, in 1911 Dr. Joseph Preuss claimed in his definitive work, *Biblical-Talmudic Medicine* that ritual circumcision imparted health benefits. Dr. P.C. Remondino was listed as his sole reference substantiating this "fact" (p. 544). Some secular Jews as well as fundamentalist Christians still justify circumcision as a divinely inspired ritual of health care, even though, traditionally, Judaism has viewed circumcision as a spiritual rite.

Nevertheless, the so-called hygienic arguments for circumcision still persuade millions of secular Jews and non-Jews to circumcise their baby boys despite the statement made by the American Academy of Pediatrics that "there is no absolute medical indication for routine circumcision of the newborn" (American Academy of Pediatrics, 1975). The American College of Obstetricians and Gynecologists followed with a similar statement in 1978 (American Academy of Pediatrics, American College of Obstetricians and Gynecologists, 1983). The desperate arguments for circumcision include prevention of penile and cervical cancer, urinary tract infections and sexually transmitted diseases. Let's examine them one at a time.

The prevention of penile cancer is certainly a desirable goal. However, when one discovers that the prevalence of penile cancer is one to three cases per million and that the studies cited did not control for hygiene, the conclusion that sexual surgery is mandated for all infant males becomes highly suspect (Wallerstein, 1985). More infants die every year in the United States as a result of circumcisions than die of penile cancer (Cole, 1993).

Circumcision as a deterrent for cervical cancer has received much publicity. This resulted from a book published in the early 1960's by Dr. S.I. McMillen who concluded that cancer of the cervix was linked to uncircumcised partners and that the Old Testament provided God-given protection against such affliction. What was not included in the research was the sexual behavior of women who tended to acquire cervical cancer. Indeed, it was later acknowledged that multiple sexual partners and intercourse at a young age were the primary influential factors in acquiring cervical cancer. The circumcision status of the partner was not significant, a conclusion which Dr. McMillen acknowledged in the second edition of his book, *None of These Diseases* (McMillen, 1984). Any connection between cancer and circumcision is dismissed in a statement by Grossman and Posner written in *Obstetrics and Gynecology* in 1981. They state, "No one today seriously promotes circumcision as a prophylactic against cancer of any form. No significant correlation between cancer and circumcision has ever been proved" (p. 245).

Urinary tract infections, also referred to as U.T.I.'s, are a somewhat more complex issue. Those who advocate circumcision as a prophylaxis against U.T.I.'s usually cite research conducted by Wiswell et. al. (1986), in a United States Army Hospital on 400,000 infants. They reported a tenfold increase in the incidence of U.T.I.'s among uncircumcised boys. That sounds significant until you look carefully at the numbers and the methodology. The increase was from 0.11 percent to 1.12 percent. Therefore, the risk for uncircumcised boys is one in one hundred. The study also included female infants who had a higher U.T.I. rate than the corresponding males. Furthermore, Wiswell had advised parents to gently retract the babies' foreskins in order to clean the glans, an action that is unnecessary, potentially irritating and an easy way to introduce bacteria to the site (Wallerstein, 1986). The study also did not control for those babies that were being breastfed. The protective bacteria ingested by a baby from its mother's milk may well have a significant prophylactic effect on the potentially pathological bacteria found in some of the infants. In European countries, in the rare instances when U.T.I.'s do develop, they are usually amenable to medical treatment and do not require surgery.

The contention that circumcision helps prevent venereal disease is completely contradicted by the facts. The Centers for Disease Control reported that the syphilis rate has increased seventy-five percent since 1985, and yet, those who have contracted the disease were born when the neonatal circumcision rate was at its highest. Likewise, the incidence of gonorrhea and genital herpes has risen sharply (Wallerstein, 1986). Neither can circumcision seriously be considered an effective prophylaxis against the transmission of HIV. American men who have been acutely vulnerable to the AIDS virus are amongst the most highly circumcised male populations in the world.

If the medical arguments for circumcision were sound, surely we would expect to see other medically advanced and technologically sophisticated societies in Europe and Japan implementing this practice, or, if not, suffering the dire consequences in statistically significant numbers which this highly flawed research would predict. Neither is true.

If a foreskin is well cared for and, therefore, does not present a medical liability, does it have any significant purpose? Our junior high classes in human sex and reproduction notwithstanding, there is epidemic ignorance about the structure and function of the normal penis. We are told, and I think most of us have believed, that the foreskin is simply an extra flap of skin of no vital significance. Yet, there are four very important functions which the foreskin serves. First, it stretches to cover the penis which increases by fifty percent in diameter and length upon erection. Without this extra skin, the skin of the circumcised penis is pulled taut when erect and sometimes is bowed, causing discomfort during erection or intercourse. Secondly, the foreskin protects the glans (the head of the penis). In infancy it shields the glans from contamination of urine and feces, and throughout life, it maintains the glans as the internal organ it was intended to be. Without the foreskin, the sensitive mucous membrane of the glans becomes dried up and is keratinized, a process of unnatural thickening that occurs and lessens sensitivity (Ritter, 1992). Thirdly, because the foreskin represents one third or more of the most erogenous tissue of the penis, having a greater concentration of fully developed, complex nerve endings than the glans, the pleasurable function of this delicate tissue is lost (Dr. John R. Taylor as cited by Bigelow, 1992). Finally, the presence of the foreskin facilitates pleasurable intercourse by increasing sensitivity and enhancing the pleasure dynamic of the couple (Ritter, 1992). Altering form inevitably alters function.

When form and function are altered, the mind and spirit are also affected. Consider, first, what happens before a circumcision can even be performed: the infant penis is usually rubbed with an antiseptic. Trustingly his little body responds to his first overtly sexual experience. Next, the most sensitive part of his fully receptive body is cut, crushed and ripped or scraped away from the head of his penis.

Mothers, pale with terror, hovering in the background, have repeatedly been told that they are "over-reacting" as they witness their newborn's piercing screams, gasps and flailing head. The instinctive terror of the mother is trivialized and the trauma to her baby is ignored. The few infants who hardly cry at all are usually those who have been sedated by the drugs administered to the mother during labor which may, according to T. Berry Brazelton, M.D. (1970), take "at least a week" for the newborn to excrete (p. 30).

Until recently, much of the medical profession denied that infants were capable of experiencing pain. Even heart and brain surgeries were performed on infants without benefit of anesthesia or sedatives within the last ten years (Lawson, 1990). According to Dr. Ronald L. Poland, chairman of the American Academy of Pediatrics' Committee on the Fetus and Newborn, unanesthetized surgery on young infants "is not a rare event" in the United States (Woods, 1987). However, science has finally confirmed what mothers have known for millennia: infants do indeed experience pain. Doctors Anand and Hickey of Harvard Medical School and Children's Hospital, Boston in an article entitled, *Pain and its effects in the human neonate and fetus*, have written the following after observing neonatal circumcisions:

> Physiologic responses to painful stimuli have been well documented in neonates of various gestational ages and are reflected in hormonal, metabolic, and cardio-respiratory changes similar to but greater than those observed in adult subjects. Other responses in newborn infants are suggestive of integrated emotional and behavioral responses to pain and are retained in memory long enough to modify subsequent behavior patterns (Anand & Hickey, 1987).

Because the centers for pain and pleasure reside in such close proximity to each other in the human brain, it has been found that flooding the neonatal brain with massive trauma creates physiological changes in brain structure (Prescott, 1989). How this may impact the maturing personality's confusion of pleasure and pain, or simply create an inexplicable anxiety relating to pleasure cannot be quantified, but remains a very serious question.

The psychological implications of circumcision may be profound. Erik Erikson has established that the first and most critical task of psychological development is trust (Erikson, 1950). He states that trust is the ground of all later development and it is focused entirely on the mother. Dr. Rima Laibow, a psychiatrist in New York, who has invented a mode of regressive therapy, points out that because the mother has been the entire universe to the infant since its life began in utero, it is imprinted to experience all pleasure and all pain as flowing from the mother. Mother controls all. Dr. Laibow states:

> Clinical work in Dyadic Repair and developmental psychology make it clear that information encoded in utero and later, is retained in somatic, cognitive and affective storage. An infant does retain significant memory traces of traumatic events. When a child is subjected to intolerable, overwhelming pain, it conceptualizes mother as both participatory and responsible regardless of mother's intent. When in fact, mother is truly complicit, as in giving permission for unanesthetized surgery, (i.e., circumcision) the perception of the infant of her culpability and willingness to have him harmed is indelibly emplaced. The consequences for impaired bonding are significant (Laibow, 1991).

Dr. Laibow states that such a trauma creates an "enormous obstacle to the development of basic trust between mother and child" which must be acknowledged to the maturing child if healing is to occur. She goes on to insist that if circumcisions are to be performed, they should be done only with the use of anesthesia (Laibow, 1991).

One of the most forceful statements opposing circumcision for its possible psychological repercussions was made by Dr. Benjamin Spock in 1976:

> I am in favor of leaving the penis alone. Pediatric opinion is swinging away from routine circumcision as unnecessary and at least mildly dangerous. I also believe that there is a po-

> tential danger of emotional harm resulting from the operation. Parents should insist on convincing reasons for circumcision—and there are no convincing reasons that I know of (as cited in Wallerstein, 1980).

The castration anxiety that is so often directed at Jewish women by Jewish men could be related to the trauma of circumcision and could be a root cause of the rampant ridicule of Jewish mothers. It may also be a contributing factor to the seemingly epidemic fears of intimacy and commitment which plague our male-female relationships. The implications are serious, serious enough to give us pause.

If circumcision cannot be justified on medical grounds, we need to probe further to understand its function in our tradition. It may be somewhat of a comfort for us to know that Jews didn't invent circumcision. It is a pre-Judaic rite originating in about the third millennia B.C.E., or perhaps even earlier, introduced into the Nile Valley by militant pastoral nomads, who were wandering cattle-raisers and aggressive warriors (De Meo, 1989).

Historically, this was a period of enormous disruption in which fundamental assumptions regarding gender and power were being challenged. The magnificent, highly developed and peaceful civilizations of the Neolithic agricultural era, which had flourished for three thousand years, were disintegrating under the impact of successive waves of Kurgan and nomadic invasions. This shift from the goddess worshipping, matrilineal, non-hierarchical cultures to the god worshipping, patriarchal, dominance and violence-based culture was actually the nexus of a cataclysmic paradigm shift whose ripples continue to resonate throughout the fabric of our contemporary secular and religious cultures. It is within this transitional historical context that circumcision emerged.

Circumcision is first mentioned in the Bible in Genesis 17:9-14. Here God gives to Abraham the injunction that circumcision shall be a sign of the covenant throughout all the generations of males, even the slaves of the household, for Abraham is about to father a new nation. Traditionally, circumcision is what connects the Jewish males to their contemporary community of Jewish men as well as to their ancient lineage of Jewish forefathers and to the Jewish God whose voice is represented in the masculine gender.

The underlying tensions of gender and power between Sarah and Abraham are expressed in the conflicts with Hagar and Ishmael and culminate in the *akedah*, the binding of Isaac. It is in the drama of the *akedah* that Abraham and Sarah's competing authority over Isaac is resolved. More than a competition between personalities, a closer examination of the text reveals a critical clash of traditions. The *akedah* is not only central as a religious text; it is, I believe, a window to an historical shift of profound proportions.

In the story contained in Genesis 22 and 23 many sacrifices take place. No one emerges whole. All are transformed but only one person is destroyed, body and soul. It is not Isaac. It is Sarah. Sarah, who is unseen and unheard during the entire episode of the binding and intended murder of her child, is casually reintroduced in the beginning of the next chapter so that the reader may learn of her death. Even though the *akedah* is central to Jewish theology and liturgy, Sarah's sacrifice is hardly noted. What happened?

Abraham is called by God to take Isaac to be a sacrifice to this new male God. Sarah is not consulted. In Hebrew Sarah's exclusion is even more clear: *Va-yomer kah-nah et bin-hah et yehid-hah asher—ahavtah et yitzhak* (Genesis 22:2). While the English pronoun "your" or "you" could refer to singular or plural, masculine or feminine subjects, in Hebrew the singular, masculine second person suffix denotes without possibility of ambiguity that God is addressing Abraham, and Abraham alone, as the sole parent of Isaac. "And he said, 'Take now your son, your only son, whom you love ... '" It is odd that Isaac is referred to as Abraham's "only son", when, in fact, Abraham also fathered Ishmael. It is Sarah for whom Isaac is truly her only son, and it is Sarah who is excluded. Her motherhood is denied by God and ignored by Abraham, as he prepares to take her only child to sacrifice for this higher cause.

Sarah's authority as a mother and her position as the grand matriarch of her people is completely undermined by this God's demand and Abraham's compliance. She is utterly disempowered by this cataclysmic event. In this context her death makes sense. It is the defeat of the matriarch, the subordination of the mother that had to precede the new covenant. Abraham passed the test. He not only was willing to obey his God's command to attempt to sacrifice his most beloved son, but he also succeeded in subverting the mother's authority over her child. He is now worthy to become the primary progenitor of a new nation. His manhood has been established in his faithfulness to his male God, his domination over his wife, his violence, albeit reluctant, towards his son and his seed will father the tribe.

Hundreds of years later, Christianity took this one step further: God loved His son so much that He not only demanded his sacrifice, He followed through with it. No sacrificial ram appeared for Jesus as had for Isaac. What does this tell us about what devoted parents, particularly fathers, are permitted, if not expected, to do to their children in the name of love? The precedent was set by the *akedah*.

I submit that this story, which lies at the nucleus of our religious and historical identity, is not only about faith. It is also, and most profoundly, about the shift of power and authority from women to men, about male domination which is always undergirded by the threat or implied threat of violence. The *akedah* is the definitive narrative of this paradigm shift.

Yet the matrilineal traditions of the biblical Jews were not so easily erased, even though patriarchy becomes established in Judaism through this story. Sarah's authority as mother of Isaac was ultimately defeated and her role as the primary progenitor of her tribe was undermined, and yet the *Torah* also reveals that those who were allowed to be buried in the cave of *Machpelah* were only Sarah's descent group. In her book *Sarah the Priestess: The First Matriarch of Genesis*, Savina Teubal (1984) explains, *"The ancestors of the Hebrews are only those whom the matriarchs accepted as members of their descent group.* As Bakan accurately points out, 'Not all the offspring of Abraham are Israelites: the Israelites stem only from Sarah. Sarah is more definitely the ancestor of the Israelites than Abraham'" (p. 95).

The survival of the matrilineal tradition and its ongoing power in the lives of our people is apparent when we look at *halachah*, Jewish law. According to Orthodox Jewish law the answer to the question of Jewish identity is quite basic: if one is born of a Jewish mother, one is a Jew.

Circumcision arose to compete with matrilineal culture. It permitted the transfer of inheritance through patrilineal descent (Teubal, 1984). Just as the *akedah* bound Isaac and Abraham to the male God, so circumcision bonds the male child to the men of his community throughout time and space and to the male God.

The circumcision we practice today is based on the passage in Genesis 17:9-14, but it is, in fact, quite different from the circumcision practiced by our biblical ancestors. Prior to the time of Hellenic and later Roman influence, Jewish circumcision consisted of cutting off that part of the foreskin which extended beyond the glans leaving much of the foreskin intact. When some Jewish men desired to compete Greek style, nude, in the athletic competitions, they were roundly ridiculed for their mutilated penises. To the Greeks, exposing the glans was a sign of vulgarity, and cutting the body in order to please God was unthinkable. Hadrian outlawed circumcision as well as castration. Circumcision became a signal for persecution. Many Jews tried to hide their circumcisions in order to assimilate into Greek culture or later, to elude persecution by the Romans.

In order to prevent Jews from hiding their circumcisions by various methods of stretching and tying their remaining foreskins, in about 140 C.E., the rabbis demanded that in order for a circumcision to meet the standard of Jewish law, radical circumcision, or *periah* must be performed. *Periah* consists of the complete stripping and shearing of the foreskin (Kohler, 1964).

It must have seemed more important to irreversibly mark and mutilate our Jewish sons, making them easy targets for oppressors, rather than to risk their survival, perhaps at the price of assimilation, with an intact body. How many thousands of Jewish boys and how many thousands of Jewish men have been lost throughout the ages because they were unable to "pass" when their lives depended on it? Was this the sacred intention of the covenant? Nevertheless, the more circumcision became associated with the terror of tribal survival, the more it became laminated to our Jewish identities. Now, to challenge circumcision is to imitate the oppressor; it is experienced as a direct assault on Jewish identity, assigning the critic instantaneous membership in the league of world class anti-Semites. And yet, challenging circumcision can be an attack on Jewish identity only if Jewish women don't count, for Jewish women have survived and kept their identities intact for millennia without any need of altering their bodies. Clearly, circumcision is serving functions far more subtle and more powerful than simply the survival and identity of the people of Israel.

The biblical injunction to circumcise speaks to a man about men. But circumcision is also a woman's issue, for on a subtle, but very potent level it is, like the *akedah*, about the primary disempowerment of the mother. At no other time is a woman so in touch with her most elemental and powerful mammalian instincts as after a birth. When her culture tells her that in order for this male baby to be a man, to be part of the masculine community and bond with the male God, the men must cut her male baby on his most sensitive male organ, this mother is inevitably in conflict with her entire life-giving feminine biology. And if a woman is made to distrust her most basic instinct to protect her newborn child, what feelings can she ever trust?

This violent disruption of the maternal-infant bond is not an accidental consequence of this ancient male bonding rite. It fits the pattern of a multitude of rituals that are prevalent cross-culturally which serve to disrupt the very delicate early hours and days of maternal-infant bonding: tight restrictive swaddling, foot binding, early baptism in cold water, smoking of the newborn and mother, ear piercing within the first hour of birth, etc. Circumcision is one of the most violent of these rituals (Odent, 1991).

When the mother is disempowered at the birth of her son, the relationship between husband and wife is artificially distorted, and that child's manhood is also transformed. Eighteen years later, the mother is often forced to relinquish him again. She has been signalled from birth by the circle of men with the knife: woman, you cannot protect this male child. This drama is repeated by military conscription, the combative and violent initiation into manhood. Once again, the mother must suppress her natural protest as her male child is ushered by the men into a larger circle of men, not with knives, but with weapons of immense destruction. In this sense circumcision foreshadows conscription.

Circumcision is also a female phenomenon, and even though it may seem unrelated, let's look for a moment at this practice. Over 84 million African and Arab girls and women in the world today have been circumcised (Hosken, 1989). Certainly, physically, psychologically and sexually, female circumcision is far more devastating than male circumcision, and yet the socially, culturally and religiously motivated forces which demand that a knife be ritually incised into a child's genitals are not so different from our own. At the Second International Symposium on Circumcision held in San Francisco in 1991, a video presentation of these procedures was shown with full close-up color views and complete audio reproduction. It was easily one of the most viscerally wrenching experiences I have ever had. The entire audience of conference attendees sobbed and shook as we witnessed the shrieking, terrorized young girls having their clitorises cut off and often their labia incised and removed... and always in the presence of their mothers. I wanted to scream, "Where is your love for your daughter? Where is your primal need to protect your beloved child?" And then, I understood: these mothers love their daughters just as we love our sons, and they, like we, are convinced that what is being done to their children is for their own good. The elemental instincts of protection of children pale before the greater forces of tribal belonging, connection to one's family, community and ancestors, their naming of holiness and the consensus of what makes one lovable.

So we use the word "circumcision," but this is a euphemism. What we are really talking about for females as well as males is culturally and religiously sanctioned sexual mutilation and child abuse. I do not believe any parent consciously inflicts this trauma on her or his child. However, our capacity to deny and rationalize is limitless and, perhaps, psychically necessary, lest we open ourselves to the immense grief that inevitably follows the awakening to the profound injury we have caused to our most beloved treasures: our beautiful, perfect babies.

This treatment of the newborn is not consistent with traditional Jewish values. Judaism places infinite value on life, particularly human life. The principal of *pikuah nefesh* is fundamental to Judaism; that is, for the sake of saving a life, even the Sabbath may be desecrated. *Sh'mirat haguf*, the protection of one's body, is a high biblical priority. Tattooing, cutting the flesh and amputation are all forbidden. Consciousness of animal suffering permeates both biblical and Talmudic thought as expressed by the concept of *tsa-ar ba-alei hayim*, or compassion for living things. In the fourth commandment, animals as well as humans are commanded to rest on the Sabbath and, according to the *Talmud*, Sabbath observance may be broken to ease the suffering of an animal. The laws of *kashrut* are specific and elaborate pertaining to permissible animal slaughter with the intention of reducing and regulating animal pain if we are to be a meat-eating people. The precept of *ba-al tashhit* also informs biblical and Rabbinic thought. We are not to destroy the fruit trees, even during a war. The notions of *sh'mitah* and *yovel*, the Sabbatical and Jubilee years, require that every seventh year, and again in the fiftieth year, the earth be allowed to rest from deliberate economic use. The message seems to be clear: we are stewards of this earth and it is our task to protect it and, more than that, *l'havdeel bain kodesh v'chol*, to make distinctions between the holy and the profane, so that we may consciously and continuously sanctify life.

Circumcision is antithetical to this very powerful life-affirming tradition. Its true intention was not unknown to the rabbis and is best revealed in the words of Rambam, the acronym for Rabbi Moses Ben Maimonides, the great twelfth century Jewish philosopher, physician and Judaic scholar, so revered in Jewish tradition that it is said, "From Moses to Moses there was no one like Moses." Here is what Rambam wrote in his well known and widely influential work, *The Guide of the Perplexed* (1190):

> Similarly with regard to *circumcision*, one of the reasons for it is, in my opinion, the wish to bring about a decrease in sexual intercourse and a weakening of the organ in question, so that this activity be diminished and the organ be in as quiet a state as possible. It has been thought that circumcision perfects what is defective congenitally. This gave the possibility to everyone to raise an objection and to say: How can natural things be defective so that they need to be perfected from outside, all the more because we know how useful the foreskin is for that member? In fact this *commandment* has not been prescribed with a view to perfecting what is defective congenitally, but to perfecting morally. The bodily pain caused to that member is the real purpose of circumcision. None of the activities necessary for the preservation of the individual is harmed thereby, nor is procreation rendered impossible, but violent concupiscence and lust that goes beyond what is needed are diminished. The fact that circumcision weakens the faculty of sexual excitement and sometimes perhaps diminishes the pleasure is indubitable. For if at birth this member has been made to bleed and has had its covering taken away from it, it must indubitably be weakened. The *Sages, may their memory be blessed*, have explicitly stated: *It is hard for a woman with whom an uncircumcised man has had sexual intercourse to separate from him* (Genesis Rabbah LXXX). In my opinion this is the strongest of reasons for circumcision (p. 609).

There they are, the twin fears: the fear of woman and the fear of pleasure. Circumcision is the antidote which both assuages and perpetuates these ancient terrors. This is the achievement and true purpose of circumcision. It achieves this by violently breaching the maternal-infant bond shortly after birth, by mutilating and marking the baby's sexual organ, by disempowering the mother at the height of her instinctual need to protect her infant, by bonding the baby to the men and the male God and by psychosexually wounding the manhood still asleep in the unsuspecting baby boy. Circumcision is fundamental to patriarchy, but it is not holy.

Recently a well-known rabbi spoke about his need to remind converts that they are entering into a religion that is not perfect, but is perfectible. Even though this comment was not made in the context of circumcision, I feel it is eminently applicable to Jewish women in the process of reweaving the fabric of Jewish tradition. Specifically, we need ceremonies to harken to the voice of Sarah so that we may honor and celebrate the traditional moments of children's separation from mothers, such as weaning and *bar mitzvah*. We also need ceremonies which will support and celebrate a woman's transformation into motherhood: ceremonies that will validate and affirm her natural and elemental life-giving and life-protecting instincts as the essence of holiness, deserving of community support and blessing. We must envision a Judaism that can welcome all of our children, nonviolently, into the *brit b'lee milah*, a covenant without circumcision. We need to support and affirm men's struggle to revise the old notion of masculinity which is rooted in fear of women. We invite men to explore ways to ritualize and celebrate masculinity and the critical passages of male bonding in ways that are life-affirming, nonviolent and protective of the sacred wholeness of men. Only in these ways will we begin the restoration of the holy and establish *tikkun*, healing, between the sexes.

Ultimately, we all must know that it is not possible to violate or suppress the sexuality of one gender without doing harm to the other. Opposing circumcision is men's work; but it is also most profoundly, women's work. Our babies know and we know: it begins with us.

REFERENCES

American academy of pediatrics committee on the fetus and newborn: Standards and recommendations for hospital care of newborn infants, Ed. 5. (1971). Evanston, IL: American Academy of Pediatrics.

American College of Obstetricians and Gynecologists. (1983). *Guidelines for Perinatal Care,* (p. 87). Chicago, IL: American Academy of Pediatrics.

Anand, K. J. S. & Hickey, P. R. (1987). Pain and its effects in the human neonate and fetus. *The New England Journal of Medicine, 317*(21), p. 1326.

Bigelow, J. (1992). *The joy of uncircumcising.* Aptos, CA: Hourglass.

Brazelton, T. B. (1970). *Doctor and child,* New York: Delacourte Press/Seymour Lawrence.

Cole, L. (1983, August 11). Sex matters: Is circumcision correct for newborn boys? *The San Francisco Examiner*, p. B-7.

De Meo, J. (1989, July/August). The geography of genital mutilations. *The Truth Seeker*, 9-13.

Denniston, G. C. (1989, July/August). First, do no harm! *The Truth Seeker*, 35-38.

Gimbutas, M. (1991). *The civilization of the goddess*. San Francisco: Harper.

Grossman, E. & Posner, N. A. (1981). Surgical circumcision of neonates: A history of its development. *Obstetrics and Gynecology, 58*, 241-246.

The Holy Scriptures. (1955). Philadelphia: Jewish Publication Society.

Hosken, F. P. (1989, July/August). Female genital mutilation — strategies for eradication. *The Truth Seeker*, 22-30.

Kohler, K. (1964). Circumcision. *The Jewish encyclopedia*. (p. 93). New York: KTAV.

Laibow, R. (1991, May). *Circumcision and it's relationship to attachment impairment.* Paper presented at the Second International Symposium on Circumcision, San Francisco, CA.

Lawson, J. R. (1990, Oct/Nov/Dec). The politics of newborn pain. *Mothering Magazine, 57*, 41-47.

Maimonides, M. (1190/1963). *The guide of the perplexed* (S. Pines, Trans.). (Vol. 2, Part 3, Chapter 49). Chicago & London: University of Chicago Press.

Odent, M. (1991, April). *Colostrum, prepuce & civilization.* Paper presented at the Second International Symposium on Circumcision, San Francisco, CA.

Prescott, J. W. (1989, July and August). Genital pain vs. genital pleasure: Why the one and not the other? *The Truth Seeker*, 14-21.

Preuss, J. (1911/1978). *Biblical-Talmudic medicine.* (F. Rosner, Trans.). Berlin: Sanhedrin Press. 544.

Remondino, P. C. (1892/1900). *History of circumcision from the earliest times to the present: Moral and physical reasons for its performance.* (pp. 254-255). New York: F.A. Davis.

Ritter, T. (1992). *Say no to circumcision!* Aptos, CA: Hourglass.

Teubal, S. (1984). *Sarah, the priestess: The first matriarch of Genesis*. Athens, OH: Swallow Press.

Valentine, R. J. (Pseudonym) (1974). Adult circumcision: A personal report. *Medical Aspects Human Sexuality, 8*, 42.

Wallerstein, E. (1980). *Circumcision: An American health fallacy.* New York: Springer.

Wallerstein, E. (1985, February). Circumcision: The uniquely American enigma. Reprint from paper presented at the Symposium conducted at the meeting of *Advances in Pediatric Urology, Urologic Clinics of North America. 12* (1).

Wallerstein, E. (1986). *Circumcision: Information, misinformation, disinformation.* San Anselmo, CA: NOCIRC.

Wiswell, T. E. & Roscelli, J. D. (1986). Corroborative evidence for the decreased incidence of urinary tract infections in circumcised male infants. *Pediatrics, 78* (1).

Woods, M. (1987, September 6). Infants undergo surgery without anesthetic aid. *Sunday Herald*, Monterey, CA. Section B, pp. 1, 4.

SPEAK OF IT: JEWISH ACTIVISM AND JEWISH IDENTITY

MICHELE CLARK

My parents weren't politically active or sophisticated; they weren't Socialists or Zionists or Bundists. They both grew up to inherit small family businesses. They voted, and still vote, Democratic; they are grateful to their country. If they have a politic it consists of asking: "Is it good for the Jews or bad for the Jews?" Despite this, as children, my brother, my sister and I developed a series of ideas which, in retrospect, came right out of the non-Zionist, Socialist position of the late 19th century. Our assumptions were: 1) All Jews know what it's like to be persecuted; 2) Jews support all other persecuted people (which meant, in our country, when I was a child, "Negroes"); 3) Jews know that if one person is persecuted it can easily be our turn next, so Jews fight for the rights of others.

We also assumed that the Conservative synagogue we attended held these beliefs. However, I can't remember ever hearing the solidarity analysis articulated by anyone in the Conservative congregation in which we grew up. In retrospect, I think some people held this view, others did not. Once, in 1959, when I was fourteen, at a United Synagogue Youth Encampment, a busload of African-American teenagers from Georgia came to stay with us overnight. Politely, warmly, we got to know each other a little. This was the only specific program in which I participated that turned into action the assumption that Jews had a primary identification with other oppressed groups.

I now see that, for me, a fourth premise of my childhood was that Jews expect that by working for social justice for all, we will be included even if we don't say a word about ourselves, don't make a peep about self-interest. So, in the early 1960's when I joined the civil rights picket lines at the local Woolworth's I did so as a Jew. I worked on campaigns for Reformed Democrats, as a Jew. When I went to folk sings in Greenwich Village or talks given by African-American leaders like Bayard Rustin and Conrad Linn, I went as a Jew. I never said that I did these things because my Jewish heritage had taught me the importance of fighting for justice. I assumed it, and I assumed others assumed it of me. In fact, I would have been ashamed to say it explicitly.

I tell this personal story because for me, as for many people, I believe it is not easy to speak publicly about Jewishness. Like all Americans, I am a product of what the psychologist Gershen Kaufman (1980/1992) calls our "shame-based culture". I fear dependence and need, I want to appear strong and in control at every moment. Kaufman describes shame as a feeling of being "...*seen* in a painfully diminished sense. The self feels exposed to itself and to anyone else present" (p. 9). For me, to say that in part, I supported civil rights because I needed protection myself, would have made me feel seen in Kaufman's sense as vulnerable and needy, instead of strong enough to extend my protection to others. In addition, there was a belief or a hope that Jews are safe in the United States; Jews have nothing to worry about here. Asking for something for myself would be to admit I was not safe. In short, I was ashamed of being afraid.

* * *

My struggles were a personalized version of the many ideological questions which have surrounded the Jewish people since the eighteenth century when the Enlightenment began to promise more tolerance and wider opportunities for all minorities. The price of Jewish entry into this wider world has always been controversial. Steven Cohen (1983), a sociologist of American Jewry writes, "...in Europe, the Jewish question divided liberals who favored Emancipation from conservatives who demanded prior Jewish acculturation, if not religious conversion, as the price of admission to the larger society" (p. 34). Historically, the number of activists in progressive causes has been disproportionately Jewish, I believe, because many Jews took the strong ethical tradition in Judaism and created a bridge between this tradition and the Enlightenment ethics of tolerance and pluralism.

There are several themes in traditional Jewish teaching which point toward an ethic of identification and solidarity with the oppressed. One is the imperative to charity and empathy as exemplified in Rabbi Akiba's injunction to love your neighbor as yourself; this is the statement which opens each morning's prayers.

Another traditional theme, honored at Passover, is the directive to be hospitable to the stranger because we are reminded "you were a stranger in a strange land." Third, there is the vision of Zion as a "light unto the nations," which implies chosen-ness as an imperative to reach out to others. Even Jews who are minimally observant will identify the meaning of being Jewish as carrying an ethical imperative to be a good, moral person (Sklare & Greenblum 1979).

In my extended family this theme is articulated in the memories and stories about my two grandfathers. My maternal grandfather, a prosperous businessman, went out searching for people in need and brought the hungry in for the Sabbath meal; he is remembered by his children primarily for this goodness rather than for his material successes. Stories of my paternal grandfather also emphasize charity. He was a garment worker who opened his small synagogue for the early prayers, every morning before work. One day he found a twenty dollar bill there; when no one claimed it, he contributed it to charity. Righteous living was the life goal of both of these men.

At the turn of the century, various Socialist movements were in ongoing disagreement over whether Jewish particularity was desirable and whether anti-Semitism would disappear with the coming of worker equality. Jewish difference was seen as, in part, a form of nationalism, and all nationalism, theoretically, was the enemy of the class struggle. Some Socialist groups felt upholding Jewish identity and particular Jewish needs was important, others dismissed these particularities or defined them as dangerous to working class identification.

Without discussion or dialogue, the New Left took the latter position. This meant that in the 1960's and 70's, it was only mainstream liberal organizations like the Anti-Defamation League which were concerned with protecting Jewish rights along with the rights of other minorities. However, over the past fifteen years, groups like Jews for Urban Justice, New Jewish Agenda, the loosely defined readership of *Tikkun* and Jews for Racial and Economic Justice (JFREJ), among others, have stressed the importance of asserting Jewish needs as well as taking progressive stands in other causes. Included in the progressive agenda is the fight against anti-Semitism as a distinct form of the larger struggle against racism. During this same fifteen years, because of the advent of an articulated and vocal multiculturalism, another need has arisen. That need is to articulate, in public, the progressive aspects of the Jewish tradition.

To understand why this articulation is important, it is necessary to understand that other oppressed groups no longer assume that Jews, because they are Jews, will be part of their coalition. Activists in their forties or older seem to have a hard time accepting this, because they feel that it is self-evident that Jews are disproportionately involved in progressive causes. Younger activists no longer make this assumption for the following reasons: 1) because of the well-publicized polarization between portions of the African-American community and portions of the Jewish community; 2) due to the Israeli-Palestinian conflict in which Jews have superior economic, political and military strength; 3) because one form of anti-Semitism is to see Jews as part of a secret, wealthy, ruling elite; 4) because of recent, vocal involvement by Jews in more conservative causes; 5) due to silence among Progressive Jews about their own tradition.

Progressive activists who have not thought and felt their way through their ideas and feelings about being Jewish seem to find it impossible to think of anything good and compassionate about the Jewish tradition, although they are, usually, ardent multiculturalists, open to and interested in, every other cultural group on earth. In *From Beirut to Jerusalem* (1989), Thomas Friedman says that, in general, both Jews and gentiles hold Jews to a higher ethical standard. Consequently, Jewish transgressions, when they occur, are viewed by both Jews and gentiles as more morally shocking and shameful. At the same time, it's sometimes difficult for Jews to take credit for good things that they do, as Jews, because the assumption of a higher ethical standard means that these good things are assumed.

Jewish progressive activists sometimes speak and act as if they are stuck between the Scylla and Charybdis of this dilemma. If one mentions something positive in the Jewish tradition, an activist who has not thought through their Jewish identity issues, may remark, "It's not just Jews who have that positive tradition," as if to praise is to boast. Or, the activist may counter by describing something negative in the Jewish tradition, or something they dislike about their mother, or they will make a derogatory remark about some policy of the Israeli government. This, I believe, comes from: 1) a deep and unexamined disappointment in the Jews and Jewishness for being imperfect; 2) an unwillingness to face one's own possible vulnerability as a Jew; 3) the fear that if Jews offer an interpersonal bridge and expect what Gershen Kaufman (1980/1992) calls mutuality of response, no one will be waiting on the other side.

* * *

In my work as a psychotherapist I use a competency-based model. I work with my client's strengths, and I believe that change is not possible from a position of feeling inadequate or hopeless. So, I have no list of pathologies which occur if Jewish identity issues go unexplored. Nor do I think such a list exists.

It's been my observation that many American Jews are mildly depressed much of the time. I believe minimizing the importance of one's Jewishness contributes to the chronically self-critical thoughts which constitute this very low level depression in Jewish adults who, if tested, might register between 7-9 on the Beck Depression Inventory.

Whether or not one is mildly depressed, however, it is my experience that, like all identity struggles, exploring unexamined feelings about Judaism and Jewishness leads to a more authentic and positive encounter with Judaism and, therefore, with the self. It is, invariably, an expansive and enhancing activity.

Damage occurs to the way we perceive ourselves, to the way others perceive us, and to the Jewish community when activists hide or don't mention their Jewish tradition. If progressive people don't allude to their Judaism, and conservative and reactionary Jews always allude to their Judaism, the public conclusion is obvious: Jewish equals conservative. This conclusion then makes progressive activists who have not thought through their Jewish identity issues more anxious and more ashamed of being Jewish, and the silence about progressive Jews deepens. The general public and the Jewish community all continue, then, to perceive the Jewish community as a conservative or reactionary one, rather than the diverse one that it is.

This perception is unfortunate for several reasons. First, because it is not accurate. Second, because silence about vibrant progressive traditions in the United States is the norm in the schools and in the media, and the silence of Jewish progressives adds to this tendency. Third, this perception contributes to insuring that each young generation of progressive Americans will have to re-invent the wheel of theory and action. Fourth, it limits the growth of creative, progressive Jewish activities. Fifth, it leaves young Jewish activists ignorant of their antecedents which weakens them and makes them more vulnerable to attacks of guilt and shame. This gap was evident at a 1992 JFREJ conference in New York City in which many "twenty-something" Jewish activists learned, for seemingly the first time, the depth of the Jewish progressive tradition. Last, someday Jews may need a mutuality of response in the face of a new persecution, and we will have no acknowledged friends among the oppressed peoples. I know that anti-Semitism has a life of its own, and all the coalition building in the world may not save us in a dire political or economic crisis. However, it can't hurt us, either.

* * *

When I say that I think activists who are Jews should act as Jews I mean something both very simple and very difficult. I mean, "Say it." Not constantly (unless you're in the mood), but occasionally. Discuss your Jewishness when anyone is interested in talking about it. If you're a public figure in your organization, find a way to put something about your Jewish tradition into your public pronouncements.

A close friend of mine works with Central American refugees and when I was helping her with a family, the issue of Jewishness arose. The adults in this family were surprised that such a thing as a Jew still existed. They had been taught Jews lived in the old days, only in the days of the Bible. An interesting discussion followed. This was an easy moment for me to talk about Judaism because the adults, who had endured many horrors, were uninformed rather than anti-Semitic. And I was the person bountiful; I was offering my hospitality to them, I was not in need and not a threat.

It can be more difficult to say something about Jewishness in a speech or at a meeting about, say, animal rights, or the protection of the rainforest, or in agitation for equality of health resources. Here you might anger other members of your organization who may see mentioning the Jewish tradition as the beginning of fragmentation in the organization. They might not understand why this seemingly extra piece of information is important. Speaking out can be used as an opening to dialogue about why this issue is important. Even if you and your group decide against a public pronouncement, you have begun an important discussion within your organization.

I know this isn't always easy to do. In another place (Clark, 1990) I have written about my own movement, as an adult, toward an active Jewish identification. For someone who has not done this for a long time, or ever, it requires a commitment of time and energy for feeling, thinking, talking and reading. It requires finding a way to engage actively with Jewishness, whatever this means to you.

For myself, after reading and talking, I joined and became active in a synagogue and participated in the organization "Women in Black." A friend of mine, after reading and talking, did a series of paintings, first, about the Holocaust, then about other, joyous aspects of Judaism, and then, although she "can't relate to religion," she enrolled her daughter in the local Hebrew School. She would rather, she says, enroll her daughter in a secular institution which stresses Jewish culture, without the religion, but there are none in central Vermont. Her daughter, by the way, is happy to attend. Recently, I've known several progressives who would identify as secular humanists and atheists, whose pre-teen children insisted on studying for *bar* or *bat mitzvah* (coming of age ritual). The children are interested in the link between Judaism and their family's values, even if their parents aren't.

* * *

In the daily prayer, *V'ahavta*, we are commanded to speak of the love of God when we walk on the road and when we return home. Similarly, I have been trying, in my daily life, to mention my Jewishness, to share something from it, when the subject comes up. I am not currently active in any political action organization. When I am teaching (I work with adults returning to college) and the subject is my students' multicultural heritage, I make sure to talk about my own. If I can find a natural way into the subject, I say something about the progressive activism of my tradition.

I believe that others, everywhere in the United States, are thinking about the importance of making this link. Recently, I received a mailing from an organization in Seattle, "The Witness Campaign," which was formed to aid Moslem women in the former Yugoslavia who have been raped as a matter of policy by the military forces of opposing armies. The letter containing the fund-raising appeal was written by a woman whose parents had been in Hitler's camps and who felt that it was this experience which, specifically, moved her to work to aid the victims of systematic violence and humiliation. I don't think such a letter would have been written ten, or even five, years ago. I think the action would have been exactly the same, but the link to Jewishness would not have been articulated. Similarly, this spring (1994) there has been a spate of letters to the editor in the *Boston Globe* in which the individual writers protest, as Jews, the treatment of Haitian refugees.

The ideal of universal understanding and tolerance is not harmed by Jews identifying as Jews in causes which fight for freedom from oppression. Rather, progressive activists who have so diligently obeyed Hillel's maxim "If I am only for myself, what am I?" must now also explore, perhaps for the first time, the beginning of Hillel's directive, "If I am not for myself, who will be for me?"

REFERENCES

Cohen, S. (1983). *American modernity & Jewish identity.* New York: Tavistock.

Clark, M. (1990). *No shuttle to central Vermont. Bridges, 1*(2), 15-21.

Friedman, T. (1989). *From Beirut to Jerusalem.* New York: Doubleday.

Kaufman, G. (1980/1992). *Shame: The power of caring.* Rochester, VT: Schenkman.

Pirke Avot, Talmud.

Sklare, M. & Greenblum, J. (1979). *Jewish identity on the suburban frontier.* (2nd ed.). Chicago: University of Chicago Press.

ANTI-SEMITISM AS TRAUMA: A THEORY OF JEWISH COMMUNAL TRAUMA RESPONSE

BARBARA U. HAMMER

INTRODUCTION

The present work has emerged from experiences in both personal and professional settings during the past five years (1989-1994). Beginning in November 1989, when the Berlin Wall was torn down and the Iron Curtain had begun to crumble in Eastern Europe and the Soviet Union, discussions of these "velvet revolutions" with friends and psychotherapist colleagues revealed important differences between the responses of Jews and non-Jews.

Everyone seemed to share the excitement of the liberation and freedom symbolically promised by these revolutions. Jews, however, both professional colleagues and those in the larger Jewish community, talked also about their fears of a rise in anti-Semitism that might follow in the wake of liberation, in the historically anti-Semitic countries that were being newly liberated.

Exploration of the psychological impact of anti-Semitism on Jews has received little attention from the psychological community, both Jewish and non-Jewish, with the exception of the study and treatment of Holocaust survivors (HS) and their children (COHS). Beyond the studies of HS and COHS, only a few published works appear in the psychological literature on the Jewish population. Moses (1993) presents papers from a conference held in 1988 that addressed the meaning of the Holocaust to those not directly affected, primarily from a psychoanalytic perspective. Rosenman & Handelsman (1990a, 1990b) discussed the impact on non-HS and non-COHS Jews of reading Holocaust memoirs and suggested that it should parallel the exchanges among HS and COHS's. The only other work to date (March 1994) which addresses the psychological sequelae of anti-Semitism within the general Jewish population comes from the Jewish feminist community. The works of Beck (1989), Burstow (1992) and Siegel and Cole (1991) discuss some of the negative experiences of Jewish women, how these might be expressed in ways that could be misunderstood by the non-Jewish observer, and the need for therapists to be sensitive to these cultural and feminist issues.

THEORY AND HYPOTHESES

Absent from these few discussions in the literature of the impact of Holocaust memoirs on readers and the Jewish experience for women in particular, is a psychological perspective of the Jewish people as a group that has suffered the impact of anti-Semitism. It appears to me that there exists within the Jewish culture the transmission of a Jewish communal trauma response. The history of traumatic persecution has left unresolved psychological sequelae within the Jewish population. This hypothesized Jewish communal trauma response needs to be addressed not only with patients in the therapy room, but culturally as well.

There are a number of examples of this communal trauma response easily discernable within the Jewish community. First and foremost is the attrition in the Jewish population that is a threat to the very existence of the community itself. A second includes the ubiquitous debate between those who are certain of the repetition of the Holocaust and those who deny that possibility, a debate that highlights the continual focus on the trauma. Third, the concomitant focus on community protection, as seen in the Jewish community's support for Israel as the "safe haven" where all Jews will always be welcomed, is typical of the trauma response. Finally, the paradoxical avoidance of Jewish religious affiliation and return to Judaism during times of increased anti-Semitic threat is an example of the dialectic of the trauma response.

The theory offered here of the impact of anti-Semitism in the Jewish cultural experience explains some of the reasons for the abandonment of Judaism and/or Jewish identity by so many Jews. In addition, it explains the underlying psychodynamics that may have produced the reactions noted in some of the papers mentioned above. It synthesizes information derived from the history of anti-Semitism, social-psychological analysis of the impact of that history on cultural identification and introjection, and the study of psychological trauma and its treatment methodology. This theory extends the work on victims of trauma, witnesses to victims of trauma, traumatic identification, and vicarious traumatization to the Jewish people as a whole.

I am hypothesizing that the loss of so many Jews through choice arises, in part, from the fact that Jews have not fully recovered from the psychological trauma of anti-Semitism. The resulting hidden, unresolved traumatic reactions have caused many Jews to go to great lengths to avoid the traumatic stimulus: Judaism and/or Jewish identity. Various other problematic response patterns have developed which need to be addressed from the cultural, social-psychological, and individual/self psychological perspectives. In addition, I am also hypothesizing that the increase in anti-Semitism in recent years is re-activating the communal trauma response.

The American Jewish population has been dwindling in numbers over the past thirty years. In the early sixties, it stood at approximately six million (Cohen, 1993). It was estimated to be five-and-a-half million in 1990 (Council of Jewish Federations, 1991). This number includes those who were born Jewish and chose Judaism as a religion, those who converted to Judaism, and those who were born Jewish but said they had no religion (Jews who call themselves secular Jews). This core Jewish population contains almost one-third more elderly persons than does the total U.S. population, thus implying that the trend is toward even greater diminution. Further, this represents a decline from three percent to two percent of the total American population.

It is often suggested that the cause of the Jewish population reduction is mainly the low birth rate within the highly educated Jewish childbearing population. This does not, however, account for the documented exodus of Jews, resulting from rejection of Judaism and/or Jewish identity.

There is a higher rate of conversion out of, as opposed to into, Judaism according to the 1990 National Jewish Population Survey (NJPS). One-fifth (1.2 million) of American born Jews celebrate Christmas (Cohen, 1993). Furthermore, Jews are highly over-represented in cults; there are estimates (some think exaggerated) that 10 to 20 percent of cult members are American-born Jews (Pressman, 1993). These Jews are desperately searching for some psycho-spiritual connection while rejecting that which could be found within their own heritage. They are doing so at a rate that is five to ten times greater than the general population.

Numerous possible explanations exist for such a large number of Jews rejecting their Judaism and/or Jewish identity. For example, many Jews who have become Buddhists report that they have left Judaism primarily because they perceived it as lacking in spirituality (Kamenetz, 1994). Another explanation for the rejection is found in the feminist community. Although in recent years women have entered the rabbinate and they, as well as lay feminist writers, have sought to transform the patriarchal liturgy of Judaism, many other women have left Judaism in response to the patriarchal sexism embodied in traditional Judaism. In fact, the 1990 NJPS reports that women are doing the most moving in and out of Judaism: two thirds of Jews by choice are women and most of those converting out of Judaism are women.

Nonetheless, according to Jewish law and *midrash* (tales), one cannot simply stop being Jewish. Less than five percent of all respondents in the 1990 NJPS "considered being Jewish solely in terms of being a member of a religious group," but 90 percent defined being Jewish as being a member of a cultural or ethnic group. Even amongst those Jews in the 1990 NJPS who converted out of Judaism, almost half (46%) said that being Jewish was important, and 40% of those born Jewish who practiced other religions also said that being Jewish was important. Thirty-nine percent of those who identified themselves as secular Jews also said that being Jewish was important to them. It appears to be extremely difficult psychologically to stop identifying oneself as a Jew even when one chooses another religion or has no religion.

There is a need to explore the motivation for such rejection of the religious part of the self while maintaining the culture to which that religion is attached, as well as the psychological functions by which this could be accomplished. This is in contrast to Christians who no longer believe in Christianity. Unlike the Jews who reject Judaism, Christians who reject Christianity do not seem to consider themselves thereafter to be Christian. Over 90 percent of respondents in the 1990 NJPS considered being Jewish to mean belonging to the Jewish community, which generally occurs by being born to a Jewish mother. Jewish beliefs and rituals are secondary and "can tolerate great diversity of theological opinion" (Kushner, 1993, p. 10).

A common observation in the Jewish community is that Jews tend to return to Judaism and/or their Jewish identities in response to anti-Semitic threats. This is viewed as another example of the way in which Jews exhibit the trauma response. Kardiner and Spiegel (1947) observed the dependency and need for group contact amongst men fighting in World War II. In fact, treatment usually focused on ways to return the traumatized soldiers quickly to their fighting units because it was believed that healing would occur most rapidly within the group setting, even if it were on the battlefield. Perhaps the Jews who return to their roots in response to anti-Semitic threats, like these traumatized soldiers, are seeking to heal the wounds of anti-Semitism when they return naturally to the "battlefield" of their religious or cultural Jewish identities.

This response to return coupled with the above mentioned avoidance of Judaism and/or Jewish identity response, seem to parallel the "dialectic of trauma" referred to by Herman (1992). This can be seen in the trauma victim's oscillation between the extremes of amnesia/avoidance and intrusive/reliving of the trauma. Pilot studies designed to test these hypotheses have been conducted and the preliminary data are supportive.

ANTI-SEMITISM

There is a marked contrast between the degree of interest in the psychological study of anti-Semitism and that in the study of the impact of anti-Semitism on its victims. A survey of the psychological literature on anti-Semitism yields hundreds of articles, books and chapters in books. Volume II in the five volume series by Bergmann entitled *Current research on anti-Semitism* (1987) contains 546 pages and is devoted entirely to psychological research on anti-Semitism. None of these articles relate to the impact of anti-Semitism on the Jewish population other than HS and COHS.

To paraphrase the poignant words on the wall of the Diaspora Museum in Tel Aviv, the history of the Jewish people is one continuous drama of destruction and rebirth. There are excellent written summaries of this history such as those by Dinnerstein (1994) and Wistrich (1991). Both of these are well documented and well written. They are especially useful records of the anti-Semitism that has most directly affected the current Jewish population: from the pogroms in Eastern Europe and Russia in the 19th century and early 20th century, through the Holocaust, as well as the less virulent versions in American society up to 1992. I will address in more detail the recent upsurge in anti-Semitism since 1989 and its psychological relevance for the Jewish community.

Since the beginning of the collapse of the Iron Curtain in late 1989, the seeds of anti-Semitism have indeed begun to sprout anew in increasingly threatening forms. Seen not just in acts of vandalism by scattered but relatively powerless groups of neo-Nazi youths, virulent anti-Semitism is today becoming a political force in all parts of the world. In Poland, where so few Jews remain, anti-Semitism has publicly surfaced anew and even the most liberal of the newly elected leaders, Lech Walesa, has not completely dissociated himself from the pervasive hatred and blaming of Jews for the ills of that society (Harden, 1990).

In 1994 alone: Fascists have again come to power in Italy and suggest that "'the New York Jewish lobby' was responsible for the country's plunging currency" (Jews Protest, 1994); anti-Semitic violence is increasing in Germany, even though attacks against non-Jewish foreigners have begun to decline; leaflets calling for the execution of "all Jews who have actively helped to damage the white race" are distributed in Britain (Bronfman, 1994).

There appeared to be a well-organized terrorist effort behind the violence in Argentina, Panama and London in July 1994. Terrorists bombed the Israeli Embassy in London and killed more than 100 Jews in Buenos Aires and Panama in separate bombings. More than 200 people were injured and the entire building that was the center of Jewish life and social services in Buenos Aires was destroyed (Benjamin, 1994). In the same month, Kurt Waldheim (the well-documented Nazi who formerly headed the U.N.) was honored by the Vatican with a papal knighthood for his "efforts for peace" as U.N. Secretary-General. During the time for which he was being honored, Waldheim oversaw the widespread anti-Israel activity of the U.N. which included the adoption of the 1975 "Zionism is racism" resolution (Cymrot, 1994). When a new statue to honor a Nazi-collaborator was erected in Romania in July 1994, Edgar Bronfman (1994) of the World Jewish Congress said: "... I shudder to think how that statue makes the Jews in that town feel..."

The upsurge in anti-Semitism has begun in the U.S. as well. In the year following the collapse of the Berlin Wall, there was a dramatic increase of 140 percent in the number of anti-Semitic incidents in the large metropolitan area centered in Washington, D.C. (Washington Jewish Week, February, 1991). Nationwide, the number of anti-Semitic incidents also reached record levels in 1990, including a steep rise in campus bigotry. By the summer of 1994 there were many more instances of hate crimes in the suburbs of our nation's capital including the discovery on August 6, 1994, of the "two-foot-high letters JEW" burned into the front lawn of a Jewish home (Aguilar, 1994).

In addition, the anti-Semitic activities of the Nation of Islam are highly stressful to Jews. The most recent expressions of hate came from that organization's spokesman, Khalid Abdul Muhammad, in his speech at Kean College, N.J. on November 29, 1993. "Muhammad's presence further angered some Jews who have been outraged since Muhammad made a widely criticized speech... in which he accused Jews of 'sucking [blacks'] blood' and suggested that the Holocaust may have been justified" (Melillo & Harris, 1994, p. B1). He also accused Jews of owning the U.S. Federal Reserve system and controlling the White House. Khalid was later removed from his position as spokesman for the Nation of Islam by its leader, Louis Farrakhan, not for making false and bigoted statements, but rather for poorly presenting his message.

ANTI-SEMITISM AS TRAUMA

The assessment and treatment of psychological trauma has been studied extensively over the past two decades. Excellent treatments of this work appear in Everstine & Everstine (1993), Figley (1985), Herman (1992) and Williams & Sommer (1994).

The construct of psychological trauma was not fully addressed until the aftermath of the Vietnam War. As a result of this expanded interest in the treatment of trauma, Holocaust victims began to be viewed from a similar perspective. Prior to that, survivors of the Holocaust had been seen as suffering "survivors' syndrome," extreme "adjustment reactions," pathological "grief responses" or extreme stress reactions. It was not until the 1960's that the mental health professions even "became involved in dealing systematically with the aftereffects of Holocaust traumatization" (Last, 1988, p. 73). The term Concentration Camp Syndrome (Chodoff, 1963) was used in the early 1960's to describe the constellation of symptoms presumed to be a reaction to the trauma of the camp experience: death anxiety, survival guilt, psychic numbing, resentment, and "a struggle for meaning, which is expressed in a continuous effort to derive significance from harmful chaotic experiences" (Last, 1988, p. 73).

Not until 1980, did the psychiatric and psychological communities give recognition to the psychological sequelae of trauma as a bona fide, correlated set of symptoms. This syndrome became labeled the post-traumatic stress disorder (PTSD); the enhanced recognition enabled treatment and research to proceed at a much faster rate.

The increased focus led to deepening understanding of the trauma response as a set of symptoms that appear to be inter-correlated as well as directly related to the occurrence of a traumatic event or stimulus. This direct linkage between a known event and a resultant psychological syndrome is unique in the field of psychopathology. It is this unique feature of the trauma response syndrome that provides for its usefulness in the treatment of trauma victims. While the clinical picture and treatment methodology of trauma victims are clearer as a result of the recent work in this area, empirical studies are needed to examine the relationship between the traumatic events and the predicted response patterns, as well as the levels of intercorrelations among the symptoms.

However, because of the intense scrutiny the field is now receiving and the usefulness of the diagnostic category, the PTSD has proven to be a highly functional prototype for research and clinical work (Foy, 1992). The criteria for the diagnostic category of PTSD (American Psychiatric Association, 1987) require that: "The person has experienced an event that is outside the range of usual human experience and that would be markedly distressing to almost anyone, e.g., serious threat to one's life or physical integrity; serious threat or harm to one's children, spouse, or other close relatives and friends; sudden destruction of one's home or community; or seeing another person who has recently been, or is being, seriously injured or killed as a result of an accident or physical violence" (p. 250).

The "sudden destruction of one's... community" is an accurate description of what happened to the world Jewish community during the Holocaust. Within a period of 6 years, from 1939 to 1945, one third of the world Jewish population, and almost the entire European Jewish population, was murdered.

There is a *midrash* that tells us that all Jews—past, present and future—stood together at Mt. Sinai when the Covenant was given to Moses, so that every meeting of Jews becomes a reunion. This, along with the family and communal values taught in Judaism, has fostered a strong sense of identification among Jews. Yet, for Jews in the path of Nazi destruction, there was, in reality, no escape from the threat of annihilation. Conversion, which before the Holocaust had been a means for escaping expulsion or death, was not even possible.

To be conscious of an identification that is associated with such terror and carries with it the threat of annihilation may be too painful for many people to endure. The psychic pain caused by this social-psychological identification may be the underlying trauma that leads to the defenses of denial and avoidance of stimuli associated with the trauma: Jewish identity and/or Judaism. In the classical psychoanalytic sense, denial of one's Jewish self may represent a form of resistance.

Traumatic identification is the process by which the individual internalizes that part of the environment that has been traumatized. For individual Jews who have not themselves been directly targeted as victims of anti-Semitism, this operates as an internalization of parental, familial or community traumas of increasing sociological distance from the individual. According to Brok (1994), understanding the historic context of the individual takes precedence over individual developmental issues. He suggests that in psychotherapy the traumatic identification needs to be resolved before individual dynamics can be addressed. Both Brok (1994) and Hopper (1994) discuss the importance of utilizing the group process for the dissolution of such traumatic identifications.

Studies in the area of social neuropsychology help us to understand the reactions of a group to the experience of other individuals within the group. Lin, Poland & Nakasaki (1993) conclude their summary of this literature stating: "There also are reasons to believe that environmental and cultural forces significantly influence neurodevelopment and possibly pathogenesis" (p. 254).

Not only do the teachings and traditions of Judaism urge a sense of "oneness" with other Jews, but the psychological processes of identification and internalization, through which all culture is transmitted, as well as traumatic identification, all converge toward a view of the Jewish people as a whole as a traumatized group. This implies that most Jews today, including those who themselves did not experience pogroms, the Holocaust, or even the pervasive discrimination in earlier 20th century America up to the 1960's, have experienced some elements of the "trauma response". Through traumatic identification, these experiences seem to have become part of Jewish cultural patterns and family dynamics that have been passed on to the succeeding generations of witnesses, leaving profound psychological effects.

TRAUMA RESPONSE IN THE JEWISH POPULATION

If anti-Semitism has generally traumatized the Jewish population, Jews as a group should exhibit symptoms of post-traumatic stress response, though likely of a lesser intensity than HS and COHS. The assessment of PTSD is, generally, a two-step process: 1) establishing that a traumatic event has occurred, and 2) determining the presence of trauma symptoms, both qualitatively and quantitatively. In the case of the Holocaust, pogroms and numerous hate crimes there is little question that the events qualify as traumatic events and most people who have experienced these events do not forget the fact that they occurred.

The primary symptoms associated with the diagnosis of PTSD are: hypervigilance and hyperarousal, intrusions, and emotional constriction or numbing, often associated with features of guilt or shame (American Psychiatric Association, 1987 & 1994). Below is a brief summary of the trauma response criteria of PTSD and illustrations of their presence within the Jewish community:

1. Hyperarousal and hypervigilance. This is the first symptom of a traumatic reaction and includes irritability and exaggerated startle reactions to low level or unexpected stimulation. Also included are states of vigilance for the return of danger, nightmares and psychosomatic complaints. Usually there is a "physiologic reactivity upon exposure to events that symbolize or resemble an aspect of the traumatic event" (American Psychiatric Association, 1987, p. 250). At least two of these behaviors are needed to qualify for the diagnosis. The hypervigilance trauma response is exhibited in one of the major organizations in contemporary American Jewish culture: the Anti-Defamation League.

2. Intrusions. "Long after the danger is past, traumatized people relive the event as though it were continually recurring in the present" (Herman, 1992, p. 37). This can occur in flashbacks and traumatic nightmares that the survivor may experience in any environment, regardless of how safe it might be. These intrusions may be triggered by minor events and are described by Freud and others as a "fixation on the trauma." Additional signs of this symptom are suddenly "acting or feeling as if the traumatic event was recurring..." and "intense psychological distress at exposure to events that symbolize or resemble an aspect of the traumatic event, including anniversaries of the trauma" (American Psychiatric Association, 1987, p. 250).

The current burgeoning of Holocaust memorials, in the years between 1990 and 1994 coinciding with the 50th anniversary of the Holocaust, are examples of intrusions called "anniversary reactions." These include the opening of the United States Holocaust Memorial Museum in the Spring of 1993 that coincided with the anniversary of the Warsaw Ghetto uprising, the opening of a Holocaust museum in Los Angeles, the movie *Schindler's List* (1993), and the reenactment of the U.S. invasion of the coast of Normandy that began the final phase of the war in June of 1944. Other examples of intrusive symptoms of Jewish communal trauma are anecdotal.

Roger Kamenetz (1994) eloquently describes his experience of intrusive symptoms when he was in Germany for the first time after deliberately avoiding "touching down on German soil" for years. He writes that upon hearing a man in the airport berating a clerk: "A few syllables of German spoken in anger and already the grainy newsreel was unwinding: Hitler at a podium, the crowds at Munich, goose-stepping soldiers, the crowd responding with a massive Heil Hitler salute.

And then, inevitably, the stacks and stacks of bodies..." (Kamenetz, 1994, p. 5). It is important to note, with respect to the presence of trauma symptoms in individuals not directly exposed to the traumatic stimulus, that Kamenetz is an American Jew, born in the U.S. at the end of the Holocaust. His grandparents arrived here having fled the pogroms at the turn of the century, not from Germany nor from the Holocaust.

Intrusions occur for American Jews not just at the scene of the Holocaust, but in their own, safe homes anywhere, often at Jewish gatherings. Six thousand miles from European soil and fifty years after the Holocaust, in Sierra Madre, California, an American Jewish mother said to her husband on the way to their daughter's wedding: "'We'll have a wedding just like the one in the movie *Fiddler on the Roof*!' When he remarked, only half-jokingly, 'With a pogrom, too?' She relates: 'I felt that sinking of the heart that being Jewish always invites. Later, at the wedding, I glanced more than once over the garden wall'" (Gerber, 1994, p. 28).

There are numerous examples of intrusion symptoms from the author's clinical practice: the American-born Jewish woman in her fifties who imagines she is observing the trains that brought Jews to the death camps whenever she sees an ordinary freight train; or the Rabbi's American-born Jewish wife in her sixties who imagines she is in the "showers" that delivered the lethal gas in the death camps whenever she takes a shower in her home in the U.S. Data on intrusions from pilot projects suggest that such symptoms are pervasive in American Jews.

3. Constriction. This represents "persistent avoidance of stimuli associated with the trauma or numbing of general responsiveness..." (American Psychiatric Association, 1987, p. 250). This persistent avoidance is the underlying process that can result in an inability to trust and form loving attachments, emotional detachment, and internalized anti-Semitism or Jewish self-hatred noted in commentaries on Jews (e.g., Burstow, 1992). At least three examples of constriction must be present for the diagnosis to be used. Seventy-seven percent in the pilot study sample met this diagnostic criterion.

Some of the most surprising, and quite troubling, examples of this avoidance or constriction response in Jews come from the community of psychotherapists. The first example occurred during a conference sponsored by a prestigious psychotherapeutic organization. The conference was titled: "External Reality and its Impact on Psychic Structure." The format of the conference was a case presentation, followed by a discussion of the case by the therapist and two senior psychotherapists, and then by audience participation in the discussion (Stern, 1994).

The patient presented was a woman in her fifties who had grown up in, and still maintained, an Orthodox Jewish home. At her request, the therapist was also a Jewish woman in her fifties. The patient dated her psychological distress to the time when her brother died and she had developed an eating disorder. When the family sought medical help for the patient's eating problem, the treatment prescribed by the physician involved feeding her a particular food that violated the kosher dietary laws. This Orthodox family complied with the prescription; eventually the patient recovered from the eating disorder but with long lasting psychological distress.

This brief description gives some of the important elements in the etiology of this patient's pathology that were a function of her Jewish identity. Yet, none of the discussants, all of whom were Jewish, nor the Jewish therapist who presented the case, spoke of the meaning and impact of this patient's Jewish cultural and religious identity and the historic context of her childhood on the etiology of her current depression and anxiety. In particular, the fact that the patient was born to an Orthodox Jewish family during the Holocaust needed to be explored. Similarly, the impact on this patient and family of following the recommendation to violate the kosher dietary laws to help their daughter overcome her eating problem needed to be explored.

In addition, the discussants did not address the meaning of the loss of the only male child in an Orthodox Jewish family, especially from the point of view of the impact on a female sibling. It was discussed only from the perspective of the impact of the loss of a child, any child, on its mother and then in a derivative manner, on the patient. After the death of the first-born son, the parents proceeded to have more children until they produced another son.

In Orthodox Judaism, the oldest son is the prime beneficiary of the birthright, and might even be the messiah—who, in Judaism, must be a first born son. He belongs to the priests until he is redeemed by a special ritual, is in the position of greatest honor and often is, therefore, the most favored child. The possible loss in this patient's self-esteem and the psychodynamic struggles that might result from this system change, especially within this family's particular religious and cultural framework, were ignored by the therapist and discussants. It is noteworthy that the particular female Jewish therapist chosen by the patient was affiliated with a women's psychotherapy center. Nonetheless, the impact of this aspect of the patient's Jewish experience, though most relevant to issues about her gender identity, was again not addressed by the therapist or the discussants. Only one discussant mentioned as significant the fact that the family violated the kosher dietary laws. Though the implications of this important issue were not addressed, it was the only time religion or culture was mentioned in the entire presentation and discussion.

When I raised questions about these issues during the discussion period, the presenting therapist reported that indeed the Holocaust must have been important to this patient since she continually referred to her life as a "Holocaust." The therapist reported that she had never asked about the importance of that communication nor discussed it, or the Holocaust, with the patient. It is strikingly ironic to witness the pervasive avoidance of the religious, cultural and historical context by these otherwise competent therapists, particularly when the title of the conference was: "External Reality and its Impact on Internal Psychic Structure."

A second example of the avoidance or constriction response in Jewish psychotherapists occurred shortly afterward at a national conference on group psychotherapy. At a workshop on the treatment of incest survivors, a Jewish therapist agreed with the presenters that incest survivors needed to focus on telling the story of their trauma, and that to interfere with that could be a retraumatization. She was concerned, however, that her patient who was a Holocaust survivor also wanted to tell her traumatic stories. She did not think that this was necessary or desirable for such patients, since she saw the Holocaust as an event that was finished whereas incest was continuous. (E.T. Beck, personal communication, March 6, 1994).

The four Jewish therapists mentioned in these two examples are not unique. Numerous other examples could be provided from the author's personal experience with colleagues. However, the above examples occurred in public meetings and are presented here particularly because they are open to verification. The examples cited are representative of the blindness of many Jewish psychotherapists to the impact of their own Jewish experience. Such blindness is not a function of incompetence; as noted in the first example, the therapists presenting and discussing the case were well known and well respected with positions of leadership in the psychotherapeutic community. These psychotherapists were exhibiting the symptom of traumatic constriction as persistent avoidance of their Jewish identities and/or religion. It is hypothesized that these aberrant behaviors on the part of these otherwise competent therapists are the result of a lack of resolution and integration of their own traumatic reactions to the Holocaust and possibly to other experiences of anti-Semitism.

While it is commonly assumed that all therapists have at least one blind spot that can potentially interfere with their effectiveness, it is particularly harmful when a therapist's blind spot is in an area of experience in which she/he would naturally be expected to be knowledgeable, empathic and well qualified. Just like the patient in the first example above, many people choose a therapist who is most like her/himself in some individually meaningful way with the expectation of receiving greater understanding and help. Indeed, research (Kelly & Strupp, 1992) has demonstrated that selecting a therapist on such a basis may be the most effective matching system. Yet in the case of Jewish patients and psychotherapists, the impact of this similarity may have a far more complicated effect, possibly resulting in reinforcement of the defenses and/or reactivation of the original trauma. This dilemma is not resolved, however, by the Jew's selection of a non-Jewish therapist, who has the potential for greater negative impact on the patient's Jewish self through Christian-centric or hidden anti-Semitic attitudes. Clearly, it is important for Jewish consumers, clients or patients to select therapists and consultants, whether Jewish or not, who have been Jewishly educated.

HEALING AND RECOVERY

In order to develop a secure sense of self, individuals need a foundation of relationship with caring people. Fifty years ago the Jewish community lost all vestiges of a sense of security in the world. "The traumatic event thus destroys the belief that one can be oneself in relation to others," writes Herman (1992, p. 53) of the trauma survivor. The Jewish self, as the victim of trauma, could no longer trust in its own safety. Amelioration of the unresolved trauma response of the Jewish population is essential for the full recovery of the community.

Recovery from trauma tends to follow an understandable path proceeding in somewhat predictable psychological stages. Initially, the rebuilding of trust, with provisions for safety and protection, is necessary for recovery. Following the Holocaust, the Jewish community lost its basic trust in the non-Jewish world as well as in its own ability to maintain its safety and security. The creation of the State of Israel by the United Nations, led by the U.S. (Schoenbaum, 1993), was the major attempt by the Jewish and non-Jewish world to provide some safety for the remaining Jewish community.

Though there were isolated attempts by some churches, individual non-Jews and secular groups to be supportive to the Jewish community, post-World War II America remained quite anti-Semitic (Dinnerstein, 1994). In fact, it was not until 1965, 20 years after the Holocaust, that the Second Vatican Council in the Declaration Nostra Aetate vehemently denounced "all hatreds, persecutions, displays of anti-Semitism leveled at any time or from any source against the Jews" (Vatican Council II, Nostra Aetate, 28 October, 1965; see also Flannery, 1981, p. 741).

Viewing the Jewish population as a group of trauma survivors leads to a variety of "treatment" activities whose usefulness could reach beyond the recovery of the community from previous anti-Semitic trauma events. Pilot studies utilizing small group psycho-educational methodology offer promising techniques for treating the Jewish communal trauma response to address the unresolved impact of anti-Semitism. Finally, it may well be that individual psychological distress that does not appear to be related to the underlying Jewish communal trauma response cannot be effectively treated until the trauma aspect of the cultural context is directly addressed.

SUMMARY

There has been significant attrition in the American Jewish population within the past 30 years that is viewed as a primary symptom of the unresolved psychological sequelae of anti-Semitism in general, and the Holocaust in particular. The theory of Jewish communal trauma response was developed to explain some of this population decrease, as well as other population and psychological characteristics of

Jews. This theory hypothesizes that the Jewish population, in general, is experiencing a post-traumatic stress response. This is a natural reaction to the traumatic experiences of the group as a whole, and is transmitted culturally through traumatic identification. Pilot studies designed to test the theory and treat the unresolved sequelae are supportive.

The theory presented here suggests that the recent surge in anti-Semitism since the beginning of the fall of the Iron Curtain in 1989 reactivates the individual trauma response and therefore retraumatizes the Jewish community. Furthermore, anti-Semitic events that have occurred repeatedly for thousands of years cannot be expected to cease even if a peace accord is reached in the Middle East in the near future. This retraumatization itself is a recurring feature of the Jewish cultural experience. Jewish as well as non-Jewish psychotherapists and consultants need to be trained to recognize, understand and treat their own, as well as others', responses to anti-Semitism.

REFERENCES

Aguilar, L. (1994, August 8). Neighbors buoy family after antisemitic attack. *The Washington Post*, p. D1.

American Psychiatric Association (1987). *Diagnostic and statistical manual of mental disorders* (3rd ed. rev.). Washington, DC: Author.

American Psychiatric Association (1994). *Diagnostic and statistical manual of mental disorders* (4th ed.). Washington, DC: Author.

American Religious Composition (1993, September 23). *Washington Jewish Week*, p. 34.

ADL sees 'dramatic' rise in anti-Semitic incidents. (1991, February). *Washington Jewish Week*, p. 22.

Anti-Defamation League. (1993). *Jew-hatred as history.* Washington, DC: Author.

Anti-Defamation League. (1994). *Minister Louis Farrakhan and the Nation of Islam claim they are moving toward moderation and increased tolerance. You Decide.* New York: Author.

Beck, E. T. (Ed.). (1989). *Nice Jewish girls: A lesbian anthology.* Boston: Beacon Press.

Benjamin, C. (1994, August 4). Experts examine bombing. *Washington Jewish Week*, p. 5.

Bergmann, W. (Ed.). (1987). *Error without trial: Psychological research on antisemitism.* Hawthorn, NY: de Gruyter.

Bronfman, E. (1994, July 8). *Recent worldwide antisemitism.* Letter. World Jewish Congress. New York: World Jewish Congress.

Brok, A. J. (1994, April). *On the dissolution of traumatic identification through the group process.* Paper presented at the Fourteenth Annual Spring meeting of Division 39, Washington, DC.

Burstow, B. (1992). *Radical feminist therapy: Working in the context of violence.* London: Sage.

Chodoff, P. (1963). Late effects of the concentration camp syndrome. *Archives of General Psychiatry, 8*, 323-333.

Cohen, D. N. (1993, December 23). Twenty percent of U.S. Jews sit in the pews. *Washington Jewish Week*, p. 23.

Council of Jewish Federations. (1991). *Highlights of the CJF 1990 National Jewish Population Survey.* New York: Author.

Cymrot, D. (1994, August 4). Waldheim's papal honor. *Washington Jewish Week*, p. 2.

Danieli, Y. (1985). The treatment and prevention of long-term effects and intergenerational transmission of victimization: A lesson from Holocaust survivors and their children. In C. R. Figley (Ed.), *Trauma and its wake.* (pp. 292-313). New York: Bruner/Mazel.

Dinnerstein, L. (1994). *Antisemitism in America.* New York: Oxford University Press.

Everstine, D. S. & Everstine, L. (1993). *The trauma response.* New York: Norton.

Figley, C. R. (Ed.). (1985). *Trauma and its wake.* New York: Brunner/Mazel.

Flannery, A. (Ed.). (1981). *Vatican Council II, The Conciliar and Post Conciliar Documents.* Northport, NY: Costello.

Foy, D. W. (1992). *Treating PTSD: Cognitive-behavioral strategies.* New York: Guilford Press.

Gerber, M. J. (1994, August/September). On being Jewish & Female. *Hadassah Magazine.* p. 28.

Harden, B. (1990, July 16). Anti-Jewish bias rising in Poland. *The Washington Post*, p. 19.

Herman, J. L. (1992). *Trauma and recovery.* New York: Basic Books.

Hopper, E. (1994, June). *Lessons for group psychotherapists from child survivors of the Holocaust.* Paper presented at the National Group Psychotherapy Institute, Washington, D.C.

Jews Protest Italian Official's Comment. (1994, August 13). *The Washington Post*, p. A18.

Kamenetz, R. (1994). *The Jew in the Lotus.* San Francisco: Harper.

Kardiner, A. & Spiegel, J. P. (1947). *Stress and neurotic illness* (Rev. ed.). New York: Hoeber.

Kelly, T. & Strupp, H. (1992). Patient and therapist values in psychotherapy: Perceived changes, assimilation, similarity, and outcome. *Journal of Clinical and Consulting Psychology, 60*, 34-40.

Kushner, H. (1993). *To life! A celebration of Jewish being and thinking.* Boston: Little, Brown & Co.

Lin, K.M., Poland, R., & Nakasaki, G. (Eds.). (1993). Psychopharmacology and Psychobiology of Ethnicity. *Progress in Psychiatry, 39.* Washington, D.C.: American Psychiatric Association.

Melillo, W. & Harris, H. R. (1994, April 20). Ex-Farrakhan aide goes to Howard U. *The Washington Post*, p. B1.

Moses, R. (Ed.). (1993). *Persistent shadows of the Holocaust: The meaning to those not directly affected.* Madison: International Universities Press.

Pressman, S. (1993, December 2). Cults a magnet to many Jews. *Washington Jewish Week*, p. 27.

Rosenman, S. & Handelsman, I. (1990a). Identity as legacy of the Holocaust: Encountering a survivor's narrative. *Journal of Psychohistory, 18*, 35-69.

Rosenman, S. & Handelsman, I. (1990b). The collective past, group psychology and personal narrative: Shaping Jewish identity by memoirs of the Holocaust. *American Journal of Psychoanalysis, 50*, 151-170.

Schoenbaum, D. (1993). *The United States and the State of Israel.* New York: Oxford University Press.

Siegel, R. J. & Cole, E. (Eds.). (1991). *Jewish women in therapy: Seen but not heard.* New York: Haworth Press.

Spielberg, S. (Producer and Director), *Schindler's List* [Film]. Hollywood, CA: Amblin Films.

Stern, D. (1994, February). *Case presentation.* Paper presented at the Conference on External Reality and It's Impact on Psychic Structure given by the Washington Psychoanalytic Foundation, Washington, DC.

Williams, M. B. & Sommer, Jr., J. F. (Eds.). (1994). *Handbook of post-traumatic therapy.* Westport, CT: Greenwood/Praeger.

Wistrich, R. S. (1991). *Antisemitism: The longest hatred.* New York: Pantheon.

ACKNOWLEDGMENTS

I am grateful to have been blessed with a loving husband of many years, Charles H. Hammer, who is also my colleague at the Jewish Psychological Centers for Psychotherapy and Consultation and who significantly added to the clarity of this paper. In addition, I appreciate the professional and emotional support of my other colleagues at the Centers: Mary Ann Dubner, Kenneth L. Fox, and Evelyn T. Beck. Evelyn T. Beck has been particularly helpful through her generous enthusiasm for this work. I am also indebted to her and to Lee Knefelkamp for their thorough and insightful review of this paper.

My participation in a group for healing the Jewish self lead by Barbara Breitman and Rabbis Devora Bartnoff, Jonathan Kligler, and Mordechai Liebling, was particularly valuable for that purpose, and as inspiration to continue the present work.

SURVIVORS NONETHELESS: TRAUMA IN WOMEN NOT DIRECTLY INVOLVED WITH THE HOLOCAUST

KAYLA MIRIYAM WEINER

The purpose of this paper is to show that many women, Jewish and non-Jewish, who may appear to have no direct connection to the Holocaust, are nonetheless traumatized by it and suffer from the effects of that trauma. There is extensive research on the subject of intergenerational transmission of trauma. In addition, a wide range of research exists on secondary trauma to mental health workers, law enforcement officials and crisis intervention workers, e.g., Diminic, et. al. (1994), Karakashian (1994), Straker and Moosa (1994), and Follette, Polusny, and Milbeck (1994). Abbott (1991) and Shabad (1993) address the intergenerational transmission of traumatic themes and negative family patterns and Nagata (1990) investigated the cross-generational impact of World War II on third generation Japanese-Americans. The literature is replete with research on the transmission of trauma to the children of Holocaust survivors, e.g., Kogan (1989), Silverman (1987), Sorscher (1992), Bogaty (1987), Chayes (1988), and Last (1988). Vogel (1994) addresses not only the intergenerational transmission of Holocaust trauma, but also the intergenerational transmission of child abuse trauma to a daughter. Yet a review of the literature indicates no research into the trauma of the Holocaust experienced by those who had no direct contact with it.

The premise of this paper is that even if one was not present during the Holocaust and had no family involved, all Jews living since the time of the Holocaust have been traumatized by it to some degree. Sexism within society compounds the trauma for Jewish women. Additionally, non-Jewish people with no direct contact to the Holocaust may also experience this trauma. Because many of these people have not themselves, nor their families, been directly involved in the Holocaust, they have not had their trauma identified or named by society. They therefore have not been able to recognize the consequences of the trauma, nor do they have the means to heal from the results of it. Therapists must be aware of this previously undesignated Holocaust trauma and consider it when working with clients. They must help each woman explore how this trauma may influence her identity and behavior. This awareness is an extra lens through which the complexity of the individual must be viewed.

INTRODUCTION

My grandparents, as young children, came to this country from Russia at the turn of the century. I have no known family members that were involved in the Holocaust, yet for many years I have considered myself to be a Holocaust survivor. I have always been afraid to say this publicly because I have felt that I didn't have a right to the designation and I didn't want to minimize "real" survivors. When I traveled to Israel and visited *Yad Vashem* (Israel's national Holocaust museum) I was profoundly moved by the exhibits. Yet, nothing I saw seemed new to me. It was as if I had seen it all before. As I watched documentaries such as *Shoah*, or movies like *Schindler's List*, or read accounts of individual's experiences, I was sad but never surprised. Somehow it always seemed familiar, and traumatic. I carried the pictures in my mind. I knew the sounds. I knew the cold. I knew the fear. I never understood exactly how I have had that knowing, but my knowledge of the Holocaust has always felt to me to be at a cellular level.

As a young girl (5-10 years old) I frequently went to the movie theater on Saturday afternoon and to religious school on Sunday morning. Although the official Nuremberg Trials were in 1945-46, trials of war criminals were still going on during the time I was attending Saturday matinees. It was standard practice in those days to include a newsreel, a summary of the news-making events of the world, before each movie. In the newsreel there was always a part about the war trials that invariably included a film clip of the liberation of the concentration camps after World War II. The pictures of people who looked like walking skeletons, the piles of shoes, the mass graves, are all burned into my mind. Each Sunday I would solidify my identity as a Jew, and each Saturday I got my dose of Holocaust trauma. The message was loud and clear, "This is what can happen to you for no other reason than that you are Jewish." I learned to live in fear and this fear required me to be constantly cautious about where I was, whom I chose as friends and how I conducted myself in the world. This fear had a direct impact on my relationships as well as all my behaviors, aspirations and goals.

THEORY DEVELOPMENT

When I was able to identify and name this unlabeled trauma within myself, I was able to more easily recognize it in others. I believe that the lives of many women of my generation, and subsequent generations not directly involved in the Holocaust, have been profoundly influenced by it due to an intergenerational transmission of trauma. This type of trauma has been transmitted through books, movies, television and overheard conversations. Fears, ideas and behaviors have also been transmitted unconsciously and unintentionally by adults themselves not directly involved in the Holocaust. Children of those who were directly involved in the Holocaust also had the trauma transmitted to them. The difference between these children and those who had no apparent direct contact with the Holocaust, is that the traumatic experience of the latter has not been validated. It is the very lack of validation that functions as a secondary trauma, permitting no means to clean the wound and purge the pain.

When the existence of this trauma is not validated, when there are no words to name the trauma, and one does not know consciously why one feels the way one does, one is left feeling an undifferentiated state of fear. In addition, the fear endemic to being a woman, forced to live in a state of constant apprehension due to our vulnerability to rape and violation, compounds our sense of endangerment. Being a Jew, cognizant of centuries of oppression to our people, adds another layer of fear. The total fear one experiences becomes exponentially greater than any single fear.

Lack of entitlement is a generalized response to fear and causes one to consider one's life at the mercy of others. Lack of entitlement is the sense of not having a right to be; not having the right to have anything of worth in one's life. The basic tenet of Judaism, *tikkun olam* (one's responsibility to heal and repair the world), when combined with a feeling of lack of entitlement and the sexist messages of our culture which require women to set everyone's needs above our own, create an individual who spends her time expending all her life energy on others. Put another way, if a woman believes she is required to improve the world, believes she is not entitled to have anything in life and has learned that her needs are secondary to the needs of others, her life may become nothing more than a joyless struggle. Finally, survivor's guilt, that guilt that exists because we know others have died and we still live, intensifies one's sense of a lack of entitlement.

At a workshop about Holocaust trauma facilitated by Joan Fisch at the Association for Women in Psychology conference in Oakland, CA (1994) each woman talked about her experience of the Holocaust. The disclosure of one woman in particular stood out for me because the woman was not Jewish. She told how one of her parents had had a professional involvement with the Nuremberg Trials and that she had been exposed to vivid pictures of the Holocaust as a child. She talked about her sense of guilt and shame, and her inability to address the pain she was experiencing because she felt she was not entitled to sympathy; it was as if she was not allowed to hurt because she wasn't Jewish. Along with the pain she felt about the Holocaust, she experienced the added pain of being invalidated. Because it is not generally acknowledged that one can be traumatized without direct contact to the Holocaust (meaning being there or having a relative there), especially if one is not Jewish, there was no acknowledgment of her Holocaust experience and pain.

The need to be constantly aware of all that is going on in our environment and the need to control our environment are reasonable responses for Jewish women who know that throughout history, and specifically within our own lifetimes, in the most so-called "civilized" countries, an attempt was made to annihilate all of our people. The need to know where our family is at all times, the need to have an adequate supply of money available and the need to have a plan of escape, are entirely appropriate responses to our reality. This hypervigilance and these control mechanisms are appropriate, adaptive responses to our environment. For many women, Jewish and non-Jewish, there is often no way to make sense of these feelings and responses. We may ultimately believe there is something wrong with us when there is no understanding or external validation for our feelings. Frequently our behaviors are labeled paranoid and controlling and are seen as unacceptable by society and the therapeutic community. When a woman with these characteristics presents for treatment, therapists have been taught to consider these as indicators of a personality or character disorder. If clinicians were trained to inquire about the ethnic background of each client, and as a matter of course assume that all Jewish women are suffering some degree of transmitted Holocaust trauma compounded by the trauma of sexism, the therapist could provide support for her experience as well as help her to understand and accept her behavior. Therapists must also remember to explore the Holocaust experience of non-Jewish women to determine the possibility of transmitted Holocaust trauma.

The following story demonstrates why it is so important that clinicians explore the possibility of a Holocaust trauma in a woman even when she appears to have no direct contact to the Holocaust. A woman I was seeing had suffered extreme emotional abuse by her father and was in a constant state of hyperarousal; she was sure that everyone was "out to get her." She told me about an experience in her childhood that helped to explain the extreme intensity of her fear and anxiety. Following are her written words about a particular period in her life. (I have edited to change identifying characteristics.)

"In the 1950's I lived with our family in Europe. As Americans living abroad at that time, we were regularly insulted for being foreigners. I always felt as if I was not safe. I felt like an outsider. When I was about eight years old I was taken to see the movie *Anne Frank*. I identified with the girl as though I was really there [in hiding] living the experience. At about the same time I read a newspaper headline that said, "War Presumed." I began to think another war was imminent and that I would be the next Anne Frank. I became overwrought and began to pray all night for world peace. I would be awake until I heard the milk truck come at about four o'clock in the morning. The milk delivery trucks had a sound that seemed the same as the siren made by the trucks used to take the Jews away in the *Anne Frank* movie and it was terrifying to me. When I heard the truck stop I expected to be taken from our home. When this did not happen, I would get a couple of hours sleep. I felt saved for another day. During this period the household staff who cared for me told stories of their lives during World War II which were stories of plunder, rape and murder.

"My early experiences living in Europe, my identification with the child in the movie *Anne Frank* and the life stories of my caretakers all contributed to the internalization of fear in my mind and body. The level of fear that I have dealt with in my adult life has often been overwhelming to me. I have reacted as though I was involved in a life and death situation, even when dealing with ordinary life stress situations."

As noted, this woman was emotionally battered by her father and essentially abandoned by her mother who did nothing to protect her. She describes her childhood as one of feeling as if she was living in a dictatorship. However, these experiences alone were not enough to explain the extreme level of her terror nor her paranoia. Her emotional intensity began to make sense when put into the context of someone suffering from a Holocaust trauma. Understanding this and naming it has made it possible for her to respond more appropriately to present stressors in her life. Because she no longer assumes everyone she meets is a mortal threat, she has also been able to improve the quality of her relationships.

CASE STUDY

Several years ago a young woman came to me for therapy. At age 26, Jane Green had come to find ways to disengage from her mother and her brother for whom she felt responsible. On her personal information form she wrote, "Very closely bonded with mother since birth. Mother's relationship with husband (my father) disintegrated after my birth. No separation from mom as child—still struggling to separate." During her initial interview she disclosed that her mother had been born Jewish but when her mother was about six years old the family became Protestant at her grandmother's insistence. Jane was raised as a Protestant until she was 15 years old. Her Catholic father had been an alcoholic all of her life and had died two years before she came into therapy. Jane described the experience of her childhood as bleak; all of her memories were of emptiness and deprivation. She reported that she rarely saw her mother eat. On the few occasions that the family would have a meal together, her mother sat off in a corner eating a bowl of cottage cheese. Jane stated that she herself had an eating disorder when she was younger but her current relationship with food, while not ideal, was acceptable to her. Her family had lived as though in poverty all of her life; she recalls her father scavenging in trash cans for food. However, when he died, she received a sizable inheritance of money he had kept from the family.

Jane's first two years of therapy were productive. She began to identify her own needs and then learned to express them to friends and family in appropriate, non-rebellious ways. Although there were some ways in which she had been parentified as a child, as her mother's confidante, she was also infantilized and not given the tools to function as an adult. Much of this period in therapy she spent learning to live in the world: getting a driver's license, car and insurance, finding a medical doctor, etc. Jane had a degree in history, but identified most deeply with her artistic talents. She was a painter and sculptor and did a great deal of writing of stories, poems and essays. During this time Jane worked in a variety of part-time jobs including providing child care, teaching art to children and working in a gift shop. Frequently she mentioned that she hated the work for which she was getting paid. It ultimately became clear that she was continuing to work even though she was financially able to live off her inheritance because she did not feel she had the right not to work for a living. She found it very difficult to consider her art as legitimate and went to extreme means to validate it by working excessively on her projects.

There are many ways Jane manifested her lack of entitlement. She rode a bicycle everywhere, in all types of weather, which in Seattle can be quite unpleasant. It took quite some time before she realized that it was possible, and permissible, for her to own a car that would allow her to have a choice about her means of transportation. She frequently appeared for her sessions disheveled, wearing clothes with patches and holes. She made several changes in her living arrangements that she said didn't bother her because most of her belongings could be easily moved by putting them in plastic bags.

Jane often made comments about always having voices in her head telling her she did not deserve to eat good food or to dress in stylish clothes or to have anything pleasing in her life. She could never exactly explain where those thoughts came from. It seemed logical for us to say that part of the messages in her head must have come from observing her mother who had been anorexic during Jane's childhood, and part must have come from observing her father who deprived himself of everything, except alcohol, all of her life. The nonverbal messages she got from her parents still did not seem to explain all the negative feelings she had about her right to exist. After two years of therapy she was beginning to reject those images but she had absolutely no success in closing the voices out of her head.

Throughout this time Jane would sometimes mention her relationship with food. One day when she saw me eating something before our session she noted how it was almost impossible for her to eat in the presence of others. At other times she would explain how she arranged her life around what she would be eating, at what time. In the third year of our work together Jane's mother became ill with lymphoma. While she was visiting her mother to care for her, in the calls Jane made to me she expressed her growing concerns about her food habits. When she returned, besides dealing with her fears due to the impending death of her mother, we began to talk about the numerous ways in which she had felt the need to deprive herself: no car, no clothes, no home, no food, etc. One day she brought in some notes of the words she heard in her head about food. She wrote, "Food will spoil you. You should always stop eating while you're still hungry and always leave the table hungry. Food is a medicine for hunger and only that. Pleasure is from men and sex, not food. You should never eat after 4 p.m. You should burn all your dinner calories before bedtime. [One of many contradictions she was trying to resolve.] Women don't need food. Eating is unattractive and inappropriate. You are ugly when you eat." I sat rather stunned after hearing this litany. She went on to say that these were only some of the voices she always heard screaming in her head. I asked her if she would be willing to draw what it felt like in her head. She seemed to jump at the offer. The instant I put out the paper and colors, she began drawing. She picked up a gray oil pastel and began putting down small circles grouped together, about one to two inches in diameter. When she had about twenty drawn she said in a breathless voice, "These are not stones, they are people." Then she began giving them superficial features: dots for eyes, nose and mouth. She continued, "There are more than I can draw. I've only drawn a few. The page is filled with them; there are thousands and thousands. They are all out there shouting at me. Some of them are in the shadows. They are all connected to me. Some of them I don't know. They are all telling me that I don't deserve anything and that I should be grateful for what I have."

As I sat and watched this woman, saw her drawing and listened to her words, I was struck by how her picture looked like some of the pictures of tortured Holocaust survivors I had seen. I mentioned that to her and we looked at each other in a kind of shock because we both realized at the same moment that one of the major things she had been carrying with her, that was creating so much pain for her, was a transmitted Holocaust trauma. At the end of the session we were both feeling very peaceful; it seemed as if we were in a state of awe. She turned to me and said, "Not that all of the other things we have done haven't been good or important, but it seems like today we found a key." I had to agree.

What follows is writing Jane did specifically as an exercise/exorcise. I have changed only identifying characteristics. Jane wrote:

"There was a whole category of things I never spoke about to Kayla. These things just never came up. I never spoke to anyone about them, not to friends, not to lovers, not to anyone in my family. They were in a cocoon, an encapsulated set of secrets I couldn't even think about. They were secret even to myself.

"I never told anyone about the warnings my father gave me. He warned me about The Germans. Often he refused to let me outside when we were at his house in Europe where he grew up, because of The Germans. Often when I did get out, he would beat me violently when he caught me. I thought the beatings were because he thought I had encountered The Germans, and that encountering The Germans was the worst thing I could possibly do. My father behaved this way in the United States also, beating me if I went outside. He never explained or discussed his behavior. The Germans were the topic of his frightening tirades yet at other times they were mentioned in offhand, unpredictable, spiteful comments. I never had any idea why he said and did these things. I truly believed there were people, The Germans, who would get me if I went outside. They would get me just because of who I am, because I am of the Green family, and for that reason alone.

"I remember this being a pervading part of my life, as far back as I can remember. The worst beatings my father gave me for being outside were when I was between six and eight years old, but the tirades against The Germans continued as long as he lived. It wasn't only The Germans. It was also The Capitalists, The Consumerists, The Bourgeoisie, and a huge mysterious nameless They. 'Maybe They've kidnapped them,' I remember my father saying one afternoon when I was nine and he and I were home alone and my mother and brother were out. He appeared to be genuinely fearful that this might be the case. I knew that if I said 'Who?' I would spark an endless tirade of rage. Or I might be beaten. So I didn't ask.

"I also knew of a whole range of topics never to be discussed with my father. I thought that if I ever mentioned any of these things, he would kill me. Included in these topics were his younger brother who had perished in Dachau, The War [World War II], and of course, The Germans. Also never to be questioned was what my father was eating or drinking or where he got his food and alcohol. My father did not buy food at a store: I think he got it from dumpsters and garbage cans. He would come home with half-eaten loaves of bread, opened containers of meats or cheese and opened packages of cold cuts. He hid his food in a cupboard high up above the stove, or outside the house. The alcohol he brought home was in opened, partially empty bottles that he also hid away.

"I never connected any of this with the World War II Holocaust. My father was not Jewish. His brother had died in Dachau because he was a partisan, an anti-fascist. Somehow the Jewish experience always seemed to be an accepted trauma, a shared experience; a truth, because it is openly remembered. My uncle's situation was instead a secret thing with no category or community behind it. Although my mother was Jewish, Judaism was not something ever offered to me as a religion or a culture. I never had any sense of belonging associated with my mother being Jewish. She was raised within another religious community and knew nothing of Jewish tradition or history.

"So whenever I thought about the Holocaust, I experienced a very confused and vague set of emotions. Loss, because my would-be uncle died at sixteen in a Nazi concentration camp. Sadness that such a thing could happen to a sixteen year old. Fear, that it happened to a Green family member and therefore it could happen to me. Anger, that no one in the world was acknowledging this, and that my uncle's internment and death were ignored in terms of its impact on the family. Fear, at the unpredictable outbursts of my father's rage, which was connected to the Holocaust in a mysterious, unexplained way. And guilt. Guilt for feeling some sense of identification with families of Holocaust victims for no good reason since I was not, in my opinion, really Jewish.

"At some point in my childhood I remember going into the bathroom and finding hundreds of tiny flies, or winged ants, in the bathtub. I don't know how they had gotten there, but I was horrified to see them, and I turned on the water and filled the tub to drown them all. But in the few seconds it took me to do this, I became equally horrified with my own action. 'This is a holocaust,' I thought. 'I have instigated a holocaust.' I directly related the insects' experience to the experience of the millions of sufferers in the Holocaust.

"The history of my father's family, and of my uncle's death in the Holocaust, is one of the things I could never address, one of the most deeply locked away and best kept secrets. Because of its specificity to my family and the lack of any clear group with which to identify, it took a long time to unravel. Although the partisans in World War II might provide a possible identification group, my own father was drafted in the fascist army and taken as a prisoner-of-war by the British; he therefore could not identify himself with the partisans. And because my uncle was not Jewish, I could not directly relate to the Jewish experience in the Holocaust. Furthermore, my uncle was turned in by fellow villagers. In a village of fewer than one thousand people, our own neighbors, I have no idea who, turned him in to the German Nazi soldiers who were conducting a search and roundup of partisans in the area. This created a feeling of alienation from, and fear of, everyone living around us. I could indirectly identify with the Jewish experience by my distant connection to the portion of my mother's family that remained Jewish. Paranoia [fear] seemed to come at me from all sides. More layers of cocooned secrets [from both parents]. I was taught to fear the people around me because they were out to get me, and tied into that message was the message that somehow I deserved to be hunted down, that I myself deserved to be captured and exterminated; that I did not deserve to live.

"It is interesting to notice that guilt is what I felt when I admitted anything that I had previously keep secret. I felt guilty when I first admitted that I'd been raped, even five years after the incident. I felt guilty when I admitted that my father had repeatedly beaten me, that my mother had fed me Valium, that I'd discovered my father had been gay and closeted. The guilt was of [my] betrayal [of the rapist, my mother, my father]. I thought I was committing a terrible treason, that I was just trying to draw attention to myself and give myself importance, validity and comfort, which I thought I did not deserve. I could hear my parents telling me I was a spoiled child, for telling such stories. Deep down, with each secret unearthed, I felt a sense of relief and of a right to my own existence. Yet it has been very difficult to get rid of the feeling that I am not entitled to exist."

DISCUSSION

There were many ways in which all of Jane's transmitted Holocaust trauma was disguised. Her initial statement about her parents' relationship after her birth was a reasonable explanation for her mother's unhealthy attachment to her. However, that attachment was much more meaningfully addressed when viewed through the filter of her father's rage and paranoia. Her disturbed eating patterns were easily attributed to her mother's anorexia, but made much more sense when put into the context of the learned fear of "Them." As Jane writes, "Get by with as little food as possible, so when they take food away, you'll be prepared. Also, 'You can't rob an empty house' theory [fits in here]. When you have nothing for a body, there's nothing to be vandalized, violated or raped." Jane's apparent need for deprivation in all areas of her life (besides depriving herself of food) when viewed in a traditional manner would imply extremely poor identity development and other pathologies. Within the context of a father who ate from dumpsters and berated her with sexist epithets, combined with her own subconscious sense of survivor's guilt, her behavior is quite understandable.

Jane left the country for several months and sublet her home to someone who subsequently leased it to someone else. While she was gone she lost the lease for the home to the sublessor. He threw away many of her belongings and put the rest into trash bags and continued to use her furniture and sleep in her bed. When she returned she was appalled by what had been done to her possessions and she was in a state of rage. She said, "It felt like what I imagine it must have felt like to the Holocaust survivors; to have all of their belongs, including their home, taken away." Understanding this violation in the context of her Holocaust experience made the intensity of her feelings understandable. Additionally, this event confirmed her feeling that she didn't have a right to anything.

Jane and I continue to address the impending death of her mother, the alcoholism in the family, the abuse that occurred, the peculiar relationships her parents had between them and with others, and the lack of worth she felt as a result of her father's sexist attitudes towards women. However, we now also include in all of our considerations the permeating influence of the transmitted trauma of the Holocaust and how this has had an impact on her life. We continue to unearth the secret traumas she has been living with and, in so doing, are finding ways to allow her to accept her right to existence and her right to a full and meaningful life.

CONCLUSION

Although one cannot extrapolate from two examples to explain all unhealthy attachment relationships, nor all eating disorders, nor the etiology of excessive fear in all women, the stories presented here clearly demonstrate the importance of recognizing generationally transmitted Holocaust trauma in those who would not ordinarily be identified as survivors of the Holocaust. Previous Holocaust trauma theory and treatment have focused on only those who have been directly involved with the Holocaust and their children. Therapists who work with clients who present with trauma symptoms are urged to look, along with the other sources of trauma one would consider, such as incest, physical abuse, alcoholism, etc., at the possibility of the Holocaust as a precipitating or complicating element in the trauma. One should screen for this possibility with Jewish and non-Jewish clients, whether or not the client appears to have any direct contact with the Holocaust. When the subconscious messages of fear and lack of entitlement are revealed, processed and replaced, the trauma survivor can move on to heal and to learn to better function in the world.

REFERENCES

Abbott, B. (1991). Family dynamics, intergenerational patterns of negative events and trauma and patterns of offending behavior: A comparison of adolescent sexual offenders and delinquent adolescents and their parents. *Dissertation Abstracts International, 51*, 8B, 4037.

Bogaty, N. (1987). The post-Holocaust family: A psychohistorical investigation in the intergenerational transmission of trauma. *Dissertation Abstracts International. Jul 48*, 1B, 256.

Chayes, M. (1988). Holocaust survivors and their children: An intergenerational study of mourning, parenting and psychological adjustment. *Dissertation Abstracts International, 48*(01), 12B, 3675.

du Diminic, I., Franciskovic, T., Delic, B., & Serdarevic, I. (1994). Traumatization of group leaders in their work with displaced persons. *Group, 18*(1), 46-54.

Follette, V., Polusny, M., & Milbeck, K. (1994). Mental health and law enforcement professionals: Trauma history, psychological symptoms, and the impact of providing services to child sexual abuse survivors. *Professional Psychology: Research & Practice*, *25*(3), 275-282.

Karakashian, M. (1994). Countertransference issues in crisis work with natural disaster victims. *Psychotherapy, 31*(2), 334-341.

Kogan, I. (1989). Working through the vicissitudes of trauma in the psychoanalysis of Holocaust survivors' offspring. *Sigmund Freud House Bulletin, 13*(2), 25-33.

Last, U. (1988). The transgenerational impact of Holocaust trauma: Current state of the evidence. *International Journal of Mental Health, 17*(4), 72-89.

Nagata, D. (1990). The Japanese American internment: Exploring the transgenerational consequences of traumatic stress. *Journal of Traumatic Stress, 3*(1), 47-49.

Straker, G. & Moosa, F. (1994). Interacting with trauma survivors in contexts of continuing trauma. *Journal of Traumatic Stress, 7*(3), 457-465.

Shabad, P. (1993). Repetition and incomplete mourning: The intergenerational transmission of traumatic themes. *Psychoanalytic Psychology, 10*(1), 61-75.

Silverman, W. (1987). Methodological issues in the study of transgenerational effects of the Holocaust: Comments on Nadler, Kav-Venaki, and Gleitman. *Journal of Consulting and Clinical Psychology, 55*(1) 125-126.

Sorscher, N. (1992). The effects of parental communication of wartime experiences on children of survivors of the Holocaust. *Dissertation Abstracts International, 52*, 8B, 4482.

Vogel, M. (1994). Gender as a factor in the transgenerational transmission of trauma. *Women and Therapy, 15*(2), 35-47.

AUTHOR'S BIOGRAPHIES

Evelyn Torton Beck, Ph.D., is Professor and Director of the Women's Studies Program at the University of Maryland, College Park, and a member of the Jewish Studies Program. She has lectured widely in Japan, Europe and across the United States and Canada on issues related to "difference." Among her books are *Kafka and the Yiddish Theater* (1971), *The Prism of Sex* (1979) and *Nice Jewish Girls: A Lesbian Anthology* (1982/1989).

Barbara Eve Breitman, M.S.W., is a psychotherapist in private practice in Philadelphia. She teaches at the University of Pennsylvania School of Social Work and conducts trainings in a variety of human service settings to promote understanding between diverse racial and cultural groups. She has been active in movements for Jewish Renewal and feminism.

Phyllis Chesler, Ph.D., was a member of Hashomer Hat'zair and Ain Harod in the 1950's; and in the 1960's, she became active in the American civil rights, anti-war and feminist movements. She is the author of seven books including, *Women and Madness* (1972), *Moth-*

ers on Trial (1986), and *Patriarchy: Notes of an Expert Witness* (1994). Phyllis is a co-founder of The Association for Women in Psychology (1969), The National Women's Health Network (1973), is a columnist for *On The Issues* magazine, and a survivor of Chronic Fatigue Immune Dysfunction Syndrome.

Michele Clark, M.Ed., lives in Vermont where she teaches psychology at Vermont College, is a psychotherapist and education specialist at Champlain Drug and Alcohol Services and is active in the Beth Jacob Synagogue in Montpelier. She worked as a therapist with the Women's Mental Health Collective in Somerville, MA for 14 years, and has written essays and reviews for *The Feminist Press, The Women's Review of Books, Bridges, Women and Therapy* and other journals.

Deborah A. Engelen-Eigles, M.S., is a doctoral student in Sociology at the University of Minnesota, with a minor in Feminist Studies. Her dissertation research compares issues of Jewish identity among *Ashkenazi* Jewish women in Argentina and in the United States.

Nora Gold, Ph.D., is an Associate Professor at the School of Social Work, McMaster University, Toronto, Canada. Her research interests include women, stress and mental health, as well as multiculturalism and anti-Semitism. She is particularly interested in the mental health of Jewish women. She is a member of the Jewish feminist community of Toronto and she loves leading prayers at her *shul*.

Barbara U. Hammer, Ph.D., has been a practicing psychologist for over 30 years, with special interests in psycho-spiritual, Jewish and gender issues. She has been an adjunct faculty member at several institutions, a consultant and supervisor at pastoral counseling centers, a leader for the professional advancement of psychology and an advocate for consumer rights.

Sara R. Horowitz, Ph.D., is Director of the Jewish Studies Program and Associate Professor of English Literature at the University of Delaware. In addition to teaching courses on film and literature, she has published books and articles on Holocaust literature, women survivors, Jewish American fiction and pedagogy. She is a founding co-editor of *Kerem: A Journal of Creative Explorations in Judaism.* She helped create and is co-host on "Storyline," a public radio program on women's literature.

Yonah Klem, Ed.D., began her career in mental health in 1977 as a dance therapist. She earned her doctorate in counseling in 1985. In her suburban Chicago private practice she specializes in working with women in recovery from the effects of severe childhood abuse, including incest and addiction related problems. She also teaches in workshop and university settings.

Arinna Moon, M.A., has been a practicing psychotherapist for the past 12 years; her career has included the provision of crisis intervention services and work in the AIDS community. Prior to that she had many years of employment in the medical health field. She has been a stepparent and a foster parent. Currently she is working in social service administration and is a cantor at her synagogue in Seattle, WA.

Miriam Pollack, M.A., has been involved in Jewish education for over 20 years as a teacher, curriculum writer, principal and educational consultant. She now owns her own business tutoring children with learning disabilities. She lives in Berkeley, CA with her two sons, Aaron, 15 and Noah, 11.

Melissa Schwartz, Ph.D., is the clinical director of the Institute of Imaginal Studies, teaches at Sonoma State University and is a clinical psychologist in private practice in Petaluma, CA. Both her research and clinical areas of specialization are the psychology of women.

Rachel Josefowitz Siegel, M.S.W., is a feminist therapist, consultant and lecturer in private practice in Ithaca, NY. She has written numerous articles and co-edited *Jewish Women in Therapy: Seen but not Heard* (1990). Born in Berlin of Lithuanian Jewish parents, she emigrated to the US in 1939. She has been an active participant and feminist critic in her Jewish community, while raising Jewish issues within her profession. She delights in being an atypical Jewish mother, grandmother and great-grandmother.

tova is a Jewish, working-class, lesbian, feminist writer. She writes poetry, fiction and nonfiction, and has had her work published in journals and anthologies. She is in the core editorial group of *Bridges: A Journal for Jewish Feminists and our Friends*.

Kayla Miriyam Weiner, Ph.D., is a psychotherapist in independent practice in Seattle, WA. She has written articles and lectured internationally on the topics of abuse and trauma, adoption and the psychology of Jewish women. She delights in her passion to travel to remote, exotic and exquisite corners of the world and to establish relationships with the people she meets on her adventures. At home she enjoys her garden, her pets (currently a cat and 6 birds) and most particularly, her loving friends.

Robin B. Zeiger, Ph.D., teaches, trains students, and writes personally and professionally. As an observant Jew, she has a particular interest in the integration of psychology and Judaism. She and her husband, Dr. Jonathan Ben-Ezra live in Richmond, Virginia with their two children, Eliana Malka and Akiva Dov, and their dog, Holly.

GLOSSARY

Agunot	Anchored women: those who, in long standing absence of husbands (due to no religious divorce, disappearance of husband, presumed death which cannot be verified), are considered married under Jewish law
Akedah	The binding and attempted sacrifice of Isaac (Gen. 22-23)
Aleph	First letter of the Hebrew alphabet
Aliyah	To be called up to the *Torah* to say a blessing (an honor)
Aliyot	Plural of *Aliyah*
Ashkenazi	Term used to denote the descendants of European and Russian Jews
Av	Hebrew month
Avot	Forefathers
Ba'al tashhit	The biblical precept forbidding the destroying of fruit trees even during war
Bar mitzvah	Coming of age ritual for boys at age 13
Bat mitzvah	Coming of age ritual for girls at age 13

Beit din	Rabbinic court
Beit midrash	Study hall
Bentsh gomel	A prayer of gratitude for narrowly escaping danger
Bima	Podium from where the service is led
B'nai Brith	Jewish social and educational organization
B'nai mitzvah	Plural of bar and/or bat mitzvah
Brit	Circumcision ceremony for the male child performed at 8 days of age
Brit b'lee milah	Male covenant ceremony without circumcision
Bubba	Grandmother
Chanukah	Festival of Lights
Chazzanim	Cantors
Chesed	Charity, kindness
Chol	Mundane, not holy
Chuppah	Marriage canopy; also, wedding
Chutzpah	Colloquial; gutsy, pushy, courageous
Daven	Pray
Dayenu	It would have been enough; song at Passover *seder*
Dreidel	Spinning toy used at *Chanukah*
D'var Torah	Scholarly/inspirational discourse on a section of *Torah*
Emahot	Foremothers
Etrog	Citron used at *Sukkot*
Frum	Orthodox; religious
Get	Jewish divorce contract
Gittin	Plural of *get*
Haftorah	Readings from the Prophets or Writings related to the *Torah* portion read on *Shabbat*
Haggadah/hagadah	Telling; also the story of the deliverance of the Jews from slavery in Egypt; read on Passover
Halakah/halachah/ halacha	Jewish law (adj. *halakhic/halachic*) as contained in Biblical and post-biblical sources
Halachot	Jewish laws
Hashem	One of the many names for God, literally The Name

Hora	Israeli folk dance
Ima	Mother
Kashrut	Jewish dietary laws, also means "the way"
Ketubah	Jewish marriage contract
Kharoses	Traditional Passover food
Khas v khulile	God forbid
Khumets	Any leavening agent
Kiddish	Prayer of sanctification typically said over a cup of wine; light meal or snack following services on *Shabbat*
Kneydlakh	Matzo ball
Kodesh	Holy
Kollel	Institute of intensive full-time Judaic studies, until recently opened exclusively to men
Kotel	Western Wall of the Second Temple left standing in Jerusalem: considered holy
L'chaim	Hebrew for "to life"; often used as a toast
Le garesh	To chase away, expel
L'havdeel bain kodesh v'chol	To make distinctions between the holy and the profane
Lulav	Special palm branches used for ritual purposes during *Sukkot*
Ma'ariv	The evening prayer
Machpelah	The cave where Jewish ancestors are said to be buried
Matzo brey	Matzo fried with egg
Midot	Characteristics
Mehitza	Visual barrier or curtain between women and men in Orthodox services
Mekhuneh	Nicknamed; commonly known as
Midrash	Tale: legends that are commentaries on biblical text
Mikvah/mikveh	A pool of natural water designated for rites of purification and renewal
Mincha	The afternoon prayer
Minyan	Congregation of ten adults needed to pray; traditionally ten men

Miskareh	Called; a Hebrew or Jewish name other than one's complete name
Mitzvah	Commandment, obligation, good deed
Mitzvot/mitzvoth	Plural of *mitzvah*
Musaf	Additional service on *Shabbat* and festivals
Na'aseh v'nishma	Do and then hear
Ne'ilah	Final section of the *Yom Kippor* service
Niggunim	Tunes
Nishma v'na'aseh	Hear and then do
Nu	Yiddish word used as a question meaning, "So?"
Parnosse	Imperative to make a living
Parsha	Weekly *Torah* reading
Periah	Complete removal of the foreskin from the glans of the penis
Pesakh	Passover
Pikuah nefesh	The rabbinic precept that the preservation of life supersedes the fulfillment of all commandments, except the prohibitions against murder, unchastity and idolatry
Purim	Holiday celebrating the saving of the Jews by Esther and Mordecai
Rav	Rabbi
Rebbe	Term of endearment for a rabbi; literally means "my teacher"
Responsa	Rabbinic literature containing questions and answers to noted Jewish scholars about problems in Jewish law
Rosh Hashannah	Jewish New Year
Rosh hodesh	New moon, first day of the Jewish (lunar) month
Seder	Order; Passover ritual
Sephardic	Descendants of Jews who lived in Spain or Portugal before 1492
Shabbat	Sabbath; Saturday; a day of rest and study; begins before sundown on Friday night and ends on Saturday evening
Shacharit	Morning service: on *Shabbat* this proceeds the *Torah* reading

Shalom	Hello, goodbye, peace
Shiduch	Arranged marriage; matchmaker
Shiva	Ritual traditionally spanning seven days following the death of a close relative
Sh'mirat haguf	Protection of the body: prohibition against tattooing the flesh
Sh'mitah	Commandment creating a "sabbath for the land" in which sowing, pruning and harvesting is forbidden every seventh year
Shoah	Holocaust
Shtetl	Jewish community of the Eastern European Pale of Settlement
Shul	Synagogue
Simhat Torah	Holiday celebrating joy and happiness in the *Torah*
Sofer	Ritual scribe
Stzenut	Modesty
Sukkah	Temporary shelter constructed during the holiday of *Sukkot*
Sukkot/Sukkos	Festival of the harvest around the time of the fall equinox
Taharat	Purity
Taharat ha'mispacha/ hamishpacha	Family purity
Tahor	Ritually pure, suitable to enter the Temple
Tallesim	Plural of *Tallis*
Tallis	Prayer shawl
Talmud	Oral law; explanation and commentaries of the *Torah*
Tehillim	Psalms
Teshuvah	Repentance
Tikkun	To heal and repair
Tikkun olam	To heal and repair the world
Tomah/tameh	Ritually defiled; not suitable to enter the Temple
Torah	Literally "the teaching"; refers to the Five Books of Moses; the Bible
Trop	Musical score for traditional prayers

Tsa'ar ba'alei hayim	Compassion for living things; cruelty is specifically forbidden
Tzedakah	Social justice or righteousness; also, charity
V'ahavta	The first paragraph of the prayer, the *Sh'mah*
Weltanschauung	Total world view
Yachid	An individual
Yad Vashem	Israel's national Holocaust museum
Yasher koach	May power be bestowed upon you
Yeshivah	School offering intensive Judaic studies historically for men, now sometimes includes women
Yichud	Union; a room where a couple retreats briefly after the wedding ceremony
Yiddishkeit	Jewish cultural behaviors, expressions, foods, etc., Judaic commitment
Yizkor	Memorial service for the dead; recited on major holy days and *Yom Kippor*
Yom Kippor/Kippur	Day of atonement and mourning; holiest day of the Jewish year
Yom tov	Holiday or holy day
Yovel	Jubilee year every 50th year after seven sabbatical years; all debts are nullified
Zaftig	Full figured

ORDER FORM

JEWISH WOMEN SPEAK OUT:
EXPANDING THE BOUNDARIES OF PSYCHOLOGY

PLEASE PRINT:

Name: ____

Shipping Address:____

City: ______________________________ State/Province: _______

Country: _________________ Zip/Mail code: _________________

Daytime phone: (_____)________________________

Please send me ______ copies at $18.95 plus $3.00 shipping and handling. WA residents add 8.2% tax.

Total enclosed: $________ (US funds only) Check: # _________

Credit Card: #___________________________ MasterCard _ Visa _

Expiration date: ____________________

Signature: ____

Make checks payable to and send or call orders to:

Phone: 206/781-4409 Fax: 206/933-9790
Canopy Press
P.O. Box 46252
Seattle, WA 98146
USA

Professional books may be tax deductible.